THE SHAKESPEARE PARALLEL TEXT SERIES, THIRD EDITION

Hamlet

by William Shakespeare

Perfection Learning© Corporation
Logan, Iowa 51546-0500

Editorial Director	Julie A. Schumacher
Senior Editor	Rebecca Christian
Series Editor	Rebecca Burke
Editorial Assistant	Kate Winzenburg
Writer, Modern Version	Wim Coleman
Design Director	Randy Messer
Design	Mark Hagenberg
Production	PerfecType
Art Research	Laura Wells
Cover Art	Brad Holland

© 2004 **Perfection Learning® Corporation**
1000 North Second Avenue, P.O. Box 500
Logan, Iowa 51546-0500
Tel: 1-800-831-4190 • Fax: 1-800-543-2745

Printed in the United States of America.

PB ISBN-13: 978-0-7891-6080-5 ISBN-10: 0-7891-6080-3
RLB ISBN-13: 978-0-7569-1483-7 ISBN-10: 0-7569-1483-3
7 8 9 10 11 PP 12 11 10 09 08

TABLE OF CONTENTS

HAMLET
VIOLENCE COMES TO THE STAGE

Hamlet is a bloody play in which only one major character, Horatio, remains alive at the end. Why is the play so violent?

It may be the influence of the Roman playwright Seneca (first century A.D.), who invented a new genre known as the "revenge tragedy."

In Shakespeare's time, playwrights used Seneca's tragedies as models. But they pandered to this era's appetite for gore by placing bloody events right onstage where the audience could see them.

The first famous Elizabethan revenge play was Thomas Kyd's *The Spanish Tragedy*, written and performed during the 1580s. It tells the story of Hieronimo, a Spanish nobleman whose son is brutally murdered and who slips in and out of madness during much of the play (although—like Hamlet's—his insanity may be a pretense).

The Spanish Tragedy was hugely popular for many years. Not surprisingly, a beginning playwright named William Shakespeare chose to imitate the formula of a hero whose personal wrongs drive him to seek bloody vengeance. His play *Titus Andronicus* (1594) is less notable for its poetry than for its scenes of rape, torture, and even cannibalism, but it was one of Shakespeare's first great successes.

Around the turn of the 17th century, Shakespeare wrote another revenge tragedy—*The Tragedy of Hamlet, Prince of Denmark*. As with

Glenn Close and Alan Bates as Gertrude and Claudius, 1990 film
directed by Franco Zeffirelli

most of Shakespeare's plays, the plot was not original. Scholars
generally agree that Shakespeare's *Hamlet* was based on Kyd's *Hamlet*
(often referred to as the *Ur-Hamlet*). He might have followed Kyd's plot
outline and even kept some of Kyd's dialogue. Recycling old plays was
simply part of the business of doing theater in Shakespeare's time.

THE LEGEND OF HAMLET

The story of Hamlet was not original to Kyd, either. He based his play
on an episode in François de Belleforest's 1576 book, *Histoires
tragiques*. Belleforest's version was, in turn, a free translation of a story
told by the Scandinavian writer Saxo Grammaticus in his *History of the
Danes*. Saxo's work, written around the year 1200, claims to be the
earliest history of Denmark. However, most of Saxo's stories are really
more folklore than history. In Saxo's version, the hero is named
Amleth.

Although Amleth is hardly a historical figure, the picture Saxo paints of Danish society is vivid and accurate. Denmark was Christianized between the 9th and 10th centuries, but the pagan Viking spirit remained alive for some time. Wars of conquest were still considered legitimate, and vengeful acts like Amleth's were not only honorable but expected.

Kyd's hero was probably more like the original Amleth than Shakespeare's "melancholy Dane." Nothing in Shakespeare's sources suggests that these models for the prince spent much time thinking deep thoughts or trying to overcome self-doubt.

A RENAISSANCE HERO

Why did Shakespeare take up this particular story around 1600? Perhaps, as one of the owners of the recently built Globe Theatre, he felt some pressure to produce a popular success. A revenge tragedy would have seemed a sure bet. But it is possible that he found himself

Sir Laurence Olivier delivers the "To be or not to be" soliloquy, 1948 film directed by Olivier

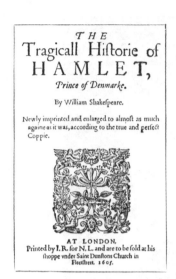

THE
Tragicall Hiftorie of
HAMLET,
Prince of Denmarke.

By William Shakefpeare.

Newly imprinted and enlarged to almoft as much
againe as it was, according to the true and perfect
Coppie.

AT LONDON,
Printed by I. R. for N. L. and are to be fold at his
fhoppe vnder Saint Dunflons Church in
Fleetflreet. 1605.

Title page of the first edition
of *Hamlet*

unwilling to crank out another one, mindful of the artistic flaws of *Titus Andronicus*. This very reluctance might have given him a stroke of inspiration. Why not transform Kyd's Hamlet into a melancholy character—a hero who felt reluctant about his task, just as Shakespeare himself did?

On the other hand, maybe too much fuss has been made about Hamlet's aversion to taking revenge on his uncle, who murdered his father, the former king. His celebrated "delay" lasts weeks in the chronology of the play, but nobody particularly noticed this fact until the 19th century. When the Romantic poets were popular, Hamlet was seen as a brooding, indecisive, and fascinating hero. Before then, scholars generally assumed that Hamlet's revenge was postponed out of dramatic necessity. Otherwise, the drama would have ended almost before it began.

So just what is Shakespeare's tragedy about? Among many other things, it is certainly a portrait of a Renaissance mind. Hamlet is very much a child of his world—the world of 16th-century Europe. To support this idea, scholars have found remarkable parallels between Hamlet's thoughts and those of the celebrated French essayist and philosopher Michel de Montaigne. Montaigne is famous for his *Essays* (1580; 1588), which some scholars think Shakespeare may have read in translation before writing *Hamlet*.

Montaigne's father raised his son to be the ideal "Renaissance man." Until

Craig Gordon as Hamlet,
painting by William Rothenstein

Kenneth Branagh and Kate Winslet as Hamlet and Ophelia, 1996

Montaigne was six years old, his tutor was allowed to speak to him only in Latin. The boy woke to the sound of fine music every morning of his childhood. He grew up studying every branch of human knowledge. Eventually, he came to the conclusion that true knowledge could only come from self-examination. So he began to write his *Essays*—a series of meditations on his own thoughts and feelings which, though seemingly private, still strike a chord of truth in almost anyone who reads them.

Montaigne was very much like Hamlet—a man who sought the great truths of the universe in his own soul. Both Hamlet and Montaigne reflected an important development in the Renaissance—a

The final scene of *Hamlet*

deepening of introspective thought. In earlier philosophy, there is nothing quite as inward-reaching as Montaigne. And as critic Harold Bloom suggests, it is perhaps impossible to find a character in all of earlier world literature who is as self-aware as Hamlet.

Shakespeare must have had some idea how Hamlet felt. The Elizabethan Age was a puzzling and ambivalent time. On one hand, it was a golden age of global exploration, artistic creativity, and scientific discovery. On the other hand, it was an age of brutality and cruelty. The Globe Theatre stood not far from the bear gardens, where bears and dogs tormented each other to death in front of bloodthirsty spectators. Public executions were perfectly ordinary. To be considered a true master, an executioner had to be able to cut out a man's heart and show it to him before he lost consciousness.

Perhaps these contradictions are reflected in Hamlet's observation that "the time is out of joint." This idea recurs throughout Shakespeare's next three tragedies—*Othello, King Lear,* and *Macbeth.* But has there ever been a time that wasn't "out of joint"? How much different is our own time from that of Shakespeare—or how much like it? One of the glories of a play like *Hamlet* is that it compels us to ask such questions.

✠ ✠ ✠

TIMELINE

1564	Shakespeare is baptized.
1568	Elizabeth I becomes Queen of England.
1572	Shakespeare begins grammar school.
1576	Opening of The Theatre, the first permanent playhouse in England.
1580	Drake sails around the world.
1582	Shakespeare marries Anne Hathaway.
1583	Shakespeare's daughter Susanna is baptized.
1585	Shakespeare's twins are baptized.
1588	Spanish Armada is defeated.
1592–94	Plague closes all of London's theaters.
1594	*Titus Andronicus* becomes first printed Shakespeare play.
1594	Shakespeare joins the Lord Chamberlain's Men.
1599	Lord Chamberlain's Men build the Globe Theatre; Shakespeare is part-owner of the building.
1609	Shakespeare's *Sonnets* published for the first time.
1610	Shakespeare retires to Stratford.
1613	Globe Theatre burns to the ground.
1616	William Shakespeare dies at the age of 52.
1623	Shakespeare's wife dies.
	First Folio published.

READING *HAMLET*

USING THIS PARALLEL TEXT

This edition of *Hamlet* is especially designed for readers who aren't familiar with Shakespeare. If you're fairly comfortable with his language, simply read the original text on the left-hand page. When you come to a confusing word or passage, refer to the modern English version on the right or the footnotes at the bottom.

If you think Elizabethan English doesn't even sound like English, read a passage of the modern version silently. Then read the same passage of the original. You'll find that Shakespeare's language begins to come alive for you. You may choose to work your way through the entire play this way.

As you read more, you'll probably find yourself using the modern version less and less. Remember, the parallel version is meant to be an aid, not a substitute for the original. If you read only the modern version, you'll cheat yourself out of Shakespeare's language—his quick-witted puns, sharp-tongued insults, and evocative images.

Keep in mind that language is a living thing, constantly growing and changing. New words are invented and new definitions for old words are added. Since Shakespeare wrote more than four hundred years ago, it is not surprising that his work seems challenging to today's readers.

Here are some other reading strategies that can increase your enjoyment of the play.

BACKGROUND

Knowing some historical background makes it easier to understand what's going on. You will find information about Shakespeare's life and Elizabethan theater at the back of the book. Reading the summaries that precede each act will also help you to follow the action of the play.

GETTING THE BEAT

Like most dramatists of his time, Shakespeare frequently used **blank verse** in his plays. In blank verse, the text is written in measured lines that do not rhyme. Look at the following speech from *Hamlet*.

> How all occasions do inform against me
> And spur my dull revenge! What is a man,
> If his chief good and market of his time
> Be but to sleep and feed? A beast, no more.

You can see that the lines above are approximately equal in length, but they do not cover the length of the whole page as the lines in a story or essay might. They are, in fact, unrhymed verse with each line containing ten or eleven syllables. Furthermore, the ten syllables can be divided into five sections called **iambs**, or feet. Each iamb contains one unstressed (U) and one stressed (/) syllable. Try reading the lines below, giving emphasis to the capitalized syllable in each iamb.

U /	U /	U /	U /	U /
If HIS	chief GOOD	and MAR	ket OF	his TIME

U /	U /	U /	U /	U /
Be BUT	to SLEEP	and FEED?	A BEAST	no MORE.

The length of a line of verse is measured by counting the stresses. This length is known as the **meter**, and when there are five stresses and the rhythm follows an unstressed/stressed pattern, it is known as **iambic pentameter**. Much of Shakespeare's work is written in iambic pentameter.

Of course, Shakespeare was not rigid about this format. He sometimes varied the lines by putting accents in unusual places, by having lines with more or fewer than ten syllables, and by varying where pauses occur. An actor's interpretation can also add variety. (Only a terrible actor would deliver lines in a way that makes the rhythm sound singsong!)

Danish castle

PROSE

In addition to verse, Shakespeare wrote speeches in **prose**, or language without rhythmic structure. Look at the dialogue in Act II, Scene ii, lines 509–533 among Hamlet, Polonius, and the Players. If you try beating out an iambic rhythm to these lines, you'll find it doesn't work because the characters are speaking in prose. Once Hamlet is left alone, however, you'll be able to find the rhythm of iambic pentameter again in his speech. Shakespeare often uses prose for comic speeches, to show madness, and for characters of lower social rank such as servants. His upper-class characters generally do not speak in prose. But these weren't hard and fast rules as far as Shakespeare was concerned. Whether characters speak in verse or prose is often a function of the situation and whom they're addressing, as well as their social status.

CONTRACTIONS

As you know, contractions are words that have been combined by substituting an apostrophe for a letter or letters that have been removed. Contractions were as common in Shakespeare's time as they are today. For example, we use *it's* as a contraction for the words *it is*. In Shakespeare's writing you will discover that *'tis* means the same thing. Shakespeare often used the apostrophe to shorten words so that they would fit into the rhythmic pattern of a line. This is especially true of verbs ending in *-ed*. Note that in Shakespeare's plays, the *-ed* at the end of a verb is usually pronounced as a separate syllable. Therefore, *walked* would be pronounced as two syllables, *walk*ed*, while *walk'd* would be only one.

SPEAK AND LISTEN

Remember that plays are written to be acted, not read silently. Reading aloud—whether in a group or alone—helps you to "hear" the meaning. Listening to another reader will also help. You might also enjoy listening to a recording of the play by professional actors.

CLUES AND CUES

Shakespeare was sparing in his use of stage directions. In fact, many of those in modern editions were added by later editors. Added stage directions are usually indicated by brackets. For example, [*aside*] tells the actor to give the audience information that the other characters can't hear. Sometimes a character's actions are suggested by the lines themselves.

THE PLAY'S THE THING

Finally, if you can't figure out every word in the play, don't get discouraged. The people in Shakespeare's audience couldn't either. At that time, language was changing rapidly and standardized spelling, punctuation, grammar, and even dictionaries did not exist. Besides, Shakespeare loved to play with words. He made up new combinations, like *fat-guts* and *mumble-news*. To make matters worse, the actors probably spoke very rapidly. But the audience didn't strain to catch every word. They went to a Shakespeare play for the same reasons we go to a movie—to get caught up in the story and the acting, to have a great laugh or a good cry.

✠ ✠ ✠

CAST OF CHARACTERS

The Royal House of Denmark

HAMLET	Prince of Denmark
CLAUDIUS	King of Denmark, Hamlet's uncle
GERTRUDE	Queen of Denmark, Hamlet's mother
GHOST	of King Hamlet, Hamlet's father

The Court of Denmark

POLONIUS Lord Chamberlain, Counsellor to the King

OPHELIA his daughter

LAERTES his son

REYNALDO his servant

OSRIC
LORDS } Courtiers
GENTLEMAN

MESSENGER and **ATTENDANTS**

VOLTEMAND
CORNELIUS } Ambassadors to Norway

MARCELLUS
BARNARDO } Officers of the Watch
FRANCISCO

SOLDIERS and **GUARDS**

Former fellow students of Hamlet

HORATIO Hamlet's friend

ROSENCRANTZ
GUILDENSTERN } Sent for by Claudius to inform on Hamlet

Norway

FORTINBRAS	Prince of Norway
CAPTAIN	in Fortinbras's army

Other characters in the play

FIRST PLAYER
OTHER PLAYERS } actors visiting Elsinore

ENGLISH AMBASSADORS

SAILORS

CLOWN gravedigger and sexton

SECOND CLOWN his assistant

PRIEST at Ophelia's funeral

Place

The Danish royal palace at Elsinore

HAMLET

ACT I

Anthony Hopkins as Claudius, Judy Parfitt as Gertrude, 1969 film directed by Tony Richardson

"SOMETHING IS ROTTEN IN THE STATE OF DENMARK."

✠ ✠ ✠

Before You Read

1. Soon after the play opens, you learn that King Hamlet, Hamlet's father, has been dead for less than three months. Within a month of the king's death, his widow has married his brother. How do you think young Hamlet might feel about his mother's quick remarriage to his uncle?

2. Note any images in Act I that might foretell a story about vengeance, double dealings, and violence.

3. *Hamlet* is a play full of questions. Beginning with Act I, keep track of some of these questions. Notice which ones get answers and which ones do not.

Literary Elements

1. **Foreshadowing** refers to hints in the text about what will occur later in the plot. In the very first scene, you learn that the castle guards have been visited by a horrible sight—a ghost. They believe this grim apparition predicts tragedy for the kingdom of Denmark.

2. A **pun** is a play on words that have similar sounds but more than one possible spelling or meaning. Hamlet remarks that he is "too much in the sun." This pun on "sun" and "son" brings attention to his difficulty as the one in the middle of many conflicting forces, as well as his problems with his new stepfather.

3. Good drama has **conflict**: struggle between opposing forces. **External conflict** involves an outer force such as nature or another character. **Internal conflict** exists inside a person. In *Hamlet*, the warring forces of Norway create much external conflict for the Danes. Prince Hamlet's internal conflict results from his inability to act quickly on disturbing news about his father's death.

4. **Imagery** is highly descriptive language that appeals to one or more of the five senses—touch, taste, hearing, smell, and sight. In Act I, Horatio describes the Ghost's effect on the night guards, who are "distilled / Almost to jelly with the act of fear."

Words to Know

The following vocabulary words appear in Act I in the original text of Shakespeare's play. However, they are words that are still used today. Read the definitions here and pay attention to the words as you read the play (they will be in boldfaced type).

ambiguous	unclear; uncertain
assail	attack with blows or words
auspicious	favorable; well-timed
contrive	invent; design
dexterity	skillfulness; proficiency
enmity	hatred; loathing
impious	unholy; blasphemous
invulnerable	secure; powerful
jocund	cheerful; happy
obsequious	overly respectful; deferential
obstinate	stubborn; unbending
perilous	dangerous; hazardous
pernicious	harmful; destructive
portentous	ominous; threatening
usurps [usurp'st]	captures; seizes

Act Summary

The play begins at midnight, outside a guard station at the royal castle in Elsinore. The Ghost of the dead King Hamlet appears to Barnardo, Marcellus, and Horatio: a bad omen for Denmark. Fortinbras of Norway wants revenge on the Danish forces, who have wronged his family and his country.

At court, the new king, Claudius, claims to grieve for his late brother, but has wasted little time marrying the king's widow, Gertrude, who is also Hamlet's mother. Now Claudius is worried about an invasion by Fortinbras.

Hamlet, played by Sir Laurence Olivier, chases the ghost of his father, 1948 film

Hamlet's moodiness is on everyone's minds. Gertrude pleads with her son to quit grieving for his father. Hamlet is angry, but he agrees to stay at court and not return to university.

After the others depart, Hamlet speaks about his despair over his mother's hasty marriage to Claudius. His religion makes him rule out suicide, but he yearns for death.

Horatio, Marcellus, and Barnardo appear and tell Hamlet about seeing his late father's ghost. Hamlet plans to join them on their next night watch, believing his father's appearance is a sign that "foul deeds will rise."

Laertes warns his sister Ophelia that Hamlet is unlikely to marry her. Hamlet is in line for the throne of Denmark and so is unable to choose his own wife. Ophelia resists her brother's bullying. Their father, Polonius, sends Laertes off to Paris with stern advice about how to behave abroad. He also forbids Ophelia to see Hamlet.

Shortly after midnight, Hamlet, Horatio, and Marcellus stand outside the castle, listening to Claudius's night carousing. The Ghost appears and beckons Hamlet to follow him. Hamlet threatens Horatio and Marcellus with death if they get in his way. Still, they follow him.

The Ghost orders Hamlet to avenge his father's "foul and unnatural murder." Hamlet swears Horatio and Marcellus to secrecy. He warns them that he may act strangely in the near future and asks them to pretend ignorance.

ACT I, SCENE I

A guard platform of the castle. Enter BARNARDO *and* FRANCISCO, *two sentinels.*

BARNARDO
Who's there?

FRANCISCO
Nay, answer me. Stand and unfold yourself.

BARNARDO
Long live the King!

FRANCISCO
Barnardo?

BARNARDO
5   He.

FRANCISCO
You come most carefully upon your hour.

BARNARDO
'Tis now struck twelve. Get thee to bed, Francisco.

FRANCISCO
For this relief much thanks. 'Tis bitter cold,
And I am sick at heart.

BARNARDO
10   Have you had quiet guard?

FRANCISCO
Not a mouse stirring.

BARNARDO
Well, good night.
If you do meet Horatio and Marcellus,
The rivals of my watch, bid them make haste.

Enter HORATIO *and* MARCELLUS.

FRANCISCO
15   I think I hear them.—Stand, ho! Who is there?

HORATIO
Friends to this ground.

ACT 1, SCENE 1

A guard platform of the castle. BARNARDO *and* FRANCISCO, *two watch guards, enter.*

BARNARDO
Who's there?

FRANCISCO
No, *you* answer *me.* Stop and say who you are.

BARNARDO
Long live the King!

FRANCISCO
Barnardo?

BARNARDO
Yes.   5

FRANCISCO
You've come right on time.

BARNARDO
The clock has now struck twelve. Go on to bed, Francisco.

FRANCISCO
Thanks so much for relieving me. It's bitter cold,
and I feel heartsick.

BARNARDO
Have things been quiet on your watch?   10

FRANCISCO
Not a mouse has stirred.

BARNARDO
Well, good night.
If you meet Horatio and Marcellus,
my watch partners, tell them to hurry here.

        HORATIO *and* MARCELLUS *enter.*

FRANCISCO
I think I hear them.—Stop, you! Who's there?   15

HORATIO
Citizens of Denmark.

MARCELLUS
And liegemen to the Dane.

FRANCISCO
Give you good night.

MARCELLUS
O, farewell, honest soldier.
20   Who hath relieved you?

FRANCISCO
Barnardo hath my place.
Give you good night.

       Exit FRANCISCO.

MARCELLUS
Holla, Barnardo!

BARNARDO
Say, what, is Horatio there?

HORATIO
25   A piece of him.

BARNARDO
Welcome, Horatio.—Welcome, good Marcellus.

MARCELLUS
What, has this thing appeared again tonight?

BARNARDO
I have seen nothing.

MARCELLUS
Horatio says 'tis but our fantasy,
30   And will not let belief take hold of him
Touching this dreaded sight twice seen of us;
Therefore I have entreated him along
With us to watch the minutes of this night,
That, if again this apparition come,
35   He may approve our eyes and speak to it.

HORATIO
Tush, tush, 'twill not appear.

BARNARDO
                    Sit down awhile,

MARCELLUS
And loyal subjects to the King.

FRANCISCO
May God give you a good night.

MARCELLUS
Farewell, honest soldier.
Who has relieved you? 20

FRANCISCO
Barnardo is taking my place.
May God give you a good night.

     FRANCISCO *exits.*

MARCELLUS
Hello, Barnardo.

BARNARDO
What's this—is Horatio there?

HORATIO
Only part of him (the rest is frozen). 25

BARNARDO
Welcome, Horatio.—Welcome, good Marcellus.

HORATIO
Tell me, has this thing appeared again tonight?

BARNARDO
I have seen nothing.

MARCELLUS
Horatio says it's only our imagination,
and won't let himself believe 30
in this dreadful vision that we've seen twice now.
So I've persuaded him to come along
and keep watch with us all the long minutes of this night,
so that, if this apparition comes again,
he can confirm what we've seen and speak to it. 35

HORATIO
Nonsense, it won't appear.

BARNARDO
Sit down awhile,

And let us once again **assail** your ears,
That are so fortified against our story,
⁴⁰ What we have two nights seen.

HORATIO

Well, sit we down,
And let us hear Barnardo speak of this.

BARNARDO

Last night of all,
When yond same star that's westward from the pole
⁴⁵ Had made his course t' illume that part of heaven
Where now it burns, Marcellus and myself,
The bell then beating one—

Enter GHOST.

MARCELLUS

Peace, break thee off! Look where it comes again.

BARNARDO

In the same figure like the King that's dead.

MARCELLUS

⁵⁰ Thou art a scholar;* speak to it, Horatio.

BARNARDO

Looks 'a not like the King? Mark it, Horatio.

HORATIO

Most like. It harrows me with fear and wonder.

BARNARDO

It would be spoke to.

MARCELLUS

Speak to it, Horatio.

HORATIO

⁵⁵ What art thou that **usurp'st** this time of night,
Together with that fair and warlike form
In which the majesty of buried Denmark
Did sometimes march? By heaven I charge thee, speak.

---

⁵⁰ *scholar* Exorcisms were performed in Latin, and therefore only a scholar could
properly speak to an evil spirit.

and let's try again to overcome your disbelieving ears,
which are so strongly defended against the story
of what we've seen for two nights.   40

HORATIO

Well, we'll sit down,
and let's hear what Barnardo has to say about this.

BARNARDO

Just last night,
when the star that you now see to the west of the North Star
had traveled on its way to light up the part of the sky   45
where it now burns, the bell was just striking one o'clock,
and Marcellus and I—

   The GHOST *enters.*

MARCELLUS

Quiet, stop talking! Look, it's coming again.

BARNARDO

Looking just like the King that died.

MARCELLUS

You are a scholar, Horatio. Speak to it.   50

BARNARDO

Doesn't he look like the King? Look at it, Horatio.

HORATIO

It looks a great deal like the King. It rips through me with fear and
   wonder.

BARNARDO

It wants to be spoken to.

MARCELLUS

Speak to it, Horatio.

HORATIO

Who are you, that you should claim as your own this time of   55
   night,
along with that handsome, warlike shape
in which the majestic, late King of Denmark
used to march? By heaven, I command you to speak.

MARCELLUS

It is offended.

BARNARDO

60 See, it stalks away.

HORATIO

Stay! Speak, speak! I charge thee, speak!

Exit GHOST.

MARCELLUS

'Tis gone and will not answer.

BARNARDO

How now, Horatio? You tremble and look pale.
Is not this something more than fantasy?
65 What think you on 't?

HORATIO

Before my God, I might not this believe
Without the sensible and true avouch
Of mine own eyes.

MARCELLUS

Is it not like the King?

HORATIO

70 As thou art to thyself.
Such as the very armor he had on
When he the ambitious Norway combated.
So frowned he once, when, in an angry parle,
He smote the sledded Polacks on the ice.
75 'Tis strange.

MARCELLUS

Thus twice before, and jump at this dead hour,
With martial stalk hath he gone by our watch.

HORATIO

In what particular thought to work I know not;
But in the gross and scope of my opinion,
80 This bodes some strange eruption to our state.

MARCELLUS

Good now, sit down, and tell me, he that knows,
Why this same strict and most observant watch

MARCELLUS
It is offended.

BARNARDO
Look, it's stalking away.   60

HORATIO
Wait! Speak! Speak! I command you to speak!

The GHOST *exits.*

MARCELLUS
It's gone and will not answer.

BARNARDO
What do you say now, Horatio? You tremble and look pale.
Isn't this something more than imagination?
What do you think of it?   65

HORATIO
I swear to God, I wouldn't believe this
without the vivid, honest proof
of my own eyes.

MARCELLUS
Isn't it like the King?

HORATIO
As much as you're like yourself.   70
He was wearing that same kind of armor
when he fought against the ambitious King of Norway.
He frowned like that once during an angry war council,
when he defeated the sled-riding Poles on the ice.
This is strange.   75

MARCELLUS
Twice before like this, and right at this deathly hour,
he has gone by our post with a warlike step.

HORATIO
I don't know exactly what to make of it,
but in the general drift of my thinking,
this predicts some violent outbreak in our country.   80

MARCELLUS
Please, let's sit down; and let anyone who knows tell me:
Why are the subjects of our country

So nightly toils the subject of the land,
And why such daily cast of brazen cannon
85 And foreign mart for implements of war,
Why such impress of shipwrights, whose sore task
Does not divide the Sunday from the week,
What might be toward that this sweaty haste
Doth make the night joint-laborer with the day?
90 Who is 't that can inform me?

HORATIO
That can I.
At least the whisper goes so: our last king,
Whose image even by now appeared to us,
Was, as you know, by Fortinbras of Norway,
95 thereto pricked on by a most emulate pride,
Dared to the combat; in which our valiant Hamlet
(For so this side of our known world esteemed him)
Did slay this Fortinbras, who, by a sealed compact
Well ratified by law and heraldry,
100 Did forfeit, with his life, all those his lands
Which he stood seized of, to the conqueror;
Against the which a moiety competent
Was gaged by our king, which had returned
To the inheritance of Fortinbras,
105 Had he been vanquisher, as, by the same comart
And carriage of the article designed,
His fell to Hamlet. Now, sir, young Fortinbras,
Of unimproved mettle hot and full,
Hath in the skirts of Norway here and there
110 Sharked up a list of lawless resolutes,
For food and diet, to some enterprise
That hath a stomach in 't; which is no other,
As it doth well appear unto our state,
But to recover of us by strong hand
115 And terms compulsatory, those foresaid lands
So by his father lost; and this, I take it,
Is the main motive of our preparations,
The source of this our watch, and the chief head
Of this posthaste and rummage in the land.

so strictly kept at work throughout the night?
And why are bronze cannon being cast daily?
And why are we buying instruments of war from foreign   85
    countries?
And why are ship makers being forced to labor heavily
on Sundays as well as the rest of the week?
What expected event is provoking all this sweaty haste,
making the night as much a time for work as the day?
Which of you can tell me?   90

HORATIO
I can.
At least this is how the rumor goes: Our last king,
whose form appeared to us just a moment ago,
was, as you know, challenged to combat by King Fortinbras
    of Norway,
who was stirred by pride and envy. In this combat, our valiant   95
    Hamlet
(for so he's called throughout this part of the world)
killed Fortinbras, who left a sealed agreement,
fully ratified by law and the rules of combat;
in it, he surrendered with his life all the lands   100
he possessed to the man who defeated him.
Likewise, our own king pledged an equal quantity of land,
which would have gone to Fortinbras
if he had been the victor—just the same as   105
Fortinbras's land went to Hamlet
according to the terms of this agreement. Now, sir, young
    Fortinbras
is of an undisciplined, hot-blooded temperament,   *ı*
and he has gathered up, here and there
along the Norwegian borders, a gang of lawless desperadoes   110
to serve him in an endeavor
that demands some courage; and it's clear
to our leaders that he fully intends
to get back from us, by brute strength
and forced terms, those aforementioned lands   115
that his father lost. And this, I take it,
is the main motive for our preparations,
the reason why we keep watch, and the chief source
of all this rush and bustle throughout the land.

BARNARDO

120   I think it be no other but e'en so.
    Well may it sort that this **portentous** figure
    Comes armed through our watch so like the King
    That was and is the question of these wars.

HORATIO

    A mote it is to trouble the mind's eye.
125   In the most high and palmy state of Rome,
    A little ere the mightiest Julius fell,
    The graves stood tenantless, and the sheeted dead
    Did squeak and gibber in the Roman streets;
    As stars with trains of fire and dews of blood,
130   Disasters in the sun; and the moist star,
    Upon whose influence Neptune's empire stands,
    Was sick almost to doomsday with eclipse.
    And even the like precurse of feared events,
    As harbingers preceding still the fates
135   And prologue to the omen coming on,
    Have heaven and earth together demonstrated
    Unto our climatures and countrymen.

       Enter GHOST.

    But soft, behold, lo where it comes again!
    I'll cross it,* though it blast me.—Stay, illusion!

       It spreads his arms.

140   If thou hast any sound or use of voice,
    Speak to me.
    If there be any good thing to be done
    That may to thee do ease and grace to me,
    Speak to me.
145   If thou art privy to thy country's fate,
    Which happily foreknowing may avoid,
    O, speak!
    Or if thou hast uphoarded in thy life
    Extorted treasure in the womb of earth,

---

139   *cross it* Horatio puts himself in the Ghost's path and holds out his arms to form a cross, a means of protecting himself from an evil spirit.

BARNARDO

    I think this must be exactly right. 120
    And so it seems fitting that this ominous figure
    passes during our watch—armed, and looking like the King
    who was and is the cause of these wars.

HORATIO

    It is like a speck troubling the mind's eye.
    In the great and powerful nation of Rome, 125
    shortly before the mighty Julius Caesar was killed,
    the graves lay empty, and the enshrouded dead
    squeaked and cried shrilly in Roman streets;
    fiery-tailed comets appeared, and dew turned to blood;
    the sun made threatening signs; and the moon, 130
    which dictates the movements of the sea,
    was so deeply eclipsed that it seemed like the end of the world.
    And similar omens of dreadful events,
    like messengers arriving ahead of fate
    to predict great calamities, 135
    have been sent by heaven and earth
    to our own country and its people.

        The GHOST *enters.*

    But quiet! Look! Here it comes again!
    I'll cross its path, even if it destroys me.—Stop, illusion!

        The GHOST *spreads its arms.*

    If you can make any sound with your voice, 140
    speak to me.
    If there is any good thing to be done
    that might ease your suffering and show kindness on my part,
        speak to me.
    If you know anything about your country's fate 145
    which perhaps might be avoided if known in advance,
    oh, speak!
    Or if you hoarded and buried in the earth
    ill-gotten treasure during your life

150   For which, they say, you spirits oft walk in death,

          The cock crows.

     Speak of it. Stay and speak.—Stop it, Marcellus.

MARCELLUS
     Shall I strike at it with my partisan?*

HORATIO
     Do, if it will not stand.

BARNARDO
     'Tis here.

HORATIO
155   'Tis here.

         Exit GHOST.

MARCELLUS
     'Tis gone.
     We do it wrong, being so majestical,
     To offer it the show of violence,
     For it is as the air, **invulnerable**,
     And our vain blows malicious mockery.

BARNARDO
160   It was about to speak when the cock crew.

HORATIO
     And then it started, like a guilty thing
     Upon a fearful summons. I have heard,
     The cock, that is the trumpet to the morn,
     Doth with his lofty and shrill-sounding throat
165   Awake the god of day, and at his warning,
     Whether in sea or fire, in earth or air,*
     Th' extravagant and erring spirit hies
     To his confine; and of the truth herein
     This present object make probation.

MARCELLUS
170   It faded on the crowing of the cock.
     Some say that ever 'gainst that season comes

---

152 *partisan* a weapon made of a long wooden shaft topped by a blade with broad, horizontally projecting cutting edges

(which they say is often the cause of spirits walking after death), 150
speak of it.

> *The rooster crows.*

Stop and speak!—Stop it, Marcellus.

MARCELLUS
Should I strike it with my pike?

HORATIO
Yes, if it won't stop.

BARNARDO
It's here.

HORATIO
It's here. 155

> *The GHOST exits.*

MARCELLUS
It's gone.
It's so majestic, we do it wrong
to show violence toward it;
for it as invulnerable as the air,
and our useless blows mock our own nasty foolishness.

BARNARDO
It was about to speak when the rooster crowed. 160

HORATIO
And then it looked startled, like a guilty creature
called on some terrible errand. I have heard
that the rooster, who is the bugler of morning,
wakens the god of day with his fine,
high-pitched voice; and at his warning,
wayward and wandering spirits, 165
whether in sea, fire, earth, or air,
hurry back to captivity. The thing we've seen
seems to prove that this is true.

MARCELLUS
It disappeared when the rooster crowed. 170
Some say that just before the season arrives

---

166   *sea . . . air* refers to the belief that the world was composed of four "elements"—
earth, water, air, and fire

Wherein our Savior's birth is celebrated,
This bird of dawning singeth all night long,
And then, they say, no spirit dare stir abroad,
175 The nights are wholesome,* then no planets strike,
No fairy takes, nor witch hath power to charm:
So hallowed and so gracious is that time.

HORATIO

So have I heard and do in part believe it.
But look, the morning in russet mantle clad
180 Walks o'er the dew of yon high eastward hill.
Break we our watch up, and by my advice
Let us impart what we have seen tonight
Unto young Hamlet, for upon my life
This spirit, dumb to us, will speak to him.
185 Do you consent we shall acquaint him with it,
As needful in our loves, fitting our duty?

MARCELLUS

Let's do 't, I pray, and I this morning know
Where we shall find him most convenient.

Exeunt.

---

175 *wholesome* In the medical beliefs of the time, the night air was considered unhealthy.

when our Savior's birth is celebrated,
this bird of the dawn sings all night long.
And then, they say, no spirit dares to stir in the world;
the night air is healthy; no planets exert a destructive influence; 175
fairies cannot work magic, and witches can cast no spells,
that time is so sacred and blessed.

HORATIO

I've heard so, too, and partly believe it.
But look—the dawn, wearing a reddish-brown cloak,
walks through the dew of that high, eastern hill yonder. 180
Let's leave our post; and I propose
that we inform young Hamlet
of what we have seen tonight. For I'll stake my life,
that this spirit will speak to him, even though it's silent to us.
Do you agree that we shall tell him about it, 185
as is required of our friendship and proper to our duty?

MARCELLUS

Please, let's do it. And I know where
we can find him most easily this morning.

They exit.

ACT I, SCENE II

The castle. Flourish. Enter CLAUDIUS, *King of
Denmark,* GERTRUDE *the Queen,* COUNCILORS,
POLONIUS *and his son* LAERTES, HAMLET, *cum aliis
[including* VOLTEMAND *and* CORNELIUS].

KING

    Though yet of Hamlet our* dear brother's death
    The memory be green, and that it us befitted
    To bear our hearts in grief, and our whole kingdom
    To be contracted in one brow of woe,
5   Yet so far hath discretion fought with nature
    That we with wisest sorrow think on him
    together with remembrance of ourselves.
    Therefore our sometime sister, now our Queen,
    Th' imperial jointress of this warlike state,
10   Have we, as 'twere, with a defeated joy,
    With an **auspicious** and a dropping eye,
    With mirth in funeral, and with dirge in marriage,
    In equal scale weighing delight and dole,
    Taken to wife. Nor have we herein barred
15   Your better wisdoms, which have freely gone
    With this affair along. For all, our thanks.
    Now follows that you know young Fortinbras,
    Holding a weak supposal of our worth,
    Or thinking by our late dear brother's death
20   Our state to be disjoint and out of frame,
    Colleagued with this dream of his advantage,
    He hath not failed to pester us with message,
    Importing the surrender of those lands
    Lost by his father, with all bonds of law,
25   To our most valiant brother—so much for him.
    Now for ourself and for this time of meeting.
    Thus much the business is: we have here writ
    To Norway, uncle of young Fortinbras—
    Who, impotent and bedrid, scarcely hears

---

1   *our* The King consistently uses the royal "we" in speaking about himself. The
paraphrase converts this to the normal first person singular, "I" and "me," and so
on.

ACT 1, SCENE 2

The castle. Trumpet fanfare. KING CLAUDIUS *of Denmark,*
QUEEN GERTRUDE, COUNSELLORS, POLONIUS, *his son*
LAERTES, *and* HAMLET *with others, including* VOLTEMAND
and CORNELIUS.

KING

Although the memory is still fresh
of my dear brother Hamlet's death, and it was right for me
to feel sorrow in my heart, and for my whole kingdom
to knit its brows in a single expression of grief,
I have to weigh prudence against natural feeling,   5
and so I find it wisest in sorrow
to remember to think of my own affairs as well as him.
And so, my former sister, now my queen
and royal partner over this powerful nation,
I've taken as my wife.
I've done this, so to speak, with a defeated joy,   10
with one eye smiling and the other weeping,
with merriment in funeral, and with mourning in marriage,
weighing delight and sadness equally. (*to the counsellors*)
Nor have I failed to listen to your wise advice,   15
which has supported me in this matter. Thanks to you all.
You know what I'm going to discuss next. Young Fortinbras
holds a low opinion of my might,
and thinks that the nation is distracted and disorganized
after my dear brother's death.
Supported by this false notion of his superiority,   20
he hasn't failed to pester me with messages
demanding the surrender of those lands
that his father lost to my most valiant brother
according to the rule of law. I need not say more of what I
    think of Fortinbras.   25
Now for myself and the reason for this meeting
which is as follows: I have written a letter
to the King of Norway, young Fortinbras's uncle—
who, helpless and bedridden, has scarcely heard

30 Of this his nephew's purpose—to suppress
His further gait herein, in that the levies,
The lists, and full proportions are all made
Out of his subject; and we here dispatch
You, good Cornelius, and you, Voltemand,
35 For bearers of this greeting to old Norway,
Giving to you no further personal power
To business with the King, more than the scope
Of these dilated articles allow.

[*He gives them the letter.*]

Farewell, and let your haste commend your duty.

CORNELIUS / VOLTEMAND
40 In that, and all things, we will show our duty.

KING
We doubt it nothing. Heartily farewell.

Exit VOLTEMAND *and* CORNELIUS.

And now, Laertes, what's the news with you?
You told us of some suit. What is 't, Laertes?
You cannot speak of reason to the Dane
45 And lose your voice. What wouldst thou beg, Laertes,
That shall not be my offer, not thy asking?
The head is not more native to the heart,
The hand more instrumental to the mouth,
Than is the throne of Denmark to thy father.
50 What wouldst thou have, Laertes?

LAERTES
                                        My dread lord,
Your leave and favor to return to France,
From whence, though willingly I came to Denmark
To show my duty in your coronation,
55 Yet now I must confess, that duty done,
My thoughts and wishes bend again toward France
And bow them to your gracious leave and pardon.

KING
Have you your father's leave? What says Polonius?

of his nephew's plans. In this letter, I ask the King to put a stop 30
to these actions, since young Fortinbras is getting his troops
and all his money and supplies
from the King's own subjects. And so I'm sending
you, good Cornelius, and you, Voltemand,
to carry this letter of greeting to the old King of Norway. 35
I give you no further personal power
to do business with the King than the range
of these detailed documents will allow.

     He gives them the letter.

Farewell, and show yourselves dutiful by making haste.

CORNELIUS and **VOLTEMAND**
We'll show ourselves dutiful in this and all things. 40

KING
I don't doubt it. A hearty farewell.

     VOLTEMAND *and* CORNELIUS *exit.*

And now, Laertes, what's new with you?
You told me that you wanted something. What is it, Laertes?
You can't speak reasonably to the King of Denmark
and waste your voice. What could you ask of me, Laertes, 45
that I wouldn't offer you without your asking for it?
The head is not more related to the heart,
nor the hand of more service to the mouth,
than the King of Denmark is to your father.
What do you want, Laertes? 50

LAERTES
My revered Lord,
your kind permission to return to France,
from which I came willingly to Denmark
to swear my loyalty at your coronation;
yet now that my duty's done, I must confess 55
that my thoughts and wishes turn again toward France,
and I bow down and beg for your gracious permission to go back.

KING
Do you have your father's permission? What does Polonius say?

POLONIUS

    Hath, my lord, wrung from me my slow leave

60   By laborsome petition, and at last

    Upon his will I sealed my hard consent.

    I do beseech you give him leave to go.

KING

    Take thy fair hour, Laertes. Time be thine,

    And thy best graces spend it at thy will.—

65   But now, my cousin Hamlet, and my son—

HAMLET [*aside*]

    A little more than kin and less than kind!*

KING

    How is it that the clouds still hang on you?

HAMLET

    Not so, my lord. I am too much in the sun.

QUEEN

    Good Hamlet, cast thy nighted color off,

70   And let thine eye look like a friend on Denmark.

    Do not forever with thy vailed lids

    Seek for thy noble father in the dust.

    Thou know'st 'tis common; all that lives must die,

    Passing through nature to eternity.

HAMLET

75   Ay, madam, it is common.*

QUEEN

                        If it be,

    Why seems it so particular with thee?

HAMLET

    "Seems," madam? Nay, it is. I know not "seems."

    'Tis not alone my inky cloak, good mother,

80   Nor customary suits of solemn black,

---

66 *less than kind* Hamlet is "more than kin" because he is closer to Claudius than a
nephew, but "less than kind" because he doesn't feel kindly toward him, the way
a son should by nature (or "kind").

POLONIUS

My lord, he has slowly wrestled my permission from me
by stubborn pleas, and I have finally
given my consent to his wishes.
I beg you, give him permission to go.

KING

Enjoy the time of your youth. Take as much time as you wish,
and may you spend it virtuously according to your will.—
But now, my nephew Hamlet, and my son—

HAMLET *(aside)*

More than a little related, but in a less than natural way!

KING

Why do clouds of sadness still hang around you?

HAMLET

That's not true, my lord; I am in the sun too much.

QUEEN

Good Hamlet, stop wearing this black clothing,
and look upon the King of Denmark with a friendly eye.
Do not seek your noble father in the dust
forever with your lowered eyes.
You know it's normal; all living things must die,
passing through the natural world to eternity.

HAMLET

Yes, madam, it's normal.

QUEEN

If so,
Why does it seem like such a personal thing to you?

HAMLET

"Seem," madam? No, it *is*. I don't know the meaning of "seem."
Good mother, it's not just my ink-colored cloak,
my black and solemn outfit,

60

65

70

75

80

---

75   *common* Hamlet's echo of his mother's term has a double meaning. Death is
common because it is universal, but also common because it is ordinary and
even vulgar.

Nor windy suspiration of forced breath,
No, nor the fruitful river in the eye,
Nor the dejected havior of the visage,
Together with all forms, moods, shapes of grief,
85 That can denote me truly. These indeed seem,
For they are actions that a man might play,
But I have that within which passes show;
These but the trappings and the suits of woe.

KING
'Tis sweet and commendable in your nature, Hamlet,
90 To give these mourning duties to your father,
But you must know your father lost a father,
That father lost, lost his, and the survivor bound
In filial obligation for some term
To do **obsequious** sorrow. But to persever
95 In **obstinate** condolement is a course
Of **impious** stubbornness. 'Tis unmanly grief.
It shows a will most incorrect to heaven,
A heart unfortified, a mind impatient,
An understanding simple and unschooled.
100 For what we know must be and is as common
As any the most vulgar thing to sense,
Why should we in our peevish opposition
Take it to heart? Fie, 'tis a fault to heaven,
A fault against the dead, a fault to nature,
105 To reason most absurd, whose common theme
Is death of fathers, and who still hath cried,
From the first corse* till he that died today,
"This must be so." We pray you throw to earth
This unprevailing woe, and think of us
110 As of a father, for let the world take note
You are the most immediate to our throne,
And with no less nobility of love
Than that which dearest father bears his son
Do I impart toward you. For your intent
115 In going back to school in Wittenberg,
It is most retrograde to our desire,

---

107 *first corse* Abel, who was killed by his brother, Cain. See Genesis 4:1–16.

my labored and heavy sighing,
the rivers of tears from my eyes,
my downcast expression,
nor all the other outward displays of grief
that portray my true feelings. Indeed, all these things "seem,"   85
for a man might use them to pretend to grieve.
Inside, I feel something which goes beyond mere display,
while these are only the shallow appearances of sorrow.

KING

Hamlet, it's sweet and commendable in your character
to mourn your father so dutifully.   90
But you surely realize that your father lost his father,
and that your grandfather lost his father. A surviving son
is obliged to show proper sorrow
for a while. But to continue
in obstinate woe is to act   95
with stubborn irreverence. It's unmanly grief.
It shows disobedience to heaven,
a defenseless heart, an impatient mind,
an ignorant and untaught view of things.
For when we know that something must happen, and that
it's as ordinary   100
as the most common thing we can experience,
why should we, with foolish stubbornness,
take it personally? Nonsense! It's a fault against heaven,
a fault against the dead, and a fault against nature.
It's an absurdity against reason—the common message   105
of which
is that fathers die; for reason has always announced,
from the first death to the person who dies today,
"This must be so." I implore you, throw to the ground
this useless sorrow and think of me
as a father. For let the world know   110
that you are the next in the line of succession to my throne,
and I offer you a love no less noble
than that which the fondest father
feels for his son. As for your intention
of going back to school in Wittenberg,   115
it is completely against my wishes,

And we beseech you, bend you to remain
Here in the cheer and comfort of our eye,
Our chiefest courtier, cousin, and our son.

QUEEN

120 Let not thy mother lose her prayers, Hamlet.
I pray thee stay with us, go not to Wittenberg.

HAMLET

I shall in all my best obey you, madam.

KING

Why, 'tis a loving and fair reply.
Be as ourself in Denmark. Madam, come.
125 This gentle and unforced accord of Hamlet
Sits smiling to my heart, in grace whereof
No **jocund** health that Denmark drinks today,
But the great cannon to the clouds shall tell,
And the King's rouse the heaven shall bruit again,
130 Respeaking earthly thunder. Come away.

Flourish. Exeunt all but HAMLET.

HAMLET

O that this too too solid flesh would melt,
Thaw, and resolve itself into a dew,
Or that the Everlasting had not fixed
His canon 'gainst self-slaughter. O God, God!
135 How weary, stale, flat, and unprofitable
Seem to me all the uses of this world!
Fie on 't, ah, fie, 'tis an unweeded garden
That grows to seed. Things rank and gross in nature
Possess it merely. That it should come to this:
140 But two months dead, nay, not so much, not two,
So excellent a king, that was to this
Hyperion to a satyr;* so loving to my mother
That he might not between the winds of heaven
Visit her face too roughly. Heaven and earth,
145 Must I remember? Why, she would hang on him
As if increase of appetite had grown

---

142   *Hyperion to a satyr* Hyperion was the Greek god of the sun and a model of manly
beauty. Satyrs were spirits with the pointed ears, legs, and short horns of a goat
and were commonly associated with lecherous behavior.

and I beg you to agree to remain
here in the cheerful comfort of my supervision—
my favorite courtier, my kinsman, and my son.

QUEEN

Don't let your mother's prayers be for nothing, Hamlet.   120
I beg you, stay with us. Don't go to Wittenberg.

HAMLET

I'll do everything I can to obey you, madam.

KING

Why, that's a loving and agreeable reply.
Consider yourself my equal in Denmark.—Madam, let's go.
Hamlet's easy and unforced agreement   125
makes my heart smile—and in thanks for it,
every merry toast drunk in Denmark today
will be announced by great cannons firing at the clouds;
and when the King drinks deeply, the heavens will resound again,
echoing my earthly thunder. Come, let's go.   130

Trumpet fanfare. Everyone but HAMLET exits.

HAMLET

Oh, if this much too soiled flesh of mine could melt,
thaw, and dissolve into dew;
or if the Almighty hadn't
made a law against suicide. Oh God, Oh God,
how tiresome, stale, flat, and pointless   135
all the business of this world seems to me.
How I despise it all! The world's an unweeded garden
growing out of control. It is overrun by nothing
but coarse, disgusting things. That it should come to this!
He's been dead only two months—no, not that long, not two   140
    months.
And he was such an excellent king—like the sun god to a satyr,
compared to this new one. He loved my mother so much
that he wouldn't allow the winds of heaven
to strike her face too roughly. Heaven and earth,
must I remember? Why, she would cling to him   145
as if feeding on him made her

By what it fed on; and yet within a month—
Let me not think on 't; frailty, thy name is woman—
A little month, or ere those shoes were old
150 With which she followed my poor father's body
Like Niobe,* all tears, why she, even she—
O God, a beast that wants discourse of reason
Would have mourned longer—married with my uncle,
My father's brother, but no more like my father
155 Than I to Hercules.* Within a month,
Ere yet the salt of most unrighteous tears
Had left the flushing in her galled eyes,
She married. O, most wicket speed, to post
With such **dexterity** to incestuous* sheets!
160 It is not, nor cannot come to good.
But break my heart, for I must hold my tongue.

        Enter HORATIO, MARCELLUS, *and* BARNARDO.

HORATIO
Hail to your lordship!

HAMLET
I am glad to see you well.
Horatio—or I do forget myself.

HORATIO
165 The same, my lord, and your poor servant ever.

HAMLET
Sir, my good friend. I'll change that name with you.
And what make you from Wittenberg, Horatio?
Marcellus.

MARCELLUS
My good lord!

HAMLET
170 I am very glad to see you.
[*to* BARNARDO] Good even, sir.—
But what, in faith, make you from Wittenberg?

---

151   *Niobe* Punished by the gods with the death of her children, the grief-stricken
mother was changed into a stone that wept forever.

155   *Hercules* not only a superman in Greek and Roman mythology, but in Shakespeare's
time a figure who represented moral decisiveness and resolute action

hunger for him even more. And yet, within a month
(don't let me think of it—weakness, your name is woman!),
just a short month, before the shoes were old
in which she followed my poor father's body,   150
like Niobe, all in tears—why, she—yes, she—
(Oh, God, a beast that lacks the ability to reason
would have mourned longer!), married my uncle,
my father's brother, but no more like my father
than I'm like Hercules. Within a month,   155
before the salt of her unfaithful tears
had stopped reddening her sore eyes,
she married. Oh, what wicked speed, to hurry
so easily to an incestuous bed!
It isn't good, and can bring no good.   160
But I must hold my tongue, even if my heart breaks.

      HORATIO, MARCELLUS, *and* BARNARDO *enter.*

HORATIO
Hail to your lordship.

HAMLET
I am glad to see that you are well.
Why, it's Horatio—unless I've forgotten who *I* am!

HORATIO
Yes, my lord—and always your humble servant.   165

HAMLET
Sir, you're my good friend. Let *me* take the name of servant.
And what are you doing away from Wittenberg, Horatio?—
Hello, Marcellus.

MARCELLUS
My good lord.

HAMLET
I am very glad to see you. (*to* BARNARDO) Good evening, sir.   170
(*to* HORATIO) But really, why are you away from Wittenberg?

---

159   *incestuous* According to the moral theology of the time, marriage with a brother's
wife was incestuous.

HORATIO

A truant disposition, good my lord.

HAMLET

I would not hear your enemy say so,
175 Nor shall you do my ear that violence
To make it truster of your own report
Against yourself. I know you are no truant.
But what is your affair in Elsinore?
We'll teach you to drink deep ere you depart.

HORATIO

180 My lord, I came to see your father's funeral.

HAMLET

I prithee do not mock me, fellow student.
I think it was to see my mother's wedding.

HORATIO

Indeed, my lord, it followed hard upon.

HAMLET

Thrift, thrift, Horatio. The funeral baked meats
185 Did coldly furnish forth the marriage tables.
Would I had met my dearest foe in heaven
Or ever I had seen that day, Horatio!
My father—methinks I see my father.

HORATIO

Where, my lord?

HAMLET

190   In my mind's eye, Horatio.

HORATIO

I saw him once. 'A was a goodly king.

HAMLET

'A was a man, take him for all in all,
I shall not look upon his like again.

HORATIO

My lord, I think I saw him yesternight.

HAMLET

195 Saw? Who?

HORATIO

A lazy state of mind, my good lord.

HAMLET

I wouldn't allow an enemy of yours to say so,
nor will I let you do violence to my ears   175
by letting them believe your own accusation
against yourself. I know that you're no shirker.
What's your business in Elsinore?
We'll teach you to do some heavy drinking before you leave.

HORATIO

My lord, I came to see your father's funeral.   180

HAMLET

I beg you not to tease me, fellow student.
I think you came to see my mother's wedding.

HORATIO

Indeed, my lord, it happened soon afterward.

HAMLET

That was out of thrift, Horatio. The baked pies at the funeral
were served as cold leftovers at the wedding.   185
I'd rather have met my worst enemy in heaven
before I saw that day, Horatio!
My father—I think I see my father.

HORATIO

Where, my lord?

HAMLET

In my mind's eye, Horatio.   190

HORATIO

I saw him once. He was a fine king.

HAMLET

He was a man, perfect in every way.
I will not see anyone like him again.

HORATIO

My lord, I think I saw him last night.

HAMLET

Saw who?   195

HORATIO
My lord, the King your father.

HAMLET
                         The King my father?

HORATIO
Season your admiration for a while
With an attent ear till I may deliver
200   Upon the witness of these gentlemen
This marvel to you.

HAMLET
                    For God's love let me hear!

HORATIO
Two nights together had these gentlemen,
Marcellus and Barnardo, on their watch
205   In the dead waste and middle of the night
Been thus encountered. A figure like your father,
Armed at point exactly, cap-a-pe,
Appears before them, and with solemn march
Goes slow and stately by them. Thrice he walked
210   By their oppressed and fear-surprised eyes,
Within his truncheon's length, whilst they, distilled
Almost to jelly with the act of fear,
Stand dumb and speak not to him. This to me
In dreadful secrecy impart they did,
215   And I with them the third night kept the watch,
Where, as they had delivered, both in time,
Form of the thing, each word made true and good,
The apparition comes. I knew your father.
These hands are not more like.

HAMLET
220   But where was this?

MARCELLUS
My lord, upon the platform where we watched.

HAMLET
Did you not speak to it?

HORATIO

  My lord, the King your father.

HAMLET

  The King my father?

HORATIO

  Control your amazement for a moment
  and listen closely, while I report
  the amazing thing that these gentlemen and I   200
  have witnessed.

HAMLET

  For the love of God, tell me!

HORATIO

  On two successive nights, these gentlemen,
  Marcellus and Barnardo, encountered it
  during their watch in the deathly, silent   205
  middle of the night. The figure looked exactly like your father,
  fully armored from head to foot;
  he appeared before them, and with a solemn step
  passed by them—slowly and with dignity. Three times he walked
  past their stunned and terrified eyes   210
  within the length of his staff—while they, melted
  almost into jelly by the effects of fear,
  stood dumbly and didn't speak to him. They told
  me all this in frightened secrecy,
  so I kept watch with them on the third night;   215
  and just as they had reported, the apparition came
  in its expected hour and form;
  every word they'd told me was true. I knew your father (*holding up
      his hands*);
  the figure was as much like him as my hands are alike.

HAMLET

  But where did this happen?   220

MARCELLUS

  My lord, on the platform where we keep watch.

HAMLET

  Didn't you speak to it?

HORATIO

My lord, I did;
But answer made it none. Yet once methought
225   It lifted up its head and did address
Itself to motion like as it would speak:
But even then the morning cock crew loud,
And at the sound it shrunk in haste away
And vanished from our sight.

HAMLET

'Tis very strange.
230

HORATIO

As I do live, my honored lord, 'tis true,
And we did think it writ down in our duty
To let you know of it.

HAMLET

Indeed, indeed, sirs, but this troubles me.
235   Hold you the watch tonight?

ALL

We do, my lord.

HAMLET

Armed, say you?

ALL

Armed, my lord.

HAMLET

From top to toe?

ALL

240   My lord, from head to foot.

HAMLET

Then saw you not his face.

HORATIO

O, yes, my lord. He wore his beaver up.

HAMLET

What, looked he frowningly?

HORATIO

A countenance more in sorrow than in anger.

HORATIO
My lord, I did,
but it made no reply. And yet, I once thought
it lifted its head and began   225
to move, as if it meant to speak.
But right then, the morning rooster crowed loudly,
and it shrank hastily away at the sound
and vanished from our sight.

HAMLET
This is very strange.   230

HORATIO
My honored lord, it's true, as surely as I live.
And we thought it our lawful duty
to let you know about it.

HAMLET
Indeed, sirs. But this troubles me.
Are you keeping watch tonight?   235

ALL
We are, my lord.

HAMLET
He was armed, you say?

ALL
Armed, my lord.

HAMLET
From head to toe?

ALL
My lord, from head to foot.   240

HAMLET
Then you didn't see his face?

HORATIO
Oh, yes, my lord. He wore his visor up.

HAMLET
Well, then, was he frowning?

HORATIO
His expression seemed more sorrowful than angry.

HAMLET

245   Pale or red?

HORATIO

Nay, very pale.

HAMLET

                And fixed his eyes upon you?

HORATIO

Most constantly.

HAMLET

                I would I had been there.

HORATIO

250   It would have much amazed you.

HAMLET

Very like. Stayed it long?

HORATIO

While one with moderate haste might tell a hundred.

BARNARDO / MARCELLUS

Longer, longer.

HORATIO

Not when I saw 't.

HAMLET

255   His beard was grizzled, no?

HORATIO

It was as I have seen it in his life,
A sable silvered.

HAMLET

            I will watch tonight.
Perchance 'twill walk again.

HORATIO

260   I warrant it will.

HAMLET

If it assume my noble father's person,
I'll speak to it though hell itself should gape

HAMLET
Was he pale or flushed? 245

HORATIO
Indeed, very pale.

HAMLET
And he fixed his eyes straight at you?

HORATIO
The whole time.

HAMLET
I wish I had been there.

HORATIO
It would have amazed you greatly. 250

HAMLET
Undoubtedly. Did it stay long?

HORATIO
As long as it would take to count to a hundred at a moderate rate.

BARNARDO and **MARCELLUS**
Longer, longer.

HORATIO
Not when I saw it.

HAMLET
His beard was gray, was it? 255

HORATIO
It looked just like it did when I saw him alive—
black streaked with white.

HAMLET
I'll join you on your watch tonight.
Perhaps it will come again.

HORATIO
I promise that it will. 260

HAMLET
If it takes my noble father's shape,
I'll speak to it, even if hell itself should open up

And bid me hold my peace.* I pray you all,
If you have hitherto concealed this sight,
265   Let it be tenable in your silence still,
And whatsomever else shall hap tonight,
Give it an understanding but no tongue;
I will requite your loves. So fare you well.
Upon the platform 'twixt eleven and twelve
270   I'll visit you.

ALL

                Our duty to your honor.

HAMLET

Your loves, as mine to you. Farewell.

    Exeunt [all but HAMLET].

My father's spirit—in arms? All is not well.
I doubt some foul play. Would the night were come!
275   Till then sit still, my soul. Foul deeds will rise,
Though all the earth o'erwhelm them, to men's eyes.

    Exit.

---

263   *peace* Hamlet considers the possibility that the spirit may be a trick of the devil,
an evil spirit sent to tempt him.

and command me to be quiet. I beg you all,
if you have kept what you've seen a secret so far,
continue to be silent about it;   265
and whatever else should happen tonight,
bear witness to it, but say nothing about it.
I will repay your kind loyalty. So farewell.
I'll visit you upon the platform   270
between eleven and twelve.

ALL

We owe our duty to your honor.

HAMLET

And be friends with me, as I am to you. Farewell.

All except HAMLET *exit.*

My father's spirit—in armor! All is not well.
I suspect some treacherous crime. I wish night were here!
Until then, be patient, my soul. Wicked deeds will reveal   275
themselves to men's eyes, even if all the earth tries to
    cover them.

He exits.

ACT I, SCENE III

[A room.] Enter LAERTES *and* OPHELIA, *his sister.*

LAERTES

My necessaries are embarked. Farewell.
And, sister, as the winds give benefit
And convoy is assistant, do not sleep,
But let me hear from you.

OPHELIA

5   Do you doubt that?

LAERTES

For Hamlet, and the trifling of his favor,
Hold it a fashion and a toy in blood,
A violet in the youth of primy nature,
Forward, not permanent, sweet, not lasting,
10   The perfume and suppliance of a minute,
No more.

OPHELIA

        No more but so?

LAERTES

                   Think it no more.
For nature crescent does not grow alone
15   In thews and bulk, but as this temple waxes,
The inward service of the mind and soul
Grows wide withal. Perhaps he loves you now,
And now no soil nor cautel doth besmirch
The virtue of his will; but you must fear,
20   His greatness weighed, his will is not his own.
For he himself is subject to his birth.
He may not, as unvalued persons do,
Carve for himself; for on his choice depends
The safety and health of this whole state;
25   And therefore must his choice be circumscribed
Until the voice and yielding of that body
Whereof he is the head. Then if he says he loves you,
It fits your wisdom so far to believe it
As he in his particular act and place
30   May give his saying deed, which is no further

ACT 1, SCENE 3

A room. LAERTES *and his sister* OPHELIA *enter.*

LAERTES

My baggage has gone on ahead of me. Farewell.
And sister, whenever the winds are favorable
and ships are available, do not sleep
without having written to me.

OPHELIA

Do you think I'd do otherwise?   5

LAERTES

As for Hamlet's trifling affection for you,
consider it only a fleeting, amorous whim;
a springtime violet in early bloom—
eager but not permanent, sweet but not lasting;
something that sweetens and delights for a minute,   10
but nothing more.

OPHELIA

Nothing more than that?

LAERTES

Think nothing more of it.
For a person does not grow only
in strength and size; but as this human body develops,   15
the inward powers of the mind and soul
grow larger as well. Perhaps he loves you now,
and no blemishes or falsehoods yet stain
the virtue of his intentions. But you should be fearful that
his will is not his own when his high rank is considered— 20
for he himself must obey the requirements of his noble birth.
He may not choose for himself
as lesser people do, because the safety and the health
of this whole nation depend upon his choices.
And therefore, his choice of a wife must be limited   25
by the approval and agreement of the state of Denmark,
of which he is the head. So if he says that he loves you,
it's wise of you to believe him only so far as he,
in his princely position,
can back up his words with deeds—which is only as far   30

Than the main voice of Denmark goes withal.
Then weigh what loss your honor may sustain
If with too credent ear you list his songs,
Or lose your heart, or your chaste treasure open
35   To his unmastered importunity.
Fear it, Ophelia, fear it, my dear sister,
And keep you in the rear of your affection,
Out of the shot and danger of desire.
The chariest maid is prodigal enough
40   If she unmask her beauty to the moon.
Virtue itself scapes not calumnious strokes.
The canker galls the infants of the spring
Too oft before their buttons be disclosed,
And in the morn and liquid dew of youth
45   Contagious blastements are most imminent.
Be wary then; best safety lies in fear;
Youth to itself rebels, though none else near.

OPHELIA
I shall the effect of this good lesson keep
As watchman to my heart. But, good my brother,
50   Do not, as some ungracious pastors do,
Show me the steep and thorny way to heaven,
Whiles, like a puffed and reckless libertine,
Himself the primrose path of dalliance treads
And recks not his own rede.

LAERTES
55   O, fear me not.

Enter POLONIUS.

I stay too long. But here my father comes.
A double blessing is a double grace;
Occasion smiles upon a second leave.

POLONIUS
Yet here, Laertes? Aboard, aboard, for shame!
60   The wind sits in the shoulder of your sail,
And you are stayed for. There—my blessing with thee,
And these few precepts in thy memory
Look thou character. Give thy thoughts not tongue,
Nor any unproportioned thought his act.

as the majority opinion of Denmark will permit.
So consider how much of a loss your honor might suffer
if you listen to his songs with too trusting an ear,
or lose your heart and give up your virginity
to his insistent pleading.   35
Beware of it, Ophelia; beware of it, dear sister;
restrain yourself from acting according your feelings,
and stay out of the path of dangerous desires.
The most cautious virgin shows enough recklessness
when she displays her beauty by dim moonlight.   40
Even the most virtuous people don't escape gossip and lies.
Too often, the cankerworm kills young flowers of spring
before their buds can even open;
and it is in the damp morning air of youth
that infectious blights are most likely to strike.   45
So be wary; it is safest to be afraid.
Youth tends toward recklessness, even when no temptation is
    near.

OPHELIA
I shall keep this wise advice
as a watchman over my heart. But my good brother,
do not be like some ungodly pastors   50
and show me the steep and thorny path to heaven
while, like a proud and reckless libertine,
you follow the flowery path of pleasure
and ignore your own advice.

LAERTES
Oh, don't worry about me.   55

        POLONIUS *enters.*

I'm waiting too long. But here comes my father.
Getting a second blessing from him is doubly fortunate.
This new farewell is a lucky sign.

POLONIUS
Still here, Laertes? Get aboard, get aboard, for shame!
The wind is favorable,   60
and you are waited for. (*placing his hand on* LAERTES's *head*)
    There, my blessing is with you.
And be sure to write down these few sayings
in your memory. Don't speak your thoughts aloud,

65 Be thou familiar, but by no means vulgar.
Those friends thou hast, and their adoption tried,
Grapple them unto thy soul with hoops of steel,
But do not dull thy palm with entertainment
Of each new-hatched, unfledged courage. Beware
70 Of entrance to a quarrel; but being in,
Bear 't that th' opposed may beware of thee.
Give every man thine ear, but few thy voice;
Take each man's censure, but reserve thy judgment.
Costly thy habit as thy purse can buy,
75 But not expressed in fancy; rich, not gaudy,
For the apparel oft proclaims the man,
And they in France of the best rank and station
Are of a most select and generous, chief in that.
Neither a borrower nor a lender be,
80 For loan oft loses both itself and friend,
And borrowing dulleth edge of husbandry.
This above all, to thine own self be true,
And it must follow, as the night the day,
Thou canst not then be false to any man.
85 Farewell. My blessing season this in thee!

LAERTES
Most humbly do I take my leave, my lord.

POLONIUS
The time invests you. Go, you servants tend.

LAERTES
Farewell, Ophelia, and remember well
What I have said to you.

OPHELIA
90 'Tis in my memory locked,
And you yourself shall keep the key of it.

LAERTES
Farewell.

Exit LAERTES.

nor act on any unconsidered impulse.
Be friendly, but by no means indiscriminate in your friendships. 65
When you have friends who've proved their loyalty to you,
fasten them to your soul with hoops of steel;
but do not wear out your handshake to please
every immature, high-spirited young man. Beware
of getting into a quarrel; but once you're in, 70
see it through so that your opponent will beware of you.
Listen to every man, but speak to few.
Consider every man's opinion, but keep your own opinions to
    yourself.
Let your clothes be as expensive as your purse can pay for,
but wear nothing too fancy; let it be costly, not gaudy, 75
for clothes often tell much about a man,
and the finest noblemen of France
take particular care in how they dress.
Be neither a borrower nor a lender,
for when you loan money, you often lose both it and your
    friend, 80
and borrowing tends to make you less thrifty.
Above all else, be honest with yourself,
and as surely as night follows day,
you cannot then be dishonest to any man.
Farewell. May my blessing make this advice fruitful. 85

LAERTES

I most humbly leave you, my lord.

POLONIUS

You're pressed for time. Go, see to your servants.

LAERTES

Farewell, Ophelia, and remember well
what I have said to you.

OPHELIA

It's locked in my memory, 90
and you yourself will keep the key to it.

LAERTES

Farewell.

LAERTES *exits.*

POLONIUS

What is 't, Ophelia, he hath said to you?

OPHELIA

So please you, something touching the Lord Hamlet.

POLONIUS

95　Marry,* well bethought.
'Tis told me he hath very oft of late
Given private time to you, and you yourself
Have of your audience been most free and bounteous.
If it be so—as so 'tis put on me,
100　And that in way of caution—I must tell you
You do not understand yourself so clearly
As it behooves my daughter and your honor.
What is between you? Give me up the truth.

OPHELIA

He hath, my lord, of late made many tenders*
105　Of his affection to me.

POLONIUS

Affection pooh! You speak like a green girl,
Unsifted in such **perilous** circumstance.
Do you believe his tenders, as you call them?

OPHELIA

I do not know, my lord, what I should think.

POLONIUS

110　Marry, I will teach you. Think yourself a baby
That you have ta'en these tenders for true pay
Which are not sterling. Tender yourself more dearly,
Or (not to crack the wind of the poor phrase)
Tend'ring it thus you'll tender me a fool.

OPHELIA

115　My lord, he hath importuned me with love
In honorable fashion.

95　*marry* Originally the name of the Virgin Mary, the word was used as a mild oath
or introductory expression, meaning "indeed" or "to be sure."

104　*tenders* As Ophelia uses it, the word means "offers," but in what follows
Polonius plays with the sense of the phrase "legal tender." In lines 110–114,

POLONIUS
What did he say to you, Ophelia?

OPHELIA
If you wish to know, it had something to do with Lord Hamlet.

POLONIUS
Indeed, I'm glad you reminded me.   95
I've heard that lately he has spent private time with you
very often, and that you yourself
have been very kind and generous in your attention to him.
If this is true (and so I've been told,
in a warning way), I must tell you   100
that you don't understand yourself as well
as is proper for my daughter and your honor.
What's going on between you? Tell me the truth.

OPHELIA
My lord, he has lately made many offers
of affection to me.   105

POLONIUS
Affection! Pah! You're talking like an inexperienced girl,
naive in such a dangerous situation.
Do you believe his "offers," as you call them?

OPHELIA
My lord, I do not know what I should think.

POLONIUS
Indeed, I will teach you. Think of yourself as a baby   110
for having taken these "offers" for true pay,
when they aren't even legitimate currency. Offer yourself at
   greater value,
or else (not to run an old saying so hard
that I leave it breathless), you'll offer yourself to me as a fool.

OPHELIA
My lord, he has wooed me lovingly,   115
and in an honorable fashion—

---

he plays with "tender," so that "you'll tender me a fool" may have three
meanings: make me look foolish, show me that you are a fool, present me with
a fool (i.e., an illegitimate child).

POLONIUS

Ay, fashion you may call it. Go to, go to!

OPHELIA

And hath given countenance to his speech, my lord,
With almost all the holy vows of heaven.

POLONIUS

120 Ay, springes to catch woodcocks. I do know,
When the blood burns, how prodigal the soul
Lends the tongue vows. These blazes, daughter,
Giving more light than heat, extinct in both,
Even in their promise, as it is a-making,
125 You must not take for fire. From this time
Be something scanter of your maiden presence.
Set your entreatments at a higher rate
Than a command to parley. For Lord Hamlet,
Believe so much in him that he is young,
130 And with a larger tether may he walk
Than may be given you. In few, Ophelia,
Do not believe his vows, for they are brokers,
Not of that dye which their investments show,
But mere implorators of unholy suits,
135 Breathing like sanctified and pious bawds,
The better to beguile. This is for all:
I would not, in plain terms, from this time forth
Have you so slander any moment leisure
As to give words or talk with the Lord Hamlet.
140 Look to 't, I charge you. Come your ways.

OPHELIA

I shall obey, my lord.

Exeunt.

POLONIUS

Yes, "fashion" is the right word for it. Come now, come now!

OPHELIA

—and has supported his words, my lord,
with almost all the holy vows of heaven.

POLONIUS

Yes, and they're snares to catch stupid birds. I know   120
how generously the soul lends words to the tongue
when the blood grows hot with passion. Daughter, these
    fleeting blazes
give more light than heat, and both light and heat
go out as soon as a promise has been made;
so you mustn't mistake this for true fire. From now on,   125
be more sparing with your virgin company.
Set your interviews with him at a higher price,
rather than give in to his every wish. As for Lord Hamlet,
keep in mind that he is young,
and he has greater freedom   130
than you do. In short, Ophelia,
do not believe his vows, for they are go-betweens—
not holy, as their clothes make them appear,
but tempters toward sinful deeds,
speaking like devout, pious pimps   135
to better trick you. Once and for all,
in plain words, from now on I don't want you
to disgrace another moment of your leisure time
having words or conversation with Lord Hamlet.
See to it, I command you. Come away.   140

OPHELIA

I shall obey you, my lord.

    They exit.

ACT I, SCENE IV

[*A guard platform.*] *Enter* HAMLET, HORATIO, *and* MARCELLUS.

HAMLET
The air bites shrewdly; it is very cold.

HORATIO
It is a nipping and an eager air.

HAMLET
What hour now?

HORATIO
I think it lacks of twelve.

MARCELLUS
5   No, it is struck.

HORATIO
Indeed? I heard it not. It then draws near the season
Wherein the spirit held his wont to walk.

A flourish of trumpets, and two pieces go off.

What does this mean, my lord?

HAMLET
The King doth wake tonight and takes his rouse,
10   Keeps wassail, and the swagg'ring upspring reels,
And as he drains his draughts of Rhenish down
The kettledrum and trumpet thus bray out
The triumph of his pledge.

HORATIO
Is it a custom?

HAMLET
15   Ay, marry, is 't.
But to my mind, though I am native here
And to the manner born, it is a custom
More honored in the breach than the observance.
This heavy-headed revel east and west
20   Makes us traduced and taxed of other nations.
They clepe us drunkards and with swinish phrase

ACT 1, SCENE 4

A guard platform. HAMLET, HORATIO, *and* MARCELLUS *enter.*

HAMLET
The air bites bitterly; it is very cold.

HORATIO
It is a nipping, sharp wind.

HAMLET
What time is it now?

HORATIO
I think it is just before twelve.

MARCELLUS
No, the clock has already struck.   5

HORATIO
Indeed, I didn't hear it. Then it is near the time
when the spirit is accustomed to come by.

> *A trumpet fanfare; then two cannons are fired.*

What does this mean, my lord?

HAMLET
The King is staying awake tonight—drinking,
partying, and dancing a wild German dance;   10
and as he drains his cups of Rhine wine,
the kettledrums and trumpets announce
his success at chugging down each cup at one try.

HORATIO
Is this a custom?

HAMLET
Yes, indeed it is;   15
but in my opinion (though I'm a native here
and used to it from birth), it is a custom
better honored by breaking it than observing it.
All this excessive drinking causes us Danes to be
blamed and criticized by other nations, east and west.   20
They call us drunkards, and stain our honor

Soil our addition, and indeed it takes
From our achievements, though performed at height,
The pith and marrow of our attribute.
25 So oft it chances in particular men
That for some vicious mole of nature in them,
As in their birth, wherein they are not guilty,
(Since nature cannot choose his origin)
By the o'ergrowth of some complexion,
30 Oft breaking down the pales and forts of reason,
Or by some habit that too much o'erleavens
The form of plausive manners, that (these men,
Carrying, I say, the stamp of one defect,
Being nature's livery, or fortune's star)
35 Their virtues else, be they as pure as grace,
As infinite as man may undergo,
Shall in the general censure take corruption
From that particular fault. The dram of evil
Doth all the noble substance of a dout
40 To his own scandal.

       Enter GHOST.

HORATIO
                Look, my lord, it comes.

HAMLET
Angels and ministers of grace defend us!
Be thou a spirit of health or goblin damned,
Bring with thee airs from heaven or blasts from hell,
45 Be they intents wicked or charitable,
Thou com'st in such a questionable shape
That I will speak to thee. I'll call thee "Hamlet,"
"King," "Father," "Royal Dane." O, answer me!
Let me not burst in ignorance, but tell
50 Why thy canonized bones, hearsed in death,
Have burst their cerements, why the sepulcher
Wherein we saw thee quietly interred
Hath oped his ponderous and marble jaws
To cast thee up again. What may this mean
55 That thou, dead corse, again in complete steel,
Revisits thus the glimpses of the moon,

by comparing us to pigs. And indeed, despite
our greatest achievements, this custom robs us
to the very heart of our reputation.
Likewise, it often happens that an individual man   25
suffers from some unlucky natural flaw—
for example, because of his birth, of which he is not guilty,
since no one can choose his parentage;
or because some fault in his personality
too often overcomes his reason;   30
or because some habit radically alters
his formerly pleasant character. Such a man,
I say, has been stamped by one defect
which he got from nature or simple bad luck;
but all his virtues, even if they're as pure as heaven   35
and as plentiful as one man may possess,
will come under general criticism, corrupted
by that single fault. Just a small drop of evil
often wipes away all traces of nobility,
bringing disrepute.   40

     The GHOST *enters.*

HORATIO
Look, my lord—it has come.

HAMLET
Angels and messengers of God, defend us!
Whether you're a good spirit, or an evil one suffering damnation;
whether you bring breezes from heaven or blasts from hell;
whether your intentions are wicked or kindly;   45
it appears that you can be asked questions,
so I will speak to you. I'll call you "Hamlet,"
"King," "Father," "Royal Dane." Oh, answer me!
Don't let me burst in ignorance, but tell me
why your bones, blessed by Christian burial in a coffin,   50
have burst from their shroud; why the tomb
where we saw you quietly laid to rest
has opened its heavy marble jaws
to cast you out again. What does it mean
that you, dead corpse, again fully armored,   55
have come out into the moonlight,

Making night hideous, and we fools of nature*
So horridly to shake our disposition
With thoughts beyond the reaches of our souls?
60   Say, why is this? Wherefore? What should we do?

GHOST *beckons* HAMLET.

HORATIO
It beckons you to go away with it,
As if it some impartment did desire
To you alone.

MARCELLUS
                            Look with what courteous action
65   It waves you to a more removed ground.
But do not go with it.

HORATIO
                            No, by no means.

HAMLET
It will not speak. Then I will follow it.

HORATIO
Do not, my lord.

HAMLET
70   Why, what should be the fear?
I do not set my life at a pin's fee,
And for my soul, what can it do to that,
Being a thing immortal as itself?
It waves me forth again. I'll follow it.

HORATIO
75   What if it tempt you toward the flood, my lord,
Or to the dreadful summit of the cliff
That beetles o'er his base into the sea,
And there assume some other horrible form,
Which might deprive your sovereignty of reason
80   And draw you into madness? Think of it.
The very place puts toys of desperation,
Without more motive, into every brain

57   *fools of nature* A fool of nature normally meant an idiot, but Hamlet uses the
term to include everyone who is merely "natural" and therefore baffled by the
supernatural.

making the night frightful, and causing us weak mortals
to wrack our minds so horribly
with thoughts beyond our souls' grasp?
Tell me, why is this? What is the reason? What should we do?   60

The GHOST *makes a gesture to* HAMLET.

HORATIO

It summons you to go away with it,
as if it wished to say something
to you alone.

MARCELLUS

Look—with a courteous gesture
it waves for you to go to a place farther off.   65
But do not go with it.

HORATIO

No, by no means.

HAMLET

It will not speak. So I will follow it.

HORATIO

Do not, my lord.

HAMLET

Why, what's there to be afraid of?   70
I don't consider my life to be worth a pin.
And as for my soul, what can it do to hurt that,
since it's an immortal thing like itself?
It waves me toward him again. I'll follow it.

HORATIO

What if it lures you toward the ocean, my lord,   75
or to the fearful summit of a cliff
that juts far out over the sea,
and then takes on some other horrible form
which might deprive you of your powers of reason
and plunge you into madness? Think about it.   80
Even without any other motive, such a place
puts suicidal impulses into the mind of anyone

That looks so many fathoms to the sea
And hears it roar beneath.

HAMLET

85 It waves me still.—Go on, I'll follow thee.

MARCELLUS

You shall not go, my lord.

HAMLET

                              Hold off your hands!

HORATIO

Be ruled. You shall not go.

HAMLET

                              My fate cries out
90 And makes each petty arture in this body
As hardy as the Nemean lion's* nerve.
Still am I called! Unhand me, gentlemen.
By heaven, I'll make a ghost of him that lets me!
I say, away!—Go on. I'll follow thee.

        Exit GHOST, *and* HAMLET.

HORATIO

95 He waxes desperate with imagination.

MARCELLUS

Let's follow. 'Tis not fit thus to obey him.

HORATIO

Have after! To what issue will this come?

MARCELLUS

Something is rotten in the state of Denmark.

HORATIO

Heaven will direct it.

MARCELLUS

                              Nay, let's follow him.

        Exeunt.

---

91 *Nemean lion* One of the twelve labors of Hercules was the killing of this beast,
    which no weapon could harm. Hercules choked it to death.

who looks into the depths of the sea
and hears it roaring beneath him.

HAMLET
It keeps waving to me. (*to the* GHOST) Go on, I'll follow you.　　85

MARCELLUS
You will not go, my lord.

　　　　MARCELLUS and HORATIO *hold* HAMLET *back.*

HAMLET
Get your hands off me.

HORATIO
Do as we say. You will not go.

HAMLET
My fate cries out,
making each little ligament in this body　　90
as strong as the Nemean lion's muscles.
I'm still being called. Unhand me, gentlemen.
By heaven, I'll kill anyone who hinders me!
Get away, I say! (*to the* GHOST) Go on. I'll follow you.

　　　　The GHOST *and* HAMLET *exit.*

HORATIO
His imagination is driving him to desperation.　　95

MARCELLUS
Let's follow him. It's not right to obey him.

HORATIO
I will follow. How is this going to end?

MARCELLUS
Something is rotten in the state of Denmark.

HORATIO
Heaven will set things straight.

MARCELLUS
Even so, let's follow him.　　100

　　　　They exit.

ACT I, SCENE V

[*The battlements.*] *Enter* GHOST *and* HAMLET.

HAMLET
Whither wilt thou lead me? Speak; I'll go no further.

GHOST
Mark me.

HAMLET
   I will.

GHOST
      My hour is almost come,
5 When I to sulf'rous and tormenting flames
Must render up myself.

HAMLET
        Alas, poor ghost.

GHOST
Pity me not, but lend thy serious hearing
To what I shall unfold.

HAMLET
10 Speak. I am bound to hear.

GHOST
So art thou to revenge, when thou shalt hear.

HAMLET
What?

GHOST
I am thy father's spirit,
Doomed for a certain term to walk the night
15 And for the day confined to fast in fires,
Till the foul crimes done in my days of nature
Are burnt and purged away. But that I am forbid
To tell the secrets of my prison house,
I could a tale unfold whose lightest word
20 Would harrow up thy soul, freeze thy young blood,
Make thy two eyes like stars start from their spheres,
Thy knotted and combined locks to part,
And each particular hair to stand on end
Like quills upon the fearful porpentine.

ACT 1, SCENE 5

The battlements. The GHOST *and* HAMLET *enter.*

HAMLET
Where do you wish to lead me? Speak; I'll go no farther.

GHOST
Listen to me.

HAMLET
I will.

GHOST
The hour has almost come
when I must return to tormenting flames   5
of burning sulfur.

HAMLET
Alas, poor ghost!

GHOST
Do not pity me, but pay serious attention
to what I'm about to tell you.

HAMLET
Speak. I am ready to hear it.   10

GHOST
And you'll be obliged to take revenge, once you've heard it.

HAMLET
What?

GHOST
I am your father's spirit,
doomed for a certain length of time to walk the night,
and during the day to be held captive in fire, and repent   15
until the foul sins committed during my mortal life
are burned and purged away. If I weren't forbidden
to tell the secrets of my prison,
I could tell a tale, the most cheerful word of which
would rip your soul apart, freeze your young blood,   20
make your two eyes leap out of their proper spheres like stars,
and cause your combed and bound-up hair to part,
and each individual hair to stand on end
like quills on a frightened porcupine.

25 But this eternal blazon must not be
    To ears of flesh and blood. List, list, O, list!
    If thou didst ever thy dear father love—

HAMLET
    O God!

GHOST
    Revenge his foul and most unnatural murder.

HAMLET
30 Murder?

GHOST
    Murder most foul, as in the best it is,
    But this most foul, strange, and unnatural.

HAMLET
    Haste me to know 't, that I, with wings as swift
    As meditation or the thoughts of love,
35 May sweep to my revenge.

GHOST
                                I find thee apt,
    And duller shouldst thou be than the fat weed
    That roots itself in ease on Lethe wharf,*
    Wouldst thou not stir in this. Now, Hamlet, hear.
40 'Tis given out that, sleeping in my orchard,
    A serpent stung me. So the whole ear of Denmark
    Is by a forged process of my death
    Rankly abused. But know, thou noble youth,
    The serpent that did sting thy father's life
45 Now wears his crown.

HAMLET
    O my prophetic soul! My uncle?

GHOST
    Ay, that incestuous, that adulterate beast,
    With witchcraft of his wits, with traitorous gifts—
    O wicked wit and gifts, that have the power
50 So to seduce!—won to his shameful lust
    The will of my most seeming-virtuous queen.

---

38 *Lethe wharf* the bank of the river of forgetfulness in Hades

But this description of eternity must not be spoken   25
to ears of flesh and blood. Listen, listen, oh listen!
If you ever loved your dear father—

HAMLET
Oh, God!

GHOST
—revenge his foul and most abnormal murder.

HAMLET
Murder?   30

GHOST
A very foul murder—as murder is even at its best.
But this one is unusually foul, strange, and abnormal.

HAMLET
Tell me about it quickly, so I may
fly on toward revenge with wings as swift as thought
or feelings of love.   35

GHOST
I see that you're eager;
and you'd have to be duller than the thick weed
that grows and thrives on the banks of the river Lethe
not to be stirred by this. Now, Hamlet, listen.
It's been said that a snake stung me
while I was sleeping in my garden. Every ear in Denmark   40
has been deeply misled by this false story
of my death. But know the truth, noble youth,
that the snake that stung your father's life away
now wears his crown.   45

HAMLET
Oh, my soul as much as guessed it! My uncle?

GHOST
Yes, that incestuous and adulterous beast;
with bewitching cleverness and treacherous gifts
(oh, what wicked cleverness and gifts, to have such power
to seduce!), he won over the willingness   50
of my seemingly virtuous queen to his shameful lust.

O Hamlet, what a falling-off was there,
From me, whose love was of that dignity
That it went hand in hand even with the vow
55 I made to her in marriage, and to decline
Upon a wretch whose natural gifts were poor
To those of mine.
But virtue, as it never will be moved,
Though lewdness court it in a shape of heaven,
60 So lust, though to a radiant angel linked,
Will sate itself in a celestial bed
And prey on garbage.
But soft, methinks I scent the morning air;
Brief let me be. Sleeping within my orchard,
65 My custom always of the afternoon,
Upon my secure hour thy uncle stole
With juice of cursed hebona* in a vial,
And in the porches of my ears did pour
The leperous distillment, whose effect
70 Holds such an **enmity** with blood of man
That swift as quicksilver it courses through
The natural gates and alleys of the body,
And with a sudden vigor it doth posset
And curd, like eager droppings into milk,
75 The thin and wholesome blood. So did it mine,
And a most instant tetter barked about
Most lazarlike with vile and loathsome crust
All my smooth body.
Thus was I, sleeping, by a brother's hand
80 Of life, of crown, of queen at once dispatched,
Cut off even in the blossoms of my sin,
Unhouseled, disappointed, unaneled,
No reck'ning made, but sent to my account
With all my imperfections on my head.
85 O, horrible! O, horrible! Most horrible!
If thou hast nature in thee, bear it not.
Let not the royal bed of Denmark be
A couch for luxury and damned incest.
But howsomever thou pursues this act,
90 Taint not my mind, not let thy soul **contrive**

---

67   *hebona* literally, "ebony," but Shakespeare apparently equates it with "henbane,"
a poison

Oh, Hamlet, what a moral failure was hers!
My love for her was so proper
that it went perfectly hand in hand with the vow
I made when I married her; but then she lowered herself   55
to a wretch whose physical attractions were so poor
compared to mine.
Virtue can never be seduced
even if lechery woos it in a heavenly shape;
but lust, even if it is married to a radiant angel,   60
will grow tired of a lawful, holy bed
and feed on garbage.
But wait—I think I smell the morning air.
Let me be brief. While I was sleeping in my garden
which was always my custom in the afternoon,   65
your uncle crept in during that unsuspecting moment
carrying the accursed juice of hebona in a bottle,
and he poured the leprosy-causing liquid
within the rim of my ear. Its effect
is so hostile to a man's blood   70
that it rushes as swiftly as quicksilver
through all the natural openings and passages of the body;
and suddenly and vigorously, it clots
and curdles the thin and healthy blood,
like acid when dropped into milk. It did that to my blood;
and instantly, as if I were a leper,   75
scabs appeared like tree bark all over my smooth body,
forming a vile and loathsome crust.
That's how, while I was sleeping, I was robbed by a brother's hand
of life, crown, and queen all at once.   80
And I was cut down while my sins were in full bloom,
without holy communion, absolution, or last rites;
I could make no confession, but was sent to my judgment
with all my misdeeds on my conscience.
Oh, horrible! Oh, horrible! Most horrible!   85
If you have any natural feelings, don't tolerate it.
Don't let the royal bed of Denmark be
a couch for lust and damned incest.
But however you go about this act,
keep your mind pure, and do not allow your soul to plot   90

Against thy mother aught. Leave her to heaven
And to those thorns that in her bosom lodge
To prick and sting her. Fare thee well at once.
The glowworm shows the matin to be near
95 And 'gins to pale his uneffectual fire.
Adieu, adieu, adieu. Remember me.

        Exit.

HAMLET
O all you host of heaven! O earth! What else?
And shall I couple hell? O fie! Hold, hold, my heart,
And you, my sinews, grow not instant old,
100 But bear me stiffly up. Remember thee?
Ay, thou poor ghost, whiles memory holds a seat
In this distracted globe. Remember thee?
Yea, from the table* of my memory
I'll wipe away all trivial fond records,
105 All saws of books, all forms, all pressures past
That youth and observation copied there,
And thy commandment all alone shall live
Within the book and volume of my brain,
Unmixed with baser matter. Yes, by heaven!
110 O most **pernicious** woman!
O villain, villain, smiling damned villain!
My tables—meet it is I set it down
That one may smile, and smile, and be a villain.
At least I am sure it may be so in Denmark.

        [*Writes.*]

115 So, uncle, there you are. Now to my word:
It is "Adieu, adieu, remember me."
I have sworn 't.

        Enter HORATIO *and* MARCELLUS.

HORATIO
My lord, my lord!

MARCELLUS
Lord Hamlet!

HORATIO
120 Heavens secure him!

---

103 *table* a small writing tablet or memorandum book

any deed against your mother. Leave her to God's judgment,
and let the thorns of remorse that are caught in her breast
prick and sting her. Farewell at once.
The glowworm shows that morning is near,
for his heatless light is beginning to fade. 95
Good-bye, good-bye, good-bye. Remember me.

He exits.

HAMLET
Oh, all you angels of heaven! Oh, earth! What else?
Should I add hell? Oh, no! Be still, be still, my heart,
and you, my muscles, do not grow old in an instant,
but hold me up firmly. Remember you? 100
Yes, poor ghost—as long as memory has its place
in my troubled head. Remember you?
Indeed, from the notebook of my memory,
I'll erase all trivial, foolish writings—
all sayings from books, all opinions, all past impressions 105
that I wrote down there from youthful observation,
and allow only your command to live
within the spacious book of my brain,
unmixed with lesser stuff. Yes, by heaven!
Oh, most destructive woman! 110
Oh, villain, villain, smiling damned villain!
Here's my notebook—it's proper that I write down
that one may smile and smile, and still be a villain.
At least I'm sure that this may be so in Denmark.

He writes in his notebook.

So much for you, uncle. Now for my promise. 115
It is, "Good-bye, good-bye, remember me."
I've sworn to do it.

HORATIO *and* MARCELLUS *enter.*

HORATIO
My lord, my lord!

MARCELLUS
Lord Hamlet!

HORATIO
May heaven protect him. 120

HAMLET
So be it!

MARCELLUS
Illo, ho, ho, ho, my lord!

HAMLET
Hillo, ho, ho boy! Come, bird, come.*

MARCELLUS
How is 't, my noble lord?

HORATIO
125   What news, my lord?

HAMLET
O, wonderful!

HORATIO
Good my lord, tell it.

HAMLET
                              No, you will reveal it.

HORATIO
Not I, my lord, by heaven.

MARCELLUS
130   Nor I, my lord.

HAMLET
How say you then? Would heart of man once think it?
But you'll be secret?

HORATIO / MARCELLUS
Ay, by heaven, my lord.

HAMLET
There's never a villain dwelling in all Denmark
135   But he's an arrant knave.

HORATIO
There needs no ghost, my lord, come from the grave
To tell us this.

---

123   *Come, bird, come* Hamlet answers Marcellus with the cry used by falconers to call their hawks.

HAMLET
(*aside*) May it, indeed!

MARCELLUS
Hey, hey, where are you, my lord!

HAMLET
Hey, hey you, boy! Come here, bird, come here!

MARCELLUS
What's happened, my noble lord?

HORATIO
What's the news, my lord?   125

HAMLET
Oh, it's amazing!

HORATIO
My good lord, tell us about it.

HAMLET
No, you will reveal it.

HORATIO
By heaven, my lord, I won't.

MARCELLUS
Nor I, my lord.

HAMLET
What do you say, then? Could any man ever imagine such   130
   a thing?
But you'll keep it secret?

HORATIO and **MARCELLUS**
By heaven, we will, my lord.

HAMLET
There's not a villain living in all of Denmark
who isn't a complete scoundrel.   135

HORATIO
My lord, no ghost needs to come from the grave
to tell us this.

HAMLET

> Why, right, you are in the right;
> And so, without more circumstance at all,
> I hold it fit that we shake hands and part:
> You, as your business and desire shall point you,
> For every man hath business and desire
> Such as it is, and for my own poor part,
> I will go pray.

140

HORATIO

> These are but wild and whirling words, my lord.

145

HAMLET

> I am sorry they offend you, heartily;
> Yes, faith, heartily.

HORATIO

> There's no offense, my lord.

HAMLET

> Yes, by Saint Patrick,* but there is, Horatio,
> And much offense too. Touching this vision here,
> It is an honest ghost—that let me tell you.
> For your desire to know what is between us,
> O'ermaster 't as you may. And now, good friends,
> As you are friends, scholars, and soldiers,
> Give me one poor request.

150

155

HORATIO

> What is 't, my lord? We will.

HAMLET

> Never make known what you have seen tonight.

HORATIO / MARCELLUS

> My lord, we will not.

HAMLET

> Nay, but swear 't.

HORATIO

> In faith, my lord, not I.

160

---

149   *Saint Patrick* thought to be the keeper of Purgatory, from where the Ghost has
      come. He was also the patron saint of confusion and mistakes.

HAMLET
　Why, you're right—you are quite right.
　And so, without any further fuss,
　I think it best that we shake hands and part;　　　　140
　you go wherever your business and desires direct you
　(for all men have business and desires,
　such as they are); and as for poor me,
　I will go pray.

HORATIO
　These are nothing but wild and perplexing words, my lord.　　145

HAMLET
　I am sincerely sorry if they offend you.
　Yes, indeed—sincerely.

HORATIO
　There's no offense, my lord.

HAMLET
　By Saint Patrick, yes, there is, Horatio—
　a great deal of offense, too. As for this vision here,　　150
　it is a genuine ghost—that much I can tell you.
　As for your desire to know what happened between us,
　overcome it however you may. And now, good friends
　(for you *are* friends—and scholars and soldiers),
　grant me one small request.　　155

HORATIO
　What is it, my lord? We'll do it.

HAMLET
　Never make known what you have seen tonight.

HORATIO and **MARCELLUS**
　My lord, we will not.

HAMLET
　No, swear to it.

HORATIO
　I swear, my lord, I won't.　　160

MARCELLUS

Nor I, my lord, in faith.

HAMLET

Upon my sword.

MARCELLUS

We have sworn, my lord, already.

HAMLET

Indeed, upon my sword, indeed.

GHOST *cries under the stage.*

165   Swear.

HAMLET

Ha, ha, boy, say'st thou so? Art thou there, truepenny?
Come on. You hear this fellow in the cellarage.
Consent to swear.

HORATIO

Propose the oath, my lord.

HAMLET

170   Never to speak of this that you have seen.
Swear by my sword.

GHOST [*beneath*]

Swear.

HAMLET

Hic et ubique? Then we'll shift our ground.
Come hither, gentlemen,
175   And lay your hands again upon my sword.
Swear by my sword
Never to speak of this that you have heard.

GHOST [*beneath*]

Swear by his sword.

HAMLET

Well said, old mole! Canst work i' th' earth so fast?
180   A worthy pioner! Once more remove, good friends.

MARCELLUS
Nor I, my lord, I swear.

HAMLET
Swear upon my sword.

MARCELLUS
My lord, we have sworn already.

HAMLET
But truly, swear upon my sword; do it.

GHOST (*calling from under the stage*)
Swear. 165

HAMLET
(*to the* GHOST) Ha, ha, boy—you say so, too? Are you there,
    honest chap?
(*to* MARCELLUS *and* HORATIO) Come on, you heard this fellow
    below us.
Agree to swear.

HORATIO
Propose the oath, my lord.

HAMLET
Never to speak of what you have seen here; 170
swear by my sword.

GHOST (*under the stage*)
Swear.

HAMLET
Here and everywhere? Then we'll move somewhere else.
Come over here, gentlemen,
and lay your hands upon my sword again. 175
Swear by my sword
never to speak what you have heard here.

GHOST (*under the stage*)
Swear by his sword.

HAMLET
Well said, old mole. Can you dig through the earth so fast?
An excellent miner! Let's move once again, good friends. 180

HORATIO
O day and night, but this is wondrous strange.

HAMLET
And therefore as a stranger give it welcome.
There are more things in heaven and earth, Horatio,
Than are dreamt of in your philosophy.
185 But come:
Here as before, never, so help you mercy,
How strange or odd so'er I bear myself
(As I perchance hereafter shall think meet
To put an antic disposition on)
190 That you, at such times seeing me, never shall
With arms encumb'red thus, or this headshake,
Or by pronouncing of some doubtful phrase,
As "Well, well, we know," or "We could, an if we would,"
Or "If we list to speak," or "There be, an if they might,"
195 Or such **ambiguous** giving out, to note
That you know aught of me—this do swear,
So grace and mercy at your most need help you.

GHOST [*beneath*]
Swear.

[*They swear.*]

HAMLET
Rest, rest, perturbed spirit.—So, gentlemen,
200 With all my love I do commend me to you,
And what so poor a man as Hamlet is
May do t' express his love and friending to you,
God willing, shall not lack. Let us go in together,
And still your fingers on your lips, I pray.
205 The time is out of joint. O cursed spite,
That ever I was born to set it right!—
Nay, come, let's go together.

Exeunt.

HORATIO

Oh, day and night, but this is amazingly strange.

HAMLET

So welcome it, as you should welcome any stranger.
There are more things in heaven and earth, Horatio,
than philosophy has ever dreamed of. But come on.   185
Swear to this now, just like before, if you hope for God's
    mercy: No matter
how strangely or oddly I conduct myself
(since it's possible that I'll soon think it best
to behave in a fantastic manner),
you will never, seeing me at such times,   190
fold your arms like this, or shake your head knowingly,
or say anything suggestive,
like "Well, well, we know about it," or "We could say something if
    we would,"
or "If we chose to speak," or "There are those who could explain,"
or any such ambiguous hint, indicating   195
that you know anything about me. Swear to this,
so that you'll have God's blessing and mercy when you need it
    most.

GHOST (*under the stage*)

Swear.

> MARCELLUS *and* HORATIO *swear.*

HAMLET

Rest, rest, troubled spirit.—So gentlemen,
I entrust myself to you with all my love,   200
and whatever a man as poor as Hamlet
may do to express his love and friendship toward you
will not be lacking, God willing. Let us go in together—
and always keep your fingers to your lips, I beg you.
These days are in complete disorder. Oh, how spiteful of fate,   205
that I was ever born to set things right!

> As they start to exit, MARCELLUS and HORATIO respectfully
> walk behind HAMLET.

No, come on, let's go together.

> They all exit side by side.

Act I Review

Discussion Questions

1. What current events are discussed as the men await the Ghost in Scene i?

2. What background information is supplied by the speech Claudius makes as Scene ii begins?

3. What do we learn about Hamlet's thoughts and feelings from his soliloquy in Scene ii?

4. Describe Hamlet's personality when he is with Horatio.

5. What is the significance of Polonius's advice to Laertes in Scene iii, lines 62–85?

6. In Scene iii, Laertes and Polonius advise Ophelia on her relationship with Hamlet. What does this scene reveal about all three characters?

7. What does Hamlet realize after talking with the Ghost in Scene v?

8. How would you judge Queen Gertrude's guilt?

Literary Elements

1. **Foreshadowing** is the use of hints or clues about what will happen later in the plot. Name some images or details in Scene i that foreshadow madness and violence later in the play.

2. A **pun** is a play on words that have similar sounds but more than one possible spelling or meaning. Find some puns in Act I and explain their dual (or triple) meanings.

3. **Conflict** refers to struggle between opposing forces. Right from the

beginning, what do you learn about Hamlet's internal conflicts? Describe any external conflicts that threaten him as well.

4. **Imagery** refers to vivid sensory descriptions that allow readers to make an emotional connection with the writing. Point out any strong images in the dialogue between the Ghost and Hamlet in Scene v. How do they enhance the play?

Writing Prompts

1. Write a description of Hamlet based on what you have learned about him so far. Use specific quotes from the play to support your writing.

2. Assume that you write an advice column for a newspaper or magazine. A modern-day Hamlet writes to you asking for your advice. He explains the recent events in his family and also mentions the potential for war in his country. First write his letter, and then write your response.

3. The Ghost tells Hamlet that the murder of King Hamlet by Claudius was "most foul, strange, and unnatural." What are some of the ways in which the death fits this description? Write out your answer in a short essay.

4. Rewrite the scene in which Polonius berates and advises Ophelia, giving it a contemporary setting, characters, and language. Show a modern father explaining to his daughter that the man she is in love with is unsuitable because he comes from a different social class. Try to make sure you create two individuals, not two "types."

HAMLET

ACT II

Polonius, played by Bill Murray, and Ophelia, played by Julia Stiles, in Michael Almereyda's 1999 film *Hamlet*. The film was set in New York City in the year 2000.

"THOUGH THIS BE MADNESS,
YET THERE IS METHOD IN 'T."

✠ ✠ ✠

Before You Read

1. After the revelations of the Ghost in Act I, Scene v, what do you expect Hamlet to do?

2. Some characters in *Hamlet* describe omens. What are some of these omens?

3. What part do you expect Ophelia to play in this story?

4. How might Gertrude use her power as Queen to help her son Hamlet?

5. Notice how many characters become spies in Act II. Consider what this implies about the Danish court.

Literary Elements

1. An **allusion** is a reference to a literary or historical figure or event. In Act I, Hamlet compares himself unfavorably with the Greek god Hercules, who was noted for great courage and strength. Hamlet's point is that his Uncle Claudius is no more like his father than Hamlet himself is like the powerful Hercules.

2. A **metaphor** makes a direct comparison between two unlike things that nevertheless have something in common. In *Hamlet*, "Fortune" is compared to a woman, one who treats human beings any way she chooses. This reflects the idea, in Shakespeare's time, that women were fickle and untrustworthy.

3. Shakespeare often uses **repetition** to stress a character's emotions or traits or lend urgency to a theme or idea. In Act I, Scene i, Horatio beseeches the Ghost to "speak." When repeated, this word conveys the fear and tension of the scene as well as the helplessness of those whom the Ghost does not choose to answer.

4. A **soliloquy** is a longer speech that reveals the innermost thoughts and feelings of the character who speaks it. In *Hamlet's* famous "to be or not to be" soliloquy in Act III, the Prince speaks of his inner turmoil and questions the value of life.

Words to Know

The following vocabulary words appear in Act II in the original text of Shakespeare's play. However, they are words that are still used today. Read the definitions here and pay attention to the words as you read the play (they will be in boldfaced type).

adheres	sticks; attaches
afflict	hurt; torment
brevity	economy; conciseness
discretion	carefulness; caution
endeavor	project; plan
potent	powerful; strong
profound	deep; intense
ominous	threatening; doomed
rebuke	scolding; condemnation
remorse	regret; guilt
surmise	guess; theorize
transformation	extreme change or alteration
treacherous	disloyal; unfaithful
treason	rebellion; uprising
tyrant	dictator; oppressive ruler

Act Summary

Polonius sends his servant Reynaldo to Paris to spy on Laertes. Ophelia reports that Hamlet has been acting bizarrely, frightening her. Polonius believes that Hamlet is being driven crazy by Ophelia's rejection.

Claudius asks Hamlet's boyhood friends, Rosencrantz and Guildenstern, to observe Hamlet to see why he is acting so strangely.

The King's ambassadors to Norway, Voltemand and Cornelius, return and announce that they have convinced the King of Norway to keep his nephew Fortinbras from attacking Denmark by ordering him to attack Poland instead.

Polonius gives a rambling explanation of why Hamlet has gone mad, and even though Claudius is dubious, he agrees to join Polonius to eavesdrop on Hamlet when the Prince meets privately with Ophelia.

Hamlet's wild talk seems to baffle Polonius. Hamlet hurls insults at him that he ignores or doesn't seem to understand. He departs, thinking Hamlet is mad.

Hamlet welcomes Rosencrantz and Guildenstern, and the young men banter and trade puns, but Hamlet becomes serious. Why have the two young men come to Elsinore? Guildenstern admits that Claudius sent for them. Hamlet shares with them his melancholic state of mind.

Rosencrantz announces the arrival of some traveling actors. Hamlet asks the principal actor to recite the story of Pyrrhus entering Troy from within a wooden horse, a classical story about revenge.

Hamlet asks the Players to return the following night and perform *The Murder of Gonzago*, with new lines he plans to add. Later, he soliloquizes on his delay in avenging his father. In the performance to come, his father's murder will be enacted just as the Ghost claimed it happened in real life.

ACT II, SCENE I

[*A room.*] *Enter old* POLONIUS, *with his man*
REYNALDO.

POLONIUS
Give him this money and these notes, Reynaldo.

REYNOLDO
I will, my lord.

POLONIUS
You shall do marvell's wisely, good Reynaldo,
Before you visit him, to make inquire
5   Of his behavior.

REYNALDO
                    My lord, I did intend it.

POLONIUS
Marry, well said, very well said. Look you sir,
Inquire me first what Danskers are in Paris,
And how, and who, what means, and where they keep,
10   What company, at what expense; and finding
By this encompassment and drift of question
That they do know my son, come you more nearer
Than your particular demands will touch it.
Take you as 'twere some distant knowledge of him,
15   As thus, "I know his father and his friends,
And, in part, him." Do you mark this, Reynaldo?

REYNALDO
Ay, very well, my lord.

POLONIUS
"And, in part, him, but," you may say, "not well,
But if 't be he I mean, he's very wild,
20   Addicted so and so." And there put on him
What forgeries you please; marry, none so rank
As may dishonor him—take heed of that—
But, sir, such wanton, wild, and usual slips
As are companions noted and most known
25   To youth and liberty.

ACT 2, SCENE 1

A room. Old POLONIUS *enters with his servant* REYNALDO.

POLONIUS
Give him this money and these letters, Reynaldo.

REYNALDO
I will, my lord.

POLONIUS
It would be extremely wise of you, good Reynaldo,
to inquire about his behavior
before you visit him.   5

REYNALDO
My lord, I already intended to do so.

POLONIUS
Indeed, well said, very well said. Now listen here, sir:
Ask first which Danes are living in Paris—
how they live, who they are and how well-off they are, where
   they live,
what company they keep, and how much they spend. And   10
   once you've learned
by roundabout talk and questioning
that somebody knows my son, you can find out
what you want to know without being too direct.
Pretend, say, that you've got some distant knowledge of him,
for example: "I know his father and his friends,   15
and him a little, too." Do you follow this, Reynaldo?

REYNALDO
Yes, very well, my lord.

POLONIUS
"And him a little, too." Then add, "Not well;
but if we're talking about the same man, he's very wild,
with such-and-such vices." And then charge him with   20
whatever faults you please—indeed, none offensive enough
to dishonor him, be careful of that,
but such rebellious, wild, and typical deeds
that often are known to go hand in hand
with youthful independence.   25

REYNALDO

As gaming, my lord.

POLONIUS

Ay, or drinking, fencing, swearing,
Quarreling, drabbing. You may go so far.

REYNALDO

My lord, that would dishonor him.

POLONIUS

30 Faith, no, as you may season it in the charge.
You must not put another scandal on him,
That he is open to incontinency.
That's not my meaning. But breathe his faults so quaintly
That they may seem the taints of liberty,
35 The flash and outbreak of a fiery mind,
A savageness in unreclaimed blood,
Of general assault.

REYNALDO

But, my good lord—

POLONIUS

Wherefore should you do this?

REYNALDO

40 Ay, my lord, I would know that.

POLONIUS

Marry, sir, here's my drift,
And I believe it is a fetch of warrant.
You laying these slight sullies on my son
As 'twere a thing a little soiled i' th' working,
45 Mark you, Your party in converse, him you
would sound,
Having ever seen in the prenominate crimes
The youth you breathe of guilty, be assured
He closes with you in this consequence:
50 "Good sir," or so, or "friend," or "gentleman"—
According to the phrase or the addition
Of man and country—

REYNALDO

Very good, my lord.

REYNALDO

Like gambling, my lord.

POLONIUS

Yes, or drinking, fencing, swearing,
brawling, or whoring—you may go that far.

REYNALDO

My lord, that would dishonor him.

POLONIUS.

Indeed, no—not if you soften your accusations.   30
You mustn't create any scandal about him
by suggesting that he's truly immoral.
That's not what I mean. But speak of his faults so cunningly
that they seem to be small vices of living independently,
the fiery outbreaks of a passionate personality,   35
an untamed wildness of the blood
common to all young men.

REYNALDO

But my good lord—

POLONIUS

Why should you do this?

REYNALDO

Yes, my lord, I'd like to know that.   40

POLONIUS

Indeed, sir, here's my reason—
and I believe it's a justifiable trick.
When you accuse my son of these slight faults
as if he were just a little tainted by contact with the world
(pay close attention, now!), if the person you're conversing with   45
has ever seen the youth that you're accusing
involved in the aforementioned crimes, be assured
that he will agree with you as follows:
"Good sir," he'll say, or "Friend," or "Gentleman,"   50
depending on the phrase or form of address
used by men in that country—

REYNALDO

I understand, my lord.

POLONIUS
And then, sir, does 'a this—'a does—what was I
about to say? By the Mass, I was about to say
something! Where did I leave?

REYNALDO
At "closes in the consequence," at "friend or so," and
"gentlemen."

POLONIUS
At "closes in the consequence"—ay marry!
He closes thus: "I know the gentleman.
I saw him yesterday," or "t' other day,"
Or then, or then, with such or such, "and as you say,
There was 'a gaming, there o'ertook in 's rouse,
There falling out at tennis"; or perchance,
"I saw him enter such a house of sale,"
Videlicet, a brothel, or so forth.
See you now—
Your bait of falsehood take this carp of truth,
And thus do we of wisdom and of reach,
With windlasses and with assays of bias,
By indirections find directions out.
So, by my former lecture and advice,
Shall you my son. You have me, have you not?

REYNALDO
My lord, I have.

POLONIUS
God bye ye, fare ye well.

REYNALDO
Good my lord.

POLONIUS
Observe his inclination in yourself.

REYNALDO
I shall, my lord.

POLONIUS
And let him ply his music.

REYNALDO
Well, my lord.

POLONIUS

And then, sir, this is what he does: He—what was I about
to say? Heavens, I was about to say something. Where did
I leave off?   55

REYNALDO

You said "he will agree with you as follows,"
with "friend," "gentleman," and such.

POLONIUS

At "agree with you as follows"—yes, indeed.
He'll agree with you like this: "I know the gentleman.   60
I saw him yesterday," or "the other day,"
or at some time or another, "and just as you say,
he was gambling there," or "he was drunk there,"
or "he was wasting time at tennis there." Or perhaps,
"I saw him enter a certain house of ill-repute"—   65
namely, a brothel—or some such thing. So now you see
how your bait of falsehood will catch this fish of truth.
And this is how those of us with wisdom and intelligence
indirectly arrive at the direct facts—   70
by roundabout and swerving means.
And this is how you'll find out about my son,
according to my teaching and advice. You understand me,
    don't you?

REYNALDO

My lord, I do.

POLONIUS

God be with you. Farewell.   75

REYNALDO

Good-bye, my lord.

POLONIUS

Observe his behavior firsthand.

REYNALDO

I shall, my lord.

POLONIUS

And let him go his own way.

REYNALDO

Yes, my lord.   80

POLONIUS
Farewell.

       Exit REYNALDO. *Enter* OPHELIA.

       How now, Ophelia, what's the matter?

OPHELIA
O my lord, my lord, I have been so affrighted!

POLONIUS
With what, i' th' name of God?

OPHELIA
85   My lord, as I was sewing in my closet,
Lord Hamlet, with his doublet all unbraced,
No hat upon his head, his stockings fouled,
Ungartered, and down-gyved to his ankle,
Pale as his shirt, his knees knocking each other,
90   And with a look so piteous in purport,
As if he had been loosed out of hell
To speak of horrors—he comes before me.

POLONIUS
Mad for thy love?

OPHELIA
              My lord, I do not know,
95   But truly I do fear it.

POLONIUS
              What said he?

OPHELIA
He took me by the wrist and held me hard;
Then goes he to the length of all his arm,
And with his other hand thus o'er his brow
100   He falls to such perusal of my face
As 'a would draw it. Long stayed he so.
At last, a little shaking of mine arm,
And thrice his head thus waving up and down,
He raised a sigh so piteous and **profound**
105   As it did seem to shatter all his bulk
And end his being. That done, he lets me go,
And, with his head over his shoulder turned,

POLONIUS
Farewell.

> REYNALDO *exits;* OPHELIA *enters.*

What is it, Ophelia? What's the matter?

OPHELIA
Oh, my lord, my lord, I've been so frightened!

POLONIUS
By what, in God's name?

OPHELIA
My lord, while I was sewing in my private room,   85
Lord Hamlet appeared before me—his jacket all unfastened,
no hat on his head, his stockings dirty
and not held up by garters, hanging down around his ankles;
he was as pale as his shirt; his knees knocked together;
and the expression on his face was so pitiful,   90
it was as if he had been released from hell
to tell of its horrors.

POLONIUS
Mad for your love?

OPHELIA
My lord, I do not know.
But truly, I'm afraid so.   95

POLONIUS
What did he say?

OPHELIA
He took me by the wrist and held me hard.
Then he stepped back the whole length of his arm,
and with his other hand held across his forehead like this,
he began to study my face so carefully,   100
he seemed to wish to draw it. He stayed like that for a long time.
At last, after shaking my arm a little,
and nodding his head up and down three times like this,
he let out a sigh so pitiful and deep
that it seemed to shatter his whole body   105
and end his life. Once that was done, he let me go,
and with his head still turned over his shoulder,

He seemed to find his way without his eyes,
For out o' doors he went without their helps,
And to the last bended their light on me.

POLONIUS

Come, go with me. I will go seek the King.
This is the very ecstasy of love,
Whose violent property fordoes itself
And leads the will to desperate undertakings
As oft as any passions under heaven
That does **afflict** our natures. I am sorry.
What, have you given him any hard words of late?

OPHELIA

No, my good lord; but as you did command,
I did repel his letters and denied
His access to me.

POLONIUS

       That hath made him mad.
I am sorry that with better heed and judgment
I had not quoted him. I feared he did but trifle
And meant to wrack thee; but beshrew my jealousy.
By heaven, it is as proper to our age
To cast beyond ourselves in our opinions
As it is common for the younger sort
To lack **discretion**. Come, go we to the King.
This must be known, which, being kept close, might move
More grief to hide than hate to utter love.
Come.

   Exeunt.

he seemed to find his way without his eyes,
for he went out the door without their help,
keeping them turned toward me the whole time. 110

POLONIUS

Come along with me. I will go look for the King.
This is clearly a case of madness caused by love,
the violent nature of which brings on its own destruction
and leads the will to desperate deeds,
as surely as any passionate feeling under heaven 115
that ever afflicts our minds. I am sorry.
What, have you said any harsh words to him lately?

OPHELIA

No, my good lord; but as you commanded,
I rejected his letters and refused
to let him see me. 120

POLONIUS

That has made him mad.
I am sorry I didn't observe him with better attention
and judgment. I was afraid he was only toying with you
and meant to ruin you. But curse my suspicions!
By heaven, it is as natural for old men like me 125
to jump to unfounded conclusions
as it is common for younger folk
to lack good judgment. Come, let's go to the King.
We must reveal this; for if we keep Hamlet's love a secret,
it's likely to create more grief than if we make the King angry
    by telling him about it. 130
Come on.

    They exit.

ACT II, SCENE II

[*The castle.*] *Flourish. Enter* KING *and* QUEEN, ROSENCRANTZ, *and* GUILDENSTERN [*with others*].

KING

Welcome, dear Rosencrantz and Guildenstern.
Moreover that we much did long to see you,
The need we have to use you did provoke
Our hasty sending. Something have you heard

5   Of Hamlet's **transformation**: so call it,
Sith nor th' exterior nor the inward man
Resembles that it was. What it should be,
More than his father's death, that thus hath put him
So much from th' understanding on himself,

10   I cannot dream of. I entreat you both
That, being of so young days brought up with him,
And sith so neighbored to his youth and havior,
That you vouchsafe your rest here in our court
Some little time, so by your companies

15   To draw him on to pleasures, and to gather
So much as from occasion you may glean,
Whether aught to us unknown afflicts him thus,
That opened lies within our remedy.

QUEEN

Good gentlemen, he hath much talked of you,

20   And sure I am, two men there is not living
To whom he more **adheres**. If it will please you
To show us so much gentry and good will
As to expend your time with us awhile
For the supply and profit of our hope,

25   Your visitation shall receive such thanks
As fits a king's remembrance.

ROSENCRANTZ

               Both your Majesties
Might, by the sovereign power you have of us,
Put your dread pleasures more into command

30   Than to entreaty.

ACT 2, SCENE 2

The castle. A flourish of trumpets. The KING *and* QUEEN *enter, with* ROSENCRANTZ, GUILDENSTERN, *and others.*

KING
Welcome, dear Rosencrantz and Guildenstern.
Aside from the fact that we greatly longed to see you,
our need to make use of you prompted us
to send for you so hastily. You've heard something
about Hamlet's transformation. Let's call it that,   5
since neither his outward nor his inward self
resembles what it was. Beyond his father's death,
what might have caused him to stray
so far from self-understanding
I cannot imagine. Because you were   10
brought up with him from such an early age,
and since you're familiar with his youthful behavior,
I implore you both to agree to stay here in our court
a little while, so that, by your companionship,
you can urge him toward enjoyment, and also learn   15
as fully as opportunity allows
whether anything unknown to us is troubling him—
which, if we knew about it, we could cure.

QUEEN
Good gentlemen, he has talked much about you,
and I'm sure there are not two other men living   20
to whom he feels closer. If it will please you
to show us enough generosity and goodwill
to spend your time with us awhile
in order to help us achieve our hopes,
your kindness will be rewarded in a way   25
that's fitting of a king's gratitude.

ROSENCRANTZ
By the great power
you hold over us, both of your Majesties
might have commanded rather than requested us
to carry out your revered wishes.   30

GUILDENSTERN

But we both obey,
And here give up ourselves in the full bent
To lay our service freely at your feet,
To be commanded.

KING

35 Thanks, Rosencrantz and gentle Guildenstern.

QUEEN

Thanks, Guildenstern and gentle Rosencrantz.
And I beseech you instantly to visit
My too much changed son. Go, some of you,
And bring these gentlemen where Hamlet is.

GUILDENSTERN

40 Heavens make our presence and our practices
Pleasant and helpful to him!

QUEEN

Ay, amen!

Exeunt ROSENCRANTZ *and* GUILDENSTERN [*with
some* ATTENDANTS]. *Enter* POLONIUS.

POLONIUS

Th' ambassadors from Norway, my good lord,
Are joyfully returned.

KING

45 Thou still hast been the father of good news.

POLONIUS

Have I, my lord? Assure you, my good liege,
I hold my duty, as I hold my soul,
Both to my God and to my gracious king;
And I do think, or else this brain of mine
50 Hunts not the trail of policy so sure
As it hath used to do, that I have found
The very cause of Hamlet's lunacy.

KING

O, speak of that! That do I long to hear.

POLONIUS

Give first admittance to th' ambassadors.
55 My news shall be the fruit to that great feast.

GUILDENSTERN
But we both obey,
and promise to do everything we can to help;
we lay our services freely at your feet,
to be commanded by you.

KING
Thanks, Rosencrantz and gentle Guildenstern.   35

QUEEN
Thanks, Guildenstern and gentle Rosencrantz.
And I beg you to visit my extremely transformed son
right away. Go, some of you,
and take these gentlemen where Hamlet is.

GUILDENSTERN
May heaven make our presence and our deeds   40
pleasant and helpful to him!

QUEEN
Indeed, amen!

> ROSENCRANTZ *and* GUILDENSTERN *exit with some* SERVANTS;
> POLONIUS *enters.*

POLONIUS
My good lord, the ambassadors have joyfully returned
from Norway.

KING
You've always been a bringer of good news.   45

POLONIUS
Have I, my lord? My good lord, I assure you
that I value my duty to both God
and my generous king as dearly as I value my soul.
And unless this brain of mine
has lost the knack for investigation   50
it used to have, I think that I have found
the exact cause of Hamlet's lunacy.

KING
Oh, tell me! I long to hear about that.

POLONIUS
First, let the ambassadors enter.
Then my news will be like dessert to a great feast.   55

KING

Thyself do grace to them and bring them in.

Exit POLONIUS.

He tells me, my dear Gertrude, he hath found
The head and source of all your son's distemper.

QUEEN

I doubt it is no other but the main—
60 His father's death and our o'erhasty marriage.

KING

Well, we shall sift him.

Enter POLONIUS, VOLTEMAND, *and* CORNELIUS.

Welcome, my good friends.
Say, Voltemand, what from our brother Norway?

VOLTEMAND

Most fair return of greetings and desires.
65 Upon our first, he sent out to suppress
His nephew's levies, which to him appeared
To be a preparation 'gainst the Polack;
But better looked into, he truly found
It was against your Highness. Whereat grieved,
70 That so his sickness, age, and impotence
Was falsely borne in hand, sends out arrests
On Fortinbras; which he, in brief, obeys,
Receives **rebuke** from Norway, and in fine,
Makes vow before his uncle never more
75 To give th' assay of arms against your Majesty.
Whereon old Norway, overcome with joy,
Gives him threescore thousand crowns in annual fee
And his commission to employ those soldiers,
So levied as before, against the Polack,
80 With an entreaty, herein further shown,

[*Gives a paper.*]

KING

Greet them yourself and bring them in.

POLONIUS exits.

My dear Gertrude, he tells me that he's found
The true source of your son's malady.

QUEEN

I'm sure that it is mainly because
Of his father's death and our overly hasty marriage.   60

KING

Well, we shall question Polonius carefully.

*The ambassadors VOLTEMAND and CORNELIUS enter, with
POLONIUS.*

Welcome, my good friends.
Tell me, Voltemand, what news do you bring from our brother, the
King of Norway?

VOLTEMAND

He responded favorably to both your greetings and your
wishes.
As soon as we spoke with him, he gave orders for his nephew   65
to stop assembling troops. The King had supposed all this
to be a preparation for war against Poland;
but when he looked into it, he found
that it was really against your Highness. Saddened
to have been so thoroughly deceived in his sickness, age,   70
and feebleness, he commanded Fortinbras
to put a stop to all this. To tell it briefly, Fortinbras obeyed,
was rebuked by the King, and ended up
promising his uncle never again
to make any attempt to attack your Majesty.   75
Then the old King of Norway, overcome with joy,
gave him 60,000 crowns as an annual allowance,
and commissioned him to make war against Poland,
using those soldiers he had already gathered.
He also hopes, as he writes in this letter,   80

He gives a letter to the KING.

That it might please you to give quiet pass
Through your dominions for this enterprise,
On such regards of safety and allowance
As therein are set down.

KING

85   It likes us well;
And at our more considered time we'll read,
Answer, and think upon this business.
Meantime, we thank you for your well-took labor.
Go to your rest; at night we'll feast together.
90 Most welcome home!

         Exeunt AMBASSADORS.

POLONIUS

                 This business is well ended.
My liege and madam, to expostulate
What majesty should be, what duty is,
Why day is day, night night, and time is time,
95 Were nothing but to waste night, day, and time.
Therefore, since **brevity** is the soul of wit,
And tediousness the limbs and outward flourishes,
I will be brief. Your noble son is mad.
Mad call I it, for, to define true madness,
100 What is 't but to be nothing else but mad?
But let that go.

QUEEN

           More matter, with less art.

POLONIUS

Madam, I swear I use no art at all.
That he's mad; 'tis true: 'tis true 'tis pity,
105 And pity 'tis 'tis true—a foolish figure.
But farewell it, for I will use no art.
Mad let us grant him then; and now remains
That we find out the cause of this effect,
Or rather say, the cause of this defect,
110 For this effect defective comes by cause.
Thus it remains, and the remainder thus.
Perpend.
I have a daughter: have, while she is mine,

that it will please you to allow Fortinbras's army
to pass quietly through your lands in this endeavor,
according to assurances and conditions
fully written down here.

KING

This pleases us well,   85
and at a more appropriate time, we'll read,
think over, and make a reply concerning this business.
Meanwhile, we thank you for a job well done.
Go get some rest. Tonight we'll feast together.
You're most welcome home!   90

> VOLTEMAND *and* CORNELIUS *exit.*

POLONIUS

This business has ended well.
My lord and lady, to make a speech about
what kingship should be, what duty is,
why day is day, night is night, and time is time,
would be to do nothing more than waste night, day, and time.   95
And so, since brevity is the very heart of wisdom,
and tediousness only its outward limbs and ornaments,
I will be brief. Your noble son is mad.
"Mad," I call it simply—because wouldn't it be mad
to go to the trouble of defining true madness?   100
But let's pass over that.

QUEEN

Get to the point without so much fancy talk.

POLONIUS

Madam, I swear that I'm not being fancy at all.
That he's mad is true; that it's true is a pity;
and it's a pity that it's true. That's a foolish way of putting it,   105
but forget I said it, for I'll not be fancy.
Let us grant that he is mad; we must now
find out the cause of this effect—
or let's say instead, the cause of this *de*fect,
for this defective effect must surely have some cause.   110
There's the problem—and the solution will follow.
Consider this carefully:
I have a daughter (at least until she is married)

Who in her duty and obedience, mark,
115   Hath given me this. Now gather and **surmise**.

     [*Reads the letter.*]

"To the celestial, and my soul's idol, the most beautified
     Ophelia"—
That's an ill phrase, a vile phrase; "beautified" is a vile
phrase. But you shall hear. Thus:
120   "In her excellent white bosom, these, etc."

QUEEN
Came this from Hamlet to her?

POLONIUS
Good madam, stay awhile. I will be faithful.

     [*He reads the letter.*]

"Doubt thou the stars are fire,
     Doubt that the sun doth move;
125   Doubt truth to be a liar
         But never doubt I love.
O dear Ophelia, I am ill at these numbers. I have not art
to reckon my groans; but that I love thee best, O most
best, believe it. Adieu.
130   Thine evermore, most dear lady, whilst this machine is
to him, Hamlet."

This in obedience hath my daughter shown me,
And more above hath his solicitings,
As they fell out by time, by means, and place,
135   All given to mine ear.

KING
But how hath she received his love?

POLONIUS
What do you think of me?

KING
As of a man faithful and honorable.

who—out of duty and obedience, mind you—
has given me this. Now draw your own conclusions. 115

> (*He reads the letter.*)

To the heavenly idol of my soul, the most beautified Ophelia—

> (*He stops reading.*)

That's a poor word, a disagreeable word; "beautified" is a
disagreeable word. But you will hear the rest. Here it is:

> (*He reads the letter.*)

In her lovely white breast, these, et cetera— 120

QUEEN
Was this sent to her by Hamlet?

POLONIUS
Good lady, wait a moment. I'll read it accurately.

> (*He reads the letter.*)

> > *Doubt that stars are made of fire,*
> > > *Doubt that the sun moves,*
> > *Suspect the truth itself of lying,* 125
> > > *But never doubt that I love.*
> > *Oh, dear Ophelia, I'm not good at writing in verse. I don't have*
> > *the artistic skill to convey my anguish. But oh, my best,*
> > *believe that I love you. Farewell.*
> > > *Yours forever, dearest lady, as long as I dwell in this body,* 130
> > > > *Hamlet.*

My daughter has obediently shown this to me,
and has let me hear all his other entreaties
as they've arrived—and has also told me
when, where, and how they came. 135

KING
But how has she responded to his love?

POLONIUS
What do you think of me?

KING
I think you're a faithful and honorable man.

POLONIUS
I would fain prove so. But what might you think,
When I had seen this hot love on the wing
(As I perceived it, I must tell you that,
Before my daughter told me), what might you,
Or my dear Majesty your Queen here, think,
If I had played the desk or table-book,
Or given my heart a winking, mute and dumb,
Or looked upon this love with idle sight?
What might you think? No, I went round to work
And my young mistress thus I did bespeak:
"Lord Hamlet is a prince, out of thy star.
This must not be." And then I prescripts gave her,
That she should lock herself from his resort,
Admit no messengers, receive no tokens.
Which done, she took the fruits of my advice,
And he, repelled, a short tale to make,
Fell into a sadness, then into a fast,
Thence to a lightness, and, by this declension,
Into the madness wherein now he raves,
And all we mourn for.

KING [*to the* QUEEN]
Do you think 'tis this?

QUEEN
It may be, very like.

POLONIUS
Hath there been such a time, I would fain know that,
That I have positively said " 'Tis so,"
When it proved otherwise?

KING
Not that I know.

POLONIUS [*pointing to his head and shoulder*]
Take this from this, if this be otherwise.
If circumstances lead me, I will find
Where truth is hid, though it were hid indeed
Within the center.

POLONIUS

I would like to prove myself so. But what might you have
    thought if,
when I had seen this hot love in full flight   140
—and I must tell you, I perceived it
before my daughter told me—what might you
or my dear Majesty your Queen have thought
if I had noted all this privately and secretly;
or if I had let my heart shut its eyes and keep silent about it;   145
or if I had looked upon this love and done nothing at all?
What might you have thought? No, I went right to work,
and said this to my young lady:
"Lord Hamlet is a prince, and beyond your rank.
This must not be." And then I instructed her   150
to lock herself away from his company,
receive no messengers from him, and accept no gifts.
Once I'd said this, she took my advice to heart.
And when he was rejected (to make my story short),
he fell into sadness, then stopped eating,   155
then stopped sleeping, then grew weak,
then grew light-headed—and finally declined
into the madness in which he now raves,
and for which we grieve.

KING (*to the* QUEEN)

Do you think this is true?

QUEEN

It may be; it seems likely.   160

POLONIUS

Has there ever been a time (I'd like to know!)
when I have positively said, "This is so,"
and it proved otherwise?

KING

Not that I know of.

POLONIUS (*pointing to his head and shoulder*)

Remove my head from my body if I'm wrong this time.   165
Given the right circumstances, I'll always find out
where the truth is hidden—indeed, even if is hidden
at the center of the earth.

KING

How may we try it further?

POLONIUS

170   You know sometimes he walks four hours together
Here in the lobby.

QUEEN

So he does indeed.

POLONIUS

At such a time I'll loose my daughter to him.
[*to the* KING] Be you and I behind an arras* then.
175   Mark the encounter. If he love her not,
And be not from his reason fall'n thereon,
Let me be no assistant for a state
But keep a farm and carters.

KING

We will try it.

Enter HAMLET *reading on a book.*

QUEEN

180   But look where sadly the poor wretch comes reading.

POLONIUS

Away, I do beseech you both, away.
I'll board him presently. O, give me leave.

Exit KING *and* QUEEN.

How does my good Lord Hamlet?

HAMLET

Well, God-a-mercy.

POLONIUS

185   Do you know me, my lord?

HAMLET

Excellent well. You are a fishmonger.

---

174   *arras* a hanging placed around the walls of a room to keep out dampness and
cold. It was often far enough from the wall so that a person could be concealed
behind it.

KING

How may we further prove this?

POLONIUS

You know that sometimes he walks for several hours at a time   170
right here in the hall.

QUEEN

He does so, indeed.

POLONIUS

At such a time, I'll let my daughter loose on him.
(*to the* KING) You and I will then hide behind a hanging
    tapestry.
Watch what happens when they meet. If he doesn't love her,   175
and hasn't gone mad because of it,
let me not continue to be a government minister;
instead, I'll take charge of a farm and its cart drivers.

KING

We'll try it.

        HAMLET *enters, reading a book.*

QUEEN

But look—here comes the poor, sad wretch reading.   180

POLONIUS

Go away, I beg you both—go away.
I'll confront him immediately. Oh, leave me alone with him.

        The KING *and* QUEEN *exit with their* SERVANTS.

How is my good Lord Hamlet doing?   185

HAMLET

Well, thank you.

POLONIUS

Do you know me, my lord?

HAMLET

Extremely well. You are a fish dealer.

POLONIUS

Not I, my lord.

HAMLET

Then I would you were so honest a man.

POLONIUS

Honest, my lord?

HAMLET

190 Ay, sir. To be honest, as this world goes, is to be one man
picked out of ten thousand.

POLONIUS

That's very true, my lord.

HAMLET

For if the sun breed maggots in a dead dog, being a good
kissing carrion.—Have you a daughter?

POLONIUS

195 I have, my lord.

HAMLET

Let her not walk i' th' sun.* Conception is a blessing, but
as your daughter may conceive, friend, look to 't.

POLONIUS [*aside*]

How say you by that? Still harping on my daughter. Yet he
knew me not at first. 'A said I was a fishmonger. 'A is far
200 gone, far gone. And truly in my youth I suffered much
extremity for love, very near this. I'll speak to him again.—
What do you read, my lord?

HAMLET

Words, words, words.

POLONIUS

What is the matter, my lord?

HAMLET

205 Between who?*

---

196 *sun* that is, in the sunshine of his sexual attentions, with a pun on "son." In
what follows, Hamlet is also punning on the word "conception," which means
understanding, and conceiving a child.

POLONIUS
I'm not, my lord.

HAMLET
Then I wish you were as honest a man as a fish dealer.

POLONIUS
Honest, my lord?

HAMLET
Yes, sir. In a world like ours, to be honest is to be one man out   190
of ten thousand.

POLONIUS
That's very true, my lord.

HAMLET
For if the sun breeds maggots in a dead dog, since it's a good
piece of flesh to kiss.—Do you have a daughter?

POLONIUS
I do, my lord.   195

HAMLET
Don't let her walk in the sun. Pregnancy can be a blessing. But
since your daughter might conceive a child, watch out for it.

POLONIUS (*aside*)
What do you think of that? He's still carrying on about
my daughter. And yet he didn't know me at first; he said I was
a fish dealer. He is far gone. And to tell the truth, I endured   200
much suffering for love in my own youth—very nearly like this.
I'll speak to him again. (*to* HAMLET) What are you reading, my
lord?

HAMLET
Words, words, words.

POLONIUS
What is the matter, my lord?

HAMLET
Between whom?   205

---

205   *Between who?* Hamlet pretends to misunderstand "matter," as if it meant the
basis of a dispute or quarrel.

POLONIUS

I mean the matter that you read, my lord.

HAMLET

Slanders, sir; for the satirical rogue says here that old men
have gray beards, that their faces are wrinkled, their eyes
purging thick amber and plumtree gum, and that they
210   have a plentiful lack of wit, together with most weak
hams. All which, sir, though I most powerfully and
potently believe, yet I hold it not honesty to have it thus
set down; for you yourself, sir, should be old as I am if,
like a crab, you could go backward.

POLONIUS [aside]

215   Though this be madness, yet there is method in 't. Will you
walk out of the air, my lord?

HAMLET

Into my grave?

POLONIUS

Indeed, that's out of the air. [aside] How pregnant
sometimes his replies are! A happiness that often madness
220   hits on, which reason and sanity could not so
prosperously be delivered of. I will leave him and
suddenly contrive the means of meeting between him and
my daughter.—My lord, I will take my leave of you.

HAMLET

You cannot take from me anything that I will more
225   willingly part withal—except my life, except my life, except
my life.

Enter GUILDENSTERN *and* ROSENCRANTZ.

POLONIUS

Fare you well, my lord.

HAMLET

These tedious old fools!

POLONIUS

You go to seek the Lord Hamlet? There he is.

POLONIUS

I mean your *reading* matter, my lord.

HAMLET

It's all slander, sir. For the satirical rogue writes here that old men have gray beards, that their faces are wrinkled, and that their eyes drip with thick yellowish fluid and plum-tree sap; also, that they have a great lack of understanding, and very 210 weak thighs and buttocks. Although I most deeply and strongly believe all this, sir, I still consider it impolite to write it down like this. For you yourself, sir, would grow as old as I am if you could go backwards like a crab.

POLONIUS (*aside*)

This may be madness, but it makes a kind of sense. (*to* 215 HAMLET) Would you prefer to get away from the open air, my lord?

HAMLET

Into my grave?

POLONIUS

Indeed, that's away from the open air. (*aside*) How full of meaning his replies sometimes are! Madness often hits on an apt way of putting things, while reason and sanity come up 220 short. I will leave him, and immediately arrange some way of bringing him and my daughter together. (*to* HAMLET) My lord, I now take leave of you.

HAMLET

Sir, you cannot take anything from me that I'm more willing to get rid of—except my life, except my life, except my life. 225

GUILDENSTERN *and* ROSENCRANTZ *enter.*

POLONIUS

Farewell, my lord.

HAMLET

These tedious old fools.

POLONIUS

You are seeking Lord Hamlet. There he is.

ROSENCRANTZ

230   [*to* POLONIUS] God save you, sir!

      [*Exit* POLONIUS.]

GUILDENSTERN

    My honored lord!

ROSENCRANTZ

    My most dear lord!

HAMLET

    My excellent good friends! How dost thou, Guildenstern?
    Ah, Rosencrantz! Good lads, how do you both?

ROSENCRANTZ

235   As the indifferent children of the earth.

GUILDENSTERN

    Happy in that we are not overhappy.
    On Fortune's cap we are not the very button.

HAMLET

    Nor the soles of her shoe?

ROSENCRANTZ

    Neither, my lord.

HAMLET

240   Then you live about her waist, or in the middle of her
    favors?

GUILDENSTERN

    Faith, her privates we.

HAMLET

    In the secret parts of Fortune? O, most true!
    She is a strumpet. What news?

ROSENCRANTZ

245   None, my lord, but that the world's grown honest.

HAMLET

    Then is doomsday near. But your news is not true. Let me
    question more in particular. What have you, my good
    friends, deserved at the hands of Fortune that she sends
    you to prison hither.

ROSENCRANTZ

(*to* POLONIUS) Good day to you, sir.   230

    POLONIUS *exits.*

GUILDENSTERN

My honored lord.

ROSENCRANTZ

My dearest lord.

HAMLET

My extremely good friends! How are you, Guildenstern? Ah,
Rosencrantz! Good lads, how are you both?

ROSENCRANTZ

Just like all average, ordinary fellows.   235

GUILDENSTERN

We're happy because we're not overly happy. We're not the
button at the top of Fortune's cap.

HAMLET

Nor the soles of her shoes?

ROSENCRANTZ

Not that either, my lord.

HAMLET

Then do you live around her waist—or perhaps a bit farther   240
down in her favor?

GUILDENSTERN

Indeed, we live between her legs.

HAMLET

In Fortune's private parts? Oh, how true! She is a whore. What's
new?

ROSENCRANTZ

Nothing, my lord—except that the world has grown honest.   245

HAMLET

Then the end of the world is near. But your news isn't true. Let
me ask you some specific questions. What have you done
wrong, that you should deserve to have Fortune send you
here to prison?

GUILDENSTERN

250   Prison, my lord?

HAMLET

Denmark's a prison.

ROSENCRANTZ

Then is the world one.

HAMLET

A goodly one, in which there are many confines, wards,
and dungeons, Denmark being one o' th' worst.

ROSENCRANTZ

255   We think not so, my lord.

HAMLET

Why, then 'tis none to you, for there is nothing either
good or bad but thinking makes it so. To me it is a prison.

ROSENCRANTZ

Why then your ambition makes it one. 'Tis too narrow for
your mind.

HAMLET

260   O God, I could be bounded in a nutshell and count
myself a king of infinite space, were it not that I have bad
dreams.

GUILDENSTERN

Which dreams indeed are ambition, for the very substance
of the ambitious is merely the shadow of a dream.

HAMLET

265   A dream itself is but a shadow.

ROSENCRANTZ

Truly, and I hold ambition of so airy and light a quality
that it is but a shadow's shadow.

HAMLET

Then are our beggars bodies, and our monarchs and
outstretched heroes the beggars' shadows. Shall we to th'
270   court? For, by my fay, I cannot reason.

GUILDENSTERN

Prison, my lord? 250

HAMLET

Denmark's a prison.

ROSENCRANTZ

Then the whole world is also one.

HAMLET

A genuine prison, in which there are many chambers, cells, and dungeons—and Denmark is one of the worst.

ROSENCRANTZ

We don't think so, my lord. 255

HAMLET

Why, then, it's not a prison for you. For nothing is good or bad in itself; only thinking about it makes it one or the other. To me, Denmark's a prison.

ROSENCRANTZ

Why, then, your ambition makes it one. Denmark is too small for your mind.

HAMLET

Oh, God! I could be shut up in a nutshell and still consider myself a king of infinite spaces—except that I have bad 260 dreams.

GUILDENSTERN

Ambition is such a dream. For an ambitious man's achievements are only a shadow of his dreams.

HAMLET

A dream itself is only a shadow. 265

ROSENCRANTZ

That's true. And I consider ambition to be so airy and light that it is only a shadow's shadow.

HAMLET

Then only beggars have real bodies, and all monarchs and great heroes are no more than the beggars' shadows. Shall we go to the court? For to be truthful, I'm not up to this sort 270 of conversation.

ROSENCRANTZ / GUILDENSTERN
We'll wait upon you.

HAMLET
No such matter. I will not sort you with the rest of my
servants, for, to speak to you like an honest man, I am
most dreadfully attended. But in the beaten way of
275   friendship, what make you at Elsinore?

ROSENCRANTZ
To visit you, my lord; no other occasion.

HAMLET
Beggar that I am, I am even poor in thanks, but I thank
you; and sure, dear friends, my thanks are too dear a
halfpenny. Were you not sent for? Is it your own inclining?
280   Is it a free visitation? Come, come, deal justly with me.
Come, come; nay, speak.

GUILDENSTERN
What should we say, my lord?

HAMLET
Why anything—but to th' purpose. You were sent for, and
there is a kind of confession in your looks, which your
285   modesties have not craft enough to color. I know the good
King and Queen have sent for you.

ROSENCRANTZ
To what end, my lord?

HAMLET
That you must teach me. But let me conjure you by the
rights of our fellowship, by the consonancy of our youth,
290   by the obligation of our ever-preserved love, and by what
more dear a better proposer can charge you withal, be
even and direct with me, whether you were sent for or no.

ROSENCRANTZ [*aside to* GUILDENSTERN]
What say you?

HAMLET [*aside*]
Nay then, I have an eye of you.—If you love me, hold not
295   off.

ROSENCRANTZ and **GUILDENSTERN**

We're at your service.

HAMLET

Oh, don't say that. I won't think of you as being like the rest of
my servants—for to be absolutely honest, they serve me very
poorly. But since we're such tried-and-true friends, tell me—
what are you doing at Elsinore? 275

ROSENCRANTZ

Visiting you, my lord—nothing else.

HAMLET

I'm such a beggar, I'm poor even in the thanks I'm able to give.
But I *do* thank you—although surely, dear friends, my thanks
aren't worth a halfpenny. Weren't you sent for? Are you here of
your own inclination? Is this visit made freely? Come, come, 280
speak honestly with me. Come, come. Really, speak up.

GUILDENSTERN

What should we say, my lord?

HAMLET

Anything—as long as it's not to the point! You were sent for;
there is a kind of confession in your expressions which your
feelings of shame can't cover up. I know that the good King 285
and Queen sent for you.

ROSENCRANTZ

For what purpose, my lord?

HAMLET

You must tell *me* that. But I solemnly ask you—by my rights
as a friend, by the harmony of our younger days, by the duties
of our continuing affection, and by whatever more persuasive 290
appeal a man of greater eloquence than myself might make—
be straight and direct with me. Were you sent for or not?

ROSENCRANTZ (*aside to* GUILDENSTERN)

What do you think we should say?

HAMLET (*aside*)

Indeed—now I know I'd better watch out for you! (*to*
ROSENCRANTZ *and* GUILDENSTERN*)* If you love me, don't keep
the truth to yourselves. 295

GUILDENSTERN

My lord, we were sent for.

HAMLET

I will tell you why; so shall my anticipation prevent your
discovery, and your secrecy to the King and Queen molt
no feather. I have of late, but wherefore I know not, lost
300 all my mirth, forgone all custom of exercises; and indeed,
it goes so heavily with my disposition that this goodly
frame, the earth, seems to me a sterile promontory; this
most excellent canopy, the air, look you, this brave
o'erhanging firmament, this majestical roof fretted with
305 golden fire: why, it appeareth nothing to me but a foul
and pestilent congregation of vapors. What a piece of
work is a man, how noble in reason, how infinite in
faculties, in form and moving how express and admirable,
in action how like an angel, in apprehension how like a
310 god: the beauty of the world, the paragon of animals; and
yet to me, what is this quintessence of dust? Man delights
not me; nor woman neither, though by your smiling you
seem to say so.

ROSENCRANTZ

My lord, there was no such stuff in my thoughts.

HAMLET

315 Why did ye laugh then, when I said "Man delights not me"?

ROSENCRANTZ

To think, my lord, if you delight not in man, what
Lenten* entertainment the players shall receive from you.
We coted them on the way, and hither are they coming to
offer you service.

HAMLET

320 He that plays the king shall be welcome; his Majesty shall
have tribute of me; the adventurous knight shall use his
foil and target; the lover shall not sigh gratis; the
humorous man* shall end his part in peace; the clown

---

317 *Lenten* During the forty days before Easter, abstinence from meat and periodic
fasting were the rule; the word therefore means "meager" or "sparse."

GUILDENSTERN

My lord, we were sent for.

HAMLET

I will tell you why. And so, by saying it first, I'll prevent you from
telling me—and your promise to the King and Queen will
remain unbroken. I don't know why, but lately I have lost all my
cheerfulness, and have given up my habit of regular exercise. 300
And indeed, my spirits have taken such a bad turn that this
fine structure, the earth, seems to me nothing more than a
barren cape; and (look up and see!) this superb awning of the
air; these handsome and all-covering heavens; this majestic
roof decorated with fiery, golden, heavenly bodies—why, to 305
me, it seems to be nothing but a foul and diseased gathering
of mists. What a masterpiece is man! How noble is his power
to reason! How infinite are his abilities! How in shape and
movement he is well-framed and admirable! How like an angel
he is in his deeds, how like a god in his understanding! He's the
most beautiful thing in the world, the finest of animals! And 310
yet, to me, of what use is this creature, made entirely of dust?
Man does not delight me . . . and women don't either, although
by your smiles, you would seem to say otherwise.

ROSENCRANTZ

My lord, I wasn't thinking anything like that.

HAMLET

So why did you laugh when I said, "Man does not delight me"? 315

ROSENCRANTZ

My lord, I was thinking that, if you take no delight in man, the
players will receive a very poor greeting from you. We passed
them on the way, and they are coming here to offer you their
services.

HAMLET

The actor who plays the king will be welcome—I'll pay his 320
Majesty. The adventurous knight will find use for his sword
and shield; the lover's sighs will be rewarded; the actor who
plays the overwrought character will end his role peacefully;

---

323   *humorous man* a type of character prominent in the comedies of the time (e.g., Ben
Jonson's *Every Man in His Humor*, 1598). The eccentric, "humorous" personality
was dominated by certain traits produced by an excess of one of the "humors."

shall make those laugh whose lungs are tickle o' th' sere;
and the lady shall say her mind freely, or the blank verse
shall halt for 't. What players are they?

ROSENCRANTZ

Even those you were wont to take such delight in, the
tragedians of the city.

HAMLET

How chances it they travel? Their residence, both in
reputation and profit, was better both ways.

ROSENCRANTZ

I think their inhibition comes by the means of the late
innovation.

HAMLET

Do they hold the same estimation they did when I was in
the city? Are they so followed?

ROSENCRANTZ

No indeed, are they not.

HAMLET

How comes it? Do they grow rusty?

ROSENCRANTZ

Nay, their **endeavor** keeps in the wonted pace, but there is,
sir, an aerie of children, little eyases, that cry out on the
top of question and are most tyrannically clapped for 't.
These are now the fashion, and so berattle the common
stages (so they call them) that many wearing rapiers are
afraid of goosequills and dare scarce come thither.

HAMLET

What, are they children? Who maintains 'em? How are
they escoted? Will they pursue the quality no longer than
they can sing? Will they not say afterwards, if they should
grow themselves to common players (as it is most like, if
their means are no better), their writers do them wrong to
make them exclaim against their own succession?

the clown will make people laugh who are easily amused; and
the actor playing the lady will speak her mind freely, unless   325
the blank verse turns out to be clumsy. Which players are they?

ROSENCRANTZ

Those very actors you've always taken such delight in—the
players in the city.

HAMLET

Why do they happen to be touring? For both fame and profit,
they've always found it better to stay in the city.   330

ROSENCRANTZ

I think they've been forced to travel because of recent
developments.

HAMLET

Are they still as highly regarded as they were when I was in the
city? Are they still so famous?

ROSENCRANTZ

No, indeed they are not.   335

HAMLET

Why is that? Have they grown rusty?

ROSENCRANTZ

No, they work as much as they ever did. But there is, sir, a nest
of children, little hawks, who speak their lines in high-pitched,
noisy voices and are outrageously applauded for it. These boy
actors are now in fashion; the authors who write plays for them   340
so viciously attack the public theaters (as they call them) that
many sword-wearing gentlemen scarcely go there anymore,
for fear of being stabbed by those writers' satirical pens.

HAMLET

What, are they children? Who takes care of them? How are
they supported financially? Will they continue acting only
until their voices change? Or if they become public players   345
after they've grown—which seems likely, if they can do no
better in life—won't they say that their writers wronged them
by making them criticize their own future careers?

ROSENCRANTZ

350   Faith, there has been much to-do on both sides, and the
nation holds it no sin to tar them to controversy. There
was, for a while, no money bid for argument unless the
poet and the player went to cuffs in the question.

HAMLET

Is 't possible?

GUILDENSTERN

O, there has been much throwing about of brains.

HAMLET

355   Do the boys carry it away?

ROSENCRANTZ

Ay, that they do, my lord—Hercules and his load too.*

HAMLET

It is not very strange, for my uncle is King of Denmark,
and those that would make mouths at him while my
father lived give twenty, forty, fifty, a hundred ducats
360   apiece for his picture in little. 'Sblood, there is something
in this more than natural, if philosophy could find it out.

A flourish.

GUILDENSTERN

There are the players.

HAMLET

Gentlemen, you are welcome to Elsinore. Your hands,
come then. Th' appurtenance of welcome is fashion and
365   ceremony. Let me comply with you in this garb, lest my
extent to the Players (which I tell you must show fairly
outwards) should more appear like entertainment than
yours. You are welcome. But my uncle-father and aunt-
mother are deceived.

GUILDENSTERN

370   In what, my dear lord?

---

356   *Hercules and his load too* One of the twelve labors of Hercules was holding up the
world for Atlas; the child actors are carrying off both Hercules and the world. This

ROSENCRANTZ

Indeed, there has been a great fuss on both sides, and the public doesn't think it a sin to provoke them to quarrel even more. For a while, a play would make no money unless it added to the fighting between the children's playwrights and the public players. 350

HAMLET

Is this possible?

GUILDENSTERN

Oh, there has been a great war of wits.

HAMLET

Have the boys won the war? 355

ROSENCRANTZ

Yes, they have, my lord. They've carried Hercules himself away— and his load too.

HAMLET

It's not all that strange. For my uncle is King of Denmark, and people who used to mock him while my father was alive now give twenty, forty, fifty, or one hundred ducats for a miniature portrait of him. By God, there's something to be learned about 360 human nature from all this, if only science could figure it out.

A fanfare announces the PLAYERS.

GUILDENSTERN

There are the players.

HAMLET

Gentlemen, you are welcome to Elsinore. Come, give me your hands. A proper welcome consists of polite, ceremonious behavior. So let me welcome you by shaking your hands, or 365 else the greeting I give to the Players—which, I tell you, must look outwardly warm—might seem greater than that which I give to you. You are welcome. But my uncle-father and aunt-mother are mistaken.

GUILDENSTERN

In what, my dear lord? 370

_____

may be an allusion to Shakespeare's own Globe playhouse, which is said to have had for its sign a picture of Hercules supporting the globe.

HAMLET

I am but mad north-north-west. When the wind is
southerly, I know a hawk from a handsaw.*

Enter POLONIUS.

POLONIUS

Well be with you, gentlemen.

HAMLET

Hark you, Guildenstern, and you too; at each ear a hearer.
That great baby you see there is not yet out of the
swaddling clouts.

ROSENCRANTZ

Happily he is the second time come to them, for they say
an old man is twice a child.

HAMLET

I will prophesy he comes to tell me of the Players. Mark
it.—You say right, sir; a Monday morning, 'twas then
indeed.

POLONIUS

My lord, I have news to tell you.

HAMLET

My lord, I have news to tell you. When Roscius* was an
actor in Rome—

POLONIUS

The actors are come hither, my lord.

HAMLET

Buzz, buzz.

POLONIUS

Upon my honor—

HAMLET

Then came each actor on his ass—

---

372   *hawk from a handsaw* hawk can refer to the bird but also to a kind of ax;
handsaw is a carpenter's tool, but is also a pun on hernshaw, or heron, a bird
often hunted by hawks. Rosencrantz and Guildenstern are the hawks; Hamlet is

HAMLET

I'm only mad when I'm facing north-northwest according to the compass. When the wind blows south, I know a hawk from a handsaw.

POLONIUS *enters.*

POLONIUS

Welcome to you, gentlemen.

HAMLET

Listen here, Guildenstern—and you, too, Rosencrantz! Both of you, lean close to hear me! That great baby you see over there 375 is not yet out of his swaddling clothes.

ROSENCRANTZ

Perhaps he's wearing them for the second time—for they say an old man goes through a second childhood.

HAMLET

I predict that he's come to tell me about the Players; remember that. *(talking loudly to* ROSENCRANTZ *and* GUILDENSTERN, *as if in mid-conversation with them)* You're right, sir; it was on 380 Monday morning. It was then, indeed.

POLONIUS

My lord, I have news to tell you.

HAMLET

My lord, I have news to tell *you*. When Roscius was an actor in Rome—

POLONIUS

The actors have arrived, my lord. 385

HAMLET

Old news, old news.

POLONIUS

Upon my honor—

HAMLET

Really? Then each actor arrived upon a donkey.

---

the heron, their prey. In the same way, "mad north-north-west" means that he is insane only on one point of the compass; that is, only when he wants to be.

383 *Roscius* the most famous Roman comic actor (died 62 B.C.). Hamlet hints at the staleness of Polonius's news.

POLONIUS

390 The best actors in the world, either for tragedy, comedy, history, pastoral, pastoral-comical, historical-pastoral, tragical-historical, tragical-comical-historical-pastoral; scene individable, or poem unlimited.* Seneca* cannot be too heavy, nor Plautus* too light. For the law of writ and the liberty, these are the only men.

HAMLET

395 O Jephthah,* judge of Israel, what a treasure hadst thou!

POLONIUS

What a treasure had he, my lord?

HAMLET

Why,

"One fair daughter, and no more,
The which he loved passing well."

POLONIUS [*aside*]

400 Still on my daughter.

HAMLET

Am I not i' th' right, old Jephthah?

POLONIUS

If you call me Jephthah, my lord, I have a daughter that I love passing well.

HAMLET

Nay, that follows not.

POLONIUS

405 What follows then, my lord?

HAMLET

Why,

"As by lot, God wot,"
and then, you know,
"It came to pass, as most like it was."

---

392 *poem unlimited* Some classical literary critics of the time thought that plays should observe unity of place; that is, that all the events in them should happen in one place. "Poem unlimited" refers to plays which disregarded that rule and others, like the unity of time, which insisted that all events happen within one day.

392 *Seneca* Roman Stoic philosopher and playwright (died 65 A.D.), who was considered a model of the tragic dramatist

POLONIUS

—they're the best actors in the world, whether for tragedy,
comedy, history, pastoral, pastoral-comical, historical-pastoral,   390
tragical-historical, tragical-comical-historical-pastoral,
compressed into one scene or stretched out over many.
Seneca is not too heavy for them, nor Plautus too light.
Whether for plays written according to the rules, or for ones
written more casually, these are the best men for the job.

HAMLET

Oh, Jephthah, judge of Israel, what a treasure you had!   395

POLONIUS

What treasure did he have, my lord?

HAMLET

Why,
> One pretty daughter, and only one,
> whom he loved extremely well.

POLONIUS *(aside)*

Still going on about my daughter.   400

HAMLET

Aren't I right, old Jephthah?

POLONIUS

If you call me "Jephthah," my lord, you must mean that I have
a daughter I love extremely well.

HAMLET

No, that's not what follows.   405

POLONIUS

What *does* follow, my lord?

HAMLET

Why,
> By chance, God knows—
and then, as you know,
> It happened, as was very likely—

---

393   *Plautus* Roman playwright (c. 254–184 B.C.), a model of the comic dramatist

395   *Jephthah* Hamlet refers to a 16th-century ballad about Jephthah, a judge of Israel
who sacrificed his daughter (see Judges 11:34–39). In what follows, he quotes
several lines of the ballad.

410 The first row of the pious chanson will show you more,
for look where my abridgment comes.

Enter the PLAYERS.

You are welcome, masters, welcome, all.—I am glad to see
thee well.—Welcome, good friends.—O, old friend, why,
thy face is valanced since I saw thee last. Com'st thou to
415 beard me in Denmark?—What, my young lady and
mistress?* By'r Lady, your ladyship is nearer to heaven
than when I saw you last by the altitude of a chopine. Pray
God your voice, like a piece of uncurrent gold, be not
cracked within the ring.* Masters, you are all welcome.
420 We'll e'en to 't like French falconers, fly at anything we see.
We'll have a speech straight. Come, give us a taste of your
quality. Come, a passionate speech.

1. PLAYER
What speech, my good lord?

HAMLET
I heard thee speak me a speech once, but it was never
425 acted, or if it was, not above once, for the play, I
remember, pleased not the million; 'twas caviary to the
general, but it was (as I received it, and others, whose
judgments in such matters cried in the top of mine) an
excellent play, well digested in the scenes, set down with
430 as much modesty as cunning. I remember one said there
were no sallets in the lines to make the matter savory; nor
no matter in the phrase that might indict the author of
affectation, but called it an honest method, as wholesome
as sweet, and by very much more handsome than fine.
435 One speech in 't I chiefly loved. 'Twas Aeneas's tale to Dido,
and thereabout of it especially when he speaks of Priam's*
slaughter. If it live in your memory, begin at this line—let
me see, let me see:

---

416 *mistress* Hamlet is kidding the boy actor who played the women's roles.

419 *cracked within the ring* that is, broken or changed, so that the boy can no longer
play women's parts. A gold coin was unacceptable as currency ("uncurrent") if it
was cracked from the edge through the ring surrounding the stamped head of
the sovereign.

The next stanza of this biblical song would tell you more, but   410
look—I'm about to be interrupted.

The PLAYERS *enter.*

You are welcome, masters; you are all welcome.—I am glad to
see you well.—Welcome, good friends.—Oh, my old friend!
Why, you've grown a beard since I saw you last! Have you
come to Denmark to challenge me? *(to the teenage boy who*   415
plays the women's parts) Why, here's my young lady! By the
Virgin Mary, your ladyship has grown taller than when I saw
you last, by the height of a thick-soled shoe. Let's pray to God
that your voice hasn't cracked, like a useless gold coin. Masters,
you are all welcome. We'll get right down to business—and   420
like French falconers, we'll fly after anything we see. Let's have
a speech right away. Come on, give us a sample of your work.
Come on, a fiery speech.

FIRST PLAYER
What speech, my good lord?

HAMLET
You spoke a speech for me once, but it was never acted. Or if
it was, it was only once—for the play, as I remember, didn't   425
please the populace. It was too rich for the public's taste. But it
was an excellent play—or so I thought, as did others whose
judgment in such matters was much better than mine. Its
scenes were well-arranged, and written with as much restraint
as skill. I remember, someone said that there was nothing   430
unnecessarily added to spice it up, nor anything in the
phrasing that showed pretentiousness on the author's part;
he called it honest writing—as nourishing as it was sweet, and
well-shaped rather than gaudily decorated. I chiefly loved one
speech in it. It was the story Aeneas told to Dido—and   435
especially the part where he told her about Priam's killing. If
you still remember it, start at this line—let me see, let me
see:

---

436   *Priam's* In the second book of Virgil's *Aeneid*, the Trojan hero, Aeneas, tells Dido,
the Queen of Carthage, the story of the fall of Troy. Priam, the king of Troy, is
killed during the conquest of the city of Pyrrhus, son of Achilles.

"The rugged Pyrrhus, like th' Hyrcanian beast*—"

440 'Tis not so; it begins with Pyrrhus:
"The rugged Pyrrhus, he whose sable arms,
Black as his purpose, did the night resemble
When he lay couched in th' **ominous** horse,
Hath now this dread and black complexion smeared
445 With heraldry more dismal. Head to foot
Now is he total gules, horridly tricked
With blood of fathers, mothers, daughter, sons,
Baked and impasted with the parching streets,
That lend a tyrannous and a damned light
450 To their lord's murder. Roasted in wrath and fire,
And thus o'ersized with coagulate gore,
With eyes like carbuncles, the hellish Pyrrhus
Old grandsire Priam seeks."

So, proceed you.

POLONIUS

455 Fore God, my lord, well spoken, with good accent and
good discretion.

1. PLAYER

"Anon he finds him,
Striking too short at Greeks. His antique sword,
Rebellious to his arm, lies where it falls,
460 Repugnant to command. Unequal matched,
Pyrrhus at Priam drives, in rage strikes wide,
But with the whiff and wind of his fell sword
Th' unnerved father falls. Then senseless Ilium,
Seeming to feel this blow, with flaming top
465 Stoops to his base, and with a hideous crash
Takes prisoner Pyrrhus's ear. For lo, his sword,
Which was declining on the milky head
Of reverend Priam, seemed i' th' air to stick.
So as a painted **tyrant** Pyrrhus stood,
470 And like a neutral to his will and matter
Did nothing.
But as we often see, against some storm,
A silence in the heavens, the rack stand still,

---

439 *Hyrcanian beast* Hyrcania, in the Caucasus region in southern Russia, was known
for its tigers.

> The rugged Pyrrhus, like the Hyrcanian tiger—

That's not right; but it *does* begin with Pyrrhus:　　　　　440

> The rugged Pyrrhus's black armor,
> as dark as his purpose, had looked like the night itself
> while he lay hidden in the Trojan horse;
> but now his ghastly, black expression is smeared
> with more disastrous shapes. Head to foot,　　　　　445
> he is now totally red, horribly decorated
> with the blood of fathers, mothers, daughters, and sons,
> baked and encrusted by the burning streets—
> fires which shine a cruel and damnable light　　　　　450
> on the murder of Troy's king. Roasting in rage and fire,
> and smeared all over with clotted blood,
> his eyes glowing like red jewels, the hellish Pyrrhus
> seeks out old grandfather Priam.

(to the FIRST PLAYER*)* You take it from there.

POLONIUS

By God, my lord, that was well spoken, with good accent and　　455
judgment.

FIRST PLAYER

> Soon, he finds Priam,
> who is unable to hit Greek soldiers with his blows. His antique sword,
> a rebel against his arm, lies where it has fallen,
> refusing to obey his command. More than the king's match,　　　460
> Pyrrhus charges at Priam. In his rage, Pyrrhus misses his target;
> but the weakened father is knocked down by the wind
> caused by the sword. The Trojan palace, though lacking senses,
> seems to feel this blow, and its flaming roof
> tumbles all the way to the ground; its hideous crash　　　465
> takes Pyrrhus's ear captive. For look—his sword,
> which has been falling toward the revered Priam's
> white-haired head, now seems to be stuck in mid-air.
> So looking like a tyrant's portrait, Pyrrhus stands there,
> unable to carry out his will and duty,　　　　　470
> doing nothing.
> But before a storm, we often notice
> a silence in the heavens, and the clouds stand still;

The bold winds speechless, and the orb below
475 As hush as death, anon the dreadful thunder
Doth rend the region, so after Pyrrhus's pause,
A roused vengeance sets him new awork,
And never did the Cyclops'* hammers fall
On Mars' armor, forged for proof eterne,
480 With less **remorse** than Pyrrhus's bleeding sword
Now falls on Priam.
Out, out, thou strumpet Fortune! All you gods,
In general synod take away her power,
Break all the spokes and fellies from her wheel,
485 And bowl the round nave down the hill of heaven,
As low as to the fiends."

POLONIUS
This is too long.

HAMLET
It shall to the barber's, with your beard.—Prithee say on.
He's for a jig or a tale of bawdry, or he sleeps. Say on;
490 come to Hecuba.*

1. PLAYER
"But who (ah woe!) had seen the mobled queen—"

HAMLET
"The mobled queen"?

POLONIUS
That's good, "Mobled queen" is good.

1. PLAYER
"Run barefoot up and down, threat'ning the flames
495 With bisson rheum; a clout upon that head
Where late the diadem stood, and for a robe,
About her lank and all o'erteemed loins,
A blanket in the alarm of fear caught up—
Who this had seen, with tongue in venom steeped
500 'Gainst Fortune's state would **treason** have
pronounced.

---

478 *Cyclops* in Greek and Roman mythology, giants who worked in Vulcan's forge
and made armor for the gods. Mars is the god of war.

the bold winds fall speechless, and the earth below
is as quiet as death—all this just before the dreadful thunder   475
shatters the countryside. In just this way, after Pyrrhus's pause,
his awakened desire for vengeance sets him to work anew.
The Cyclops' hammer never fell
more ruthlessly against Mars' armor,
forged to endure forever, than Pyrrhus's bloody sword   480
now falls upon Priam.
Away, away, you whore Fortune! All you gods,
by unanimous agreement, take away her power,
break all the spokes and the rim of her wheel,
and roll the round hub down the hill of heaven   485
all the way to the fiends of hell!

POLONIUS

This is too long.

HAMLET

It'll be sent to the barber's, along with your beard. *(to the
PLAYER)* Please go on. He prefers to hear a merry tune or a
bawdy story, or else he falls asleep. Go on. Come to the part
about Hecuba.   490

FIRST PLAYER

"But look—ah, woe!—at the muffled queen—"

HAMLET

"The muffled queen"?

POLONIUS

That's good. "Muffled queen" is good.

FIRST PLAYER

—running barefoot up and down, threatening to put out the flames
with blinding tears, a rag upon the head   495
that recently wore a crown; and instead of a robe,
a blanket snatched up in a fearful panic
is wrapped around her shriveled sides exhausted from
    childbirth.
Whoever saw this would surely have cried out
with treasonous and venomous words against the rule of   500
    Fortune.

---

490   *Hecuba*   Priam's wife and Queen of Troy

But if the gods themselves did see her then,
When she saw Pyrrhus make malicious sport
In mincing with his sword her husband's limbs,
The instant burst of clamor that she made
(Unless things mortal move them not at all)
Would have made milch the burning eyes of heaven
And passion in the gods."

POLONIUS

Look, whe'er he has not turned his color and has tears in 's
eyes. Prithee no more.

HAMLET

'Tis well. I'll have thee speak out the rest of this soon. Good
my lord, will you see the Players well bestowed? Do you
hear? Let them be well used, for they are the abstract and
brief chronicles of the time. After your death you were better
have a bad epitaph than their ill report while you live.

POLONIUS

My lord, I will use them according to their desert.

HAMLET

God's bodkin, man, much better! Use every man after his
desert and who shall scape whipping? Use them after your
own honor and dignity. The less they deserve, the more
merit is in your bounty. Take them in.

POLONIUS

Come, sirs.

HAMLET

Follow him, friends. We'll hear a play tomorrow. [*aside to*
PLAYER] Dost thou hear me, old friend? Can you play *The
Murder of Gonzago*?

1. PLAYER

Ay, my lord.

HAMLET

We'll ha 't tomorrow night. You could for a need study a
speech of some dozen or sixteen lines which I would set
down and insert in 't, could you not?

> *But if the gods themselves had seen her*
> *when she witnessed Pyrrhus making cruel sport*
> *of her husband's limbs by hacking them with his sword,*
> *the sudden outcry that she made* 505
> *(unless mortal matters do not move the heavens at all)*
> *would make the stars shed tears*
> *and stir the gods to pity.*

POLONIUS
Look—he's grown pale, and he has tears in his eyes. Please,
no more. 510

HAMLET
(to the PLAYER*)* That's enough. I'll have you speak the rest of
this speech soon. *(to* POLONIUS*)* My good lord, will you see
that the Players are well housed? Do you hear? Make sure they
are treated well, for they summarize and narrate the times for
us. It would be better for you to have a bad epitaph after you
die than for them to speak ill about you while you're alive. 515

POLONIUS
My lord, I will treat them as well as they deserve.

HAMLET
By God's body, man, much better! If you treat every man as he
deserves, who will escape being whipped? Treat them
according to your own honor and rank. The less they deserve,
the more generous you'll prove yourself. Lead them inside. 520

POLONIUS
Come, sirs.

HAMLET
Follow him, friends. We'll watch a play tomorrow. *(aside to the*
FIRST PLAYER*)* Do you hear me, old friend? Can your men
perform "The Murder of Gonzago"?

FIRST PLAYER
Yes, my lord. 525

HAMLET
We'll watch it tomorrow night. If necessary, could you learn a
speech of about a dozen or sixteen lines, which I'll write down
and insert into the play?

1. PLAYER
Ay, my lord.

HAMLET

530 Very well. Follow that lord, and look you mock him not.

Exeunt POLONIUS *and* PLAYERS.

[*to* ROSENCRANTZ *and* GUILDENSTERN] My good
friends, I'll leave you till night. You are welcome to Elsinore.

ROSENCRANTZ
Good my lord.

Exeunt ROSENCRANTZ *and* GUILDENSTERN.

HAMLET
Ay, so, God bye to you.—Now I am alone.

535 O, what a rogue and peasant slave am I!
Is it not monstrous that this player here,
But in a fiction, in a dream of passion,
Could force his soul so to his own conceit
That from her working all his visage waned,

540 Tears in his eyes, distraction in his aspect,
A broken voice, and his whole function suiting
With forms to his conceit? And all for nothing!
For Hecuba!
What's Hecuba to him, or he to Hecuba,

545 That he should weep for her? What would he do
Had he the motive and the cue for passion
That I have? He would drown the stage with tears
And cleave the general ear with horrid speech,
Make mad the guilty and appall the free,

550 Confound the ignorant, and amaze indeed
The very faculties of eyes and ears,
Yet I,
A dull and muddy-mettled rascal, peak
Like John-a-dreams, unpregnant of my cause,

555 And can say nothing. No, not for a king,
Upon whose property and most dear life
A damned defeat was made. Am I a coward?
Who calls me "villain"? Breaks my pate across?
Plucks off my beard and blows it in my face?

FIRST PLAYER
Yes, my lord.

HAMLET
Very well. *(to the* PLAYERS*)* Follow that lord—and be sure not
to make fun of him.   530

    The PLAYERS *exit with* POLONIUS.

(to ROSENCRANTZ *and* GUILDENSTERN*)* My good friends, I'll leave
you until night. You are welcome to Elsinore.

ROSENCRANTZ
Good-bye, my lord.

    ROSENCRANTZ *and* GUILDENSTERN *exit.*

HAMLET
Yes, good-bye to you, too.—Now I am alone.
Oh, what a rogue and spiritless coward I am!   535
Isn't it outrageous that this player here—
in nothing more than a fiction, an imagined passion—
could force his soul to work so closely with his thoughts
that his soul caused his face to grow pale,
put tears in his eyes, gave him a troubled expression,   540
broke his voice, and made his every action
match his every thought? And all for nothing!
For Hecuba!
What does Hecuba mean to him, or he mean to Hecuba,
to make him weep for her? What would he do   545
if he had the motives and causes for passion
that I have? He would drown the stage with tears
and shatter the ears of his audience with horrifying words,
madden the guilty, terrify the innocent,
perplex the ignorant—and indeed, astonish   550
the very faculties of sight and hearing. Yet I,
a dull and weak-willed rascal, mope about
like some foolish dreamer, not stirred by my cause,
and can say nothing—no, not even for a king,   555
whose royal power and precious life
were so damnably destroyed. Am I a coward?
Does anyone call me "villain"? Strike me across the head?
Pluck off my beard and blow it in my face?

560 Tweaks me by the nose? Gives me the lie i' th' throat
     As deep as to the lungs? Who does me this?
     Ha, 'swounds, I should take it, for it cannot be
     But I am pigeon-livered* and lack gall
     To make oppression bitter, or ere this
565 I should ha' fatted all the region kites
     With this slave's offal. Bloody, bawdy villain!
     Remorseless, **treacherous**, lecherous, kindless villain!
     O, vengeance!
     Why, what an ass am I! This is most brave,
570 That I, the son of a dear father murdered,
     Prompted to my revenge by heaven and hell,
     Must, like a whore, unpack my heart with words
     And fall a-cursing like a very drab,
     A scullion! Fie upon 't, foh!
575 About, my brains. Hum—I have heard
     That guilty creatures sitting at a play
     Have by the very cunning of the scene
     Been struck so to the soul that presently
     They have proclaimed their malefactions.
580 For murder, though it have no tongue, will speak
     With most miraculous organ. I'll have these players
     Play something like the murder of my father
     Before mine uncle. I'll observe his looks,
     I'll tent him to the quick. If 'a do blench,
585 I know my course. The spirit that I have seen
     May be a devil, and the devil hath power
     T' assume a pleasing shape, yea, and perhaps
     Out of my weakness and my melancholy,
     As he is very **potent** with such spirits,
590 Abuses me to damn me. I'll have grounds
     More relative than this. The play's the thing
     Wherein I'll catch the conscience of the King.

         Exit.

---

563 *pigeon-livered* Popular belief held that doves or pigeons were mild and gentle
     because their livers produced no gall.

Tweak me by the nose? Call me the most lowdown 560
and despicable of liars? Who does this to me?
Ha! By Christ's wounds, I would take it! For surely
I am pigeon-livered and cannot summon up the anger
to embitter me against injustice—or else by now
I would have fattened all the vultures hereabouts 565
with this scoundrel's guts. Murderous, obscene villain!
Pitiless, treacherous, lecherous, unnatural villain!
Oh, vengeance!
Why, what a donkey I am! This is very fine—
that I, the son of a dear, murdered father, 570
urged toward my revenge by both heaven and hell,
must, like a whore, unload my heart with nothing but words,
take to cursing like a prostitute
or a kitchen wench! Away with this! Enough!
Get to work, my brains! Hmm . . . I have heard 575
that guilty people watching a play
have, by the sheer artistry of the performance,
been so wounded to the soul that they soon
admit their wicked deeds.
For murder, though it has no tongue, will make itself heard 580
in a miraculous way. I'll have these players
perform something like the murder of my father
in front of my uncle. I'll observe his expression;
I'll probe him till he hurts. If he but flinches,
I know what I must do. The spirit that I have seen 585
might be the devil—for the devil has the power
to assume an attractive appearance. Indeed—and perhaps
due to my weakness and depression
(since the devil is very powerful when you're in such moods),
he is deceiving me in order to damn me. I need stronger 590
    evidence
than I yet have. The play's the thing
in which I'll catch the guilty conscience of the King.

He exits.

Act II Review

Discussion Questions

1. What change of mood occurs with Scene i?

2. How do you explain Hamlet's behavior toward Ophelia, as she describes it in Scene i?

3. Fortinbras is mentioned again in Scene ii, line 72. Why is he discussed repeatedly throughout the play, even though he takes no direct part in the action?

4. How does Hamlet receive Rosencrantz and Guildenstern in Scene ii?

5. Why is Hamlet excited about the Players' arrival?

6. Compare the characters of Queen Gertrude and Ophelia. Consider how the women are different and how they are alike, citing details from the texts to support your answer. Do these women wield any power in Elsinore? Explain your answer.

7. What kind of man do you think Polonius is? Find one or two lines that support your opinion.

8. Contrast Horatio with Rosencrantz and Guildenstern as longtime friends of Hamlet.

Literary Elements

1. An **allusion** is a reference to a literary or historical figure or event. What do you think is the purpose of the allusions to Pyrrhus and Priam in Scene ii?

2. A **metaphor** makes a direct comparison between two unlike things. In Scene ii, Hamlet tells Rosencrantz and Guildenstern that "Denmark's a prison." Name all the ways in which Hamlet feels his country is like a prison; then add your own comparisons. Do you think this is an appropriate metaphor?

3. The **repetition** of words and phrases is one of Shakespeare's favorite ways of increasing the tension and emotional impact of a speech or scene. Notice where Hamlet uses repetition in Scene ii, and say what you think it contributes to this scene.

4. A **soliloquy** expresses a character's private thoughts, even if other characters are on stage. In Hamlet's soliloquy in Scene ii, he berates himself for his lack of action. Is he a coward or does he just think too much? Decide for yourself after reading his self-accusations.

Writing Prompts

1. Look at Hamlet's love poem to Ophelia in Act II, Scene ii. Would the Hamlet we meet in the play still be able to write such a poem? Explain why in a short essay. You will need to decide whether the language and feelings of his poem seem to predate the tragic events at court.

2. In Act II, Scene ii, Polonius says of Hamlet, "That he is mad, 'tis true." Do you believe that Hamlet is truly mad at this point in the play? Give your reasons in writing, referring to his words, actions, and the way other people respond to him.

3. List the emotions Hamlet expresses in Act II, connecting each emotion with a line from the text.

4. *Hamlet* is Shakespeare's longest play, and it is usually cut before being produced on stage. Pretend you are a director and decide what could be eliminated from Act II. Explain your decision in a memo to the producer.

5. One of this play's most famous quotations is "for there is nothing either good or bad but thinking makes it so." Look back at the passage where Hamlet says this (Act II, Scene ii, lines 256–257), and think about the idea he is expressing. Do you agree? Explain why or why not, using your own experiences to support your opinion.

HAMLET
ACT III

Ralph Fiennes as Hamlet and Francesca Annis as Gertrude, Almeida Theatre, London, 1995

"O SHAME, WHERE IS THY BLUSH?"

✛ ✛ ✛

Before You Read

1. Based on the first two acts, what is your opinion of Hamlet? Say what you think he should do next.

2. How do you expect Hamlet to make use of the Players?

3. Do Rosencrantz and Guildenstern seem like trustworthy friends of Hamlet? Explain why or why not.

Literary Element

1. A **soliloquy** is an extended speech in which the character reveals his or her innermost thoughts and feelings. *Hamlet* contains a number of soliloquies. In a play full of spying and deception, it is fitting that Shakespeare would give the main characters so many opportunities to reveal their true feelings to the audience.

2. **Motivation** refers to the reasons why a character behaves as he or she does. In Act III, Hamlet does not kill Claudius while the King is praying, believing that doing so would automatically send Claudius to heaven.

3. **Irony** can be the opposite of what is expected. The young girl Ophelia is not as innocent as she seems. This irony becomes apparent in Act IV, Scene v, when she sings some bawdy and knowing songs.

4. The **theme** of a work of literature is the message about life that the writer wants to convey. In *Hamlet,* the Prince often wrestles with the nature of sin and salvation since he fears hell and eternal damnation.

5. **Personification** means giving human characteristics to nonhuman things or ideas. In Act III, Claudius personifies his own words, claiming "My words fly up, my thoughts remain below. / Words without thoughts never to heaven go."

Words to Know

The following vocabulary words appear in Act III in the original text of Shakespeare's play. However, they are words that are still used today. Read the definitions here and pay attention to the words as you read the play (they will be in boldfaced type).

buffets	hits; strikes
calamity	disaster; hardship
consummation	completion; fulfillment
enterprises	projects; plans
inoculate	make resistant to; immunize
insolence	disrespect; impudence
mandate	order; command
melancholy	sadness; low spirits
panders	exploits; pimps
paradox	contradiction; inconsistency
profanely	irreverently; disrespectfully
purging	purifying; cleansing
temperance	moderation; restraint
turbulent	agitated; excited
visage	face; appearance

Act Summary

Rosencrantz and Guildenstern cannot figure out the cause of Hamlet's apparent madness. So, Claudius and Polonius plan to eavesdrop on him when he is together with Ophelia. Privately, Claudius voices his guilt over murdering his brother, the former king.

In his "to be or not to be" soliloquy, Hamlet questions the value of life. When Ophelia enters, he unleashes an onslaught of insults. Though she is grief-stricken, Claudius is suspicious. He tells Polonius that he intends to send Hamlet to England. Polonius decides to spy on Hamlet when the young man meets with his mother Gertrude.

Hamlet coaches a traveling theater troupe—the Players—on how to act. He is eager to see if the King has any reaction to the specially selected play.

The play begins with a pantomime of *The Murder of Gonzago*, a revenge play which echoes the murder of Hamlet's father. When the Player King is poisoned, Claudius rushes from the room. Hamlet is thrilled by his plot's success: Claudius's guilty exit condemns him.

Claudius is anxious to get Hamlet away from the royal court. In privacy, he again expresses remorse for killing his brother. Hamlet enters and sees him praying. He draws his sword, but then resists. If he kills Claudius while the King prays, Claudius will go to heaven. Hamlet would rather kill him when he is sinning because then Claudius would surely go to hell.

Hamlet enters Gertrude's chamber and alarms her with his threatening behavior. She calls out, and Polonius echoes her from behind the wall hanging where he is hiding. In panic, Hamlet stabs the curtain and kills Polonius. Then he continues to berate his mother. Gertrude's scared pleas summon the Ghost, who reminds Hamlet that he is meant

to avenge himself on Claudius, not torture his own mother. Hamlet is obsessed with his mother's marriage to Claudius and begs her not to sleep with Claudius that night. He also warns her not to discuss his madness with Claudius. He decides to kill Rosencrantz and Guildenstern, his supposed friends, who are in league with the King to get rid of him.

Damian Lewis as Hamlet and Paul Freeman as Claudius, Open Air Theatre, London, 1994

ACT III, SCENE I

[*The castle.*] *Enter* KING, QUEEN, POLONIUS,
ROSENCRANTZ, GUILDENSTERN, LORDS.

KING
And can you by no drift of conference
Get from him why he puts on this confusion,
Grating so harshly all his days of quiet
With **turbulent** and dangerous lunacy?

ROSENCRANTZ
5   He does confess he feels himself distracted,
But from what cause 'a will by no means speak.

GUILDENSTERN
Nor do we find him forward to be sounded,
But with a crafty madness keeps aloof
When we would bring him on to some confession
10   Of his true state.

QUEEN
                              Did he receive you well?

ROSENCRANTZ
Most like a gentleman.

GUILDENSTERN
But with much forcing of his disposition.

ROSENCRANTZ
Niggard of question, but of our demands
15   Most free in his reply.

QUEEN
Did you assay him to any pastime?

ROSENCRANTZ
Madam, it so fell out that certain players
We o'erraught on the way. Of these we told him,
And there did seem in him a kind of joy
20   To hear of it. They are here about the court,
And, as I think, they have already order
This night to play before him.

ACT 3, SCENE 1

The castle. The KING *and* QUEEN, POLONIUS, OPHELIA,
ROSENCRANTZ, GUILDENSTERN, *and* LORDS *enter.*

KING
And no matter how you manage the conversation,
you can't learn from him why he's acting strangely,
disrupting his quiet days so harshly
with violent and dangerous lunacy?

ROSENCRANTZ
He confesses that he feels troubled,   5
but by no means will he say what the cause of this might be.

GUILDENSTERN
Nor do we find him eager to be questioned,
for he keeps aloof with a cunning display of madness
whenever we try to urge him to tell us
what his true condition is.   10

QUEEN
Did he greet you well?

ROSENCRANTZ
Like a true gentleman.

GUILDENSTERN
But it seemed to be against his will.

ROSENCRANTZ
He was reluctant to talk, but replied openly
to our questions.   15

QUEEN
Did you encourage him to take part in any pastimes?

ROSENCRANTZ
Madam, it just so happened that we overtook a troupe of players
on our way here. We told him about them,
and he seemed to show some joy
in hearing of them. They are here, near the court,   20
and I think they have already been ordered
to perform for him tonight.

POLONIUS

'Tis most true,
And he beseeched me to entreat your Majesties
25   To hear and see the matter.

KING

With all my heart, and it doth much content me
To hear him so inclined.
Good gentlemen, give him a further edge
And drive his purpose into these delights.

ROSENCRANTZ

30   We shall, my lord.

> *Exeunt* ROSENCRANTZ *and* GUILDENSTERN
> [*and the* LORDS].

KING

Sweet Gertrude, leave us too,
For we have closely sent for Hamlet hither,
That he, as 'twere by accident, may here
Affront Ophelia.
35   Her father and myself (lawful espials)
Will so bestow ourselves that, seeing unseen,
We may of their encounter frankly judge
And gather by him, as he is behaved,
If 't be th' affliction of his love or no
40   That thus he suffers for.

QUEEN

I shall obey you.
And for your part, Ophelia, I do wish
That your good beauties be the happy cause
Of Hamlet's wildness. So shall I hope your virtues
45   Will bring him to his wonted way again,
To both your honors.

OPHELIA

Madam, I wish it may.

> [*Exit* QUEEN.]

POLONIUS

Ophelia, walk you here.—Gracious, so please you,
We will bestow ourselves. [*to* OPHELIA] Read on this
50   book,

POLONIUS

This is very true,
and he asked me to implore your Majesties
to hear and see the play.   25

KING

I will, with all my heart. It makes me very happy
to hear that he's so inclined.
Good gentlemen, keep tempting him in this direction,
and encourage him to throw himself into these delights.

ROSENCRANTZ

We shall, my lord.   30

ROSENCRANTZ, GUILDENSTERN, *and the* LORDS *exit.*

KING

Sweet Gertrude, you leave us, too;
for I have privately sent for Hamlet to come here,
so that he might meet Ophelia face to face,
as if by accident.
Her father and I will justifiably spy on him   35
by placing ourselves where we can see him without being
    seen;
based on their encounter, we'll be able to judge clearly
and gather from his behavior
whether or not the torment of his love
is really the cause of his suffering.   40

QUEEN

I shall obey you.
As for you, Ophelia, I hope
that your great beauty is the fortunate cause
of Hamlet's strange behavior. I also hope that your virtue
will restore him to his normal ways,   45
and that both of you will gain honor from it.

OPHELIA

Madam, I hope so, too.

The QUEEN *exits.*

POLONIUS

Ophelia, you walk here. Your Majesty, if it pleases you,
let's hide ourselves. *(to* OPHELIA*)* Read this prayer book;   50

That show of such an exercise may color
Your loneliness. We are oft to blame in this,
'Tis too much proved, that with devotion's **visage**
And pious action we do sugar o'er
55　　The devil himself.

KING [*aside*]

O, 'tis too true.
How smart a lash that speech doth give my conscience!
The harlot's cheek, beautied with plast'ring art,
Is not more ugly to the thing that helps it
60　　Than is my deed to my most painted word.
O heavy burden!

POLONIUS

I hear him coming. Let's withdraw, my lord.

[*Exeunt* KING *and* POLONIUS.]

Enter HAMLET.

HAMLET

To be or not to be—that is the question:
Whether 'tis nobler in the mind to suffer
65　　The slings and arrows of outrageous fortune,
Or to take arms against a sea of troubles,
And by opposing end them. To die, to sleep—
No more—and by a sleep to say we end
The heartache and the thousand natural shocks
70　　That flesh is heir to!—'tis a **consummation**
Devoutly to be wished. To die, to sleep—
To sleep, perchance to dream: ay, there's the rub,
For in that sleep of death what dreams may come
When we have shuffled off this mortal coil,
75　　Must give us pause. There's the respect
That makes **calamity** of so long life:
For who would bear the whips and scorns of time,
Th' oppressor's wrong, the proud man's contumely,
The pangs of despised love, the law's delay,

seeming to pray will give you a plausible excuse
for being alone. All too often, we are guilty
of putting on an outward show of piety
or performing religious acts to cover up
our inward wickedness.   55

KING (*aside*)
Oh, this is too true!
What a cutting blow that remark gave my conscience!
The whore's pockmarked face, made beautiful by heavy
   makeup,
is not more ugly, compared to the paint it wears,
than my deed is, compared to the words that try to paint   60
   over it.
Oh, what a heavy burden!

POLONIUS
I hear him coming. Let's hide, my lord.

     They hide; HAMLET *enters.*

HAMLET
Is life worth living, or isn't it? That is the question.
Which is nobler? To mentally endure
the stones and arrows launched at us by unpredictable   65
   fortune?
Or to arm ourselves against a sea of troubles,
and put an end to ourselves by fighting them? To die means
   to sleep—
no more than that. And by sleeping, we could say that we
   put an end
to the heartache and the thousand blows
to which the flesh is naturally vulnerable. That's an ending 70
truly worth wishing for. To die means to sleep;
to sleep might mean to dream. Yes, *there's* the problem.
For in that sleep of death, what dreams may come
after we have rid ourselves of the turmoil of mortal life
must make us hesitate. That's the consideration   75
that makes us endure calamity throughout our long lives.
For who would tolerate the beatings and mockeries of the world,
the injustices of tyrants, the proud man's insults,
the pangs of unrequited love, the delays of the legal process,

80 The **insolence** of office, and the spurns
That patient merit of th' unworthy takes,
When he himself might his quietus make
With a bare bodkin? Who would fardels bear,
To grunt and sweat under a weary life,
85 But that the dread of something after death,
The undiscovered country, from whose bourn
No traveler returns, puzzles the will,
And makes us rather bear those ills we have,
Than fly to others that we know not of?
90 Thus conscience does make cowards of us all,
And thus the native hue of resolution
Is sicklied o'er with the pale cast of thought,
And **enterprises** of great pitch and moment,
With this regard their currents turn awry,
95 And lose the name of action.—Soft you now,
The fair Ophelia!—Nymph, in thy orisons
Be all my sins remembered.

OPHELIA

                             Good my lord,
How does your Honour for this many a day?

HAMLET
100 I humbly thank you, well, well, well.

OPHELIA
My lord, I have remembrances of yours
That I have longed to redeliver.
I pray you now, receive them.

HAMLET
No, not I. I never gave you aught.

OPHELIA
105 My honored lord, you know right well you did,
And with them words of so sweet breath composed
As made these things more rich. Their perfume lost,
Take these again, for to the noble mind
Rich gifts wax poor when givers prove unkind.
110 There, my lord.

the insolence of officeholders, and the humiliation   80
that a good person must patiently endure from the unworthy,
when he might settle his own account
with nothing more than a dagger? Who would carry loads,
grunting and sweating under life's wearisome burdens,
except that the dread of something after death,   85
the unexplored country from whose frontier
no traveler returns, paralyzes the will,
making us choose to bear the troubles we already have
rather than flee to others that we know nothing of?
And so introspection turns us all into cowards;   90
and so the naturally healthy complexion of resolution
turns sickly with the pale shade of anxiety;
and on account of this, ambitious
and important endeavors lose their direction and momentum
and are not put into action. But look—   95
the lovely Ophelia. Nymph, remember all my sins
in your prayers.

OPHELIA

My good lord,
how has your Honor been for these many days?

HAMLET

I thank you humbly—I've been well.   100

OPHELIA

My lord, I have gifts of affection from you
that I have wanted to give back for a long time.
I ask you, please accept them now.

HAMLET

No, not I. I never gave you anything.

OPHELIA

My honored lord, you know perfectly well that you did—   105
and with them, you spoke words with such a sweet breath
that they made the gifts more precious. Now that the
perfume of your words is gone,
take these gifts back again; for to someone with a noble mind,
precious gifts become cheap when their givers turn unkind.
There, my lord.   110

HAMLET

Ha, ha! Are you honest?

OPHELIA

My lord?

HAMLET

Are you fair?

OPHELIA

What means your lordship?

HAMLET

115   That if you be honest and fair, your honesty should admit
no discourse to your beauty.

OPHELIA

Could beauty, my lord, have better commerce than with
honesty?

HAMLET

Ay, truly; for the power of beauty will sooner transform
120   honesty from what it is to a bawd than the force of
honesty can translate beauty into his likeness. This was
sometime a **paradox**, but now the time gives it proof. I
did love you once.

OPHELIA

Indeed, my lord, you made me believe so.

HAMLET

125   You should not have believed me, for virtue cannot so
inoculate our old stock but we shall relish of it. I loved
you not.

OPHELIA

I was the more deceived.

HAMLET

Get thee to a nunnery. Why wouldst thou be a breeder of
130   sinners? I am myself indifferent honest, but yet I could
accuse me of such things that it were better my mother
had not borne me: I am very proud, revengeful,
ambitious, with more offenses at my beck than I have
thoughts to put them in, imagination to give them shape,
135   or time to act them in. What should such fellows as I do

HAMLET
Ha, ha, are you chaste?

OPHELIA
My lord?

HAMLET
Are you lovely?

OPHELIA
What does your lordship mean?

HAMLET
That if you are both chaste and lovely, your chastity will allow   115
no dealings with your beauty.

OPHELIA
But my lord, could beauty have any better contact than with
chastity?

HAMLET
Truly, it could. For the power of beauty can more easily change
chastity from what it is into a pimp, than the power of chastity   120
can change beauty into something more virtuous. This was
once not generally believed, but recent events have proven
it true. I did love you once.

OPHELIA
Indeed, my lord, you made me believe so.

HAMLET
You should not have believed me; for even if virtue is grafted   125
onto the sinful plant of human nature, the fruit will still
taste like sin. I did not love you.

OPHELIA
I was all the more deceived.

HAMLET
Get yourself to a convent. Why do you want to be a breeder
of sinners? I myself am reasonably virtuous, and yet I could   130
accuse myself of such terrible things that it would be better
if my mother had not given birth to me. I am very proud,
vengeful, and ambitious, and I'm prone to commit so many
crimes, I don't have enough brains to think about them,
enough imagination to plan them, nor enough time to carry   135

crawling between earth and heaven? We are arrant knaves all; believe none of us. Go thy ways to a nunnery. Where's your father?

OPHELIA

At home, my lord.

HAMLET

140 Let the doors be shut upon him, that he may play the fool nowhere but in 's own house. Farewell.

OPHELIA

O help him, you sweet heavens!

HAMLET

If thou dost marry, I'll give thee this plague for thy dowry: Be thou as chaste as ice, as pure as snow, thou shalt not
145 escape calumny. Get thee to a nunnery. Go, farewell. Or if thou wilt needs marry, marry a fool, for wise men know well enough what monsters* you make of them. To a nunnery, go, and quickly too. Farewell.

OPHELIA

Heavenly powers, restore him!

HAMLET

150 I have heard of your paintings, well enough. God hath given you one face, and you make yourselves another. You jig and amble, and you lisp; you nickname God's creatures and make your wantonness your ignorance. Go to, I'll no more on 't; it hath made me mad. I say we will have no
155 more marriage. Those that are married already—all but one*—shall live. The rest shall keep as they are. To a nunnery, go.

    Exit.

OPHELIA

O what a noble mind is here o'erthrown!
The courtier's, soldier's, scholar's, eye, tongue, sword,
160 Th' expectancy and rose of the fair state,

---

147 *monsters* alludes to the notion that the husbands of unfaithful wives grew horns. Any allusion to horns, even of the vaguest sort, was therefore a joke on cuckoldry.

156 *all but one* a reference to Claudius

them out. What are fellows like me doing, crawling between earth and heaven? We are all outright villains; don't believe any of us. Get on your way to a convent. Where's your father?

OPHELIA

At home, my lord.

HAMLET

Let him be shut up indoors, so he can act the part of the fool   140
nowhere except in his own house. Farewell.

OPHELIA

Oh, help him, you sweet heavens!

HAMLET

If you *do* marry, I'll give you this curse for your dowry: Even if you're as chaste as ice, as pure as snow, you won't escape slander. Get yourself to a convent. Farewell. Or if you really   145
must marry, marry a fool, for wise men know well enough what monsters you women make of them. To a convent, go— and quickly, too. Farewell.

OPHELIA

Heavenly powers, cure him!

HAMLET

I've also heard plenty about how you wear makeup. God has   150
given you one face, and you make yourself another. You dance, you walk and talk affectedly, you call God's creatures by silly names, and you excuse your frivolous ways by pretending to be ignorant. Enough! I'll have no more to do with it! It has driven me mad. I say that we'll have no more marriages. Those who are already married—except one—will be allowed to live.   155
All others must remain as they are. To a convent—go!

>   HAMLET *exits.*

OPHELIA

Oh, what a noble mind has been overthrown here!
The courtier's cleverness; the soldier's sword; the scholar's
    tongue;
the promising flower of our nation's future;   160

The glass of fashion, and the mold of form,
Th' observed of all observers, quite, quite down!
And I, of ladies most deject and wretched,
That sucked the honey of his musicked vows,
165 Now see that noble and most sovereign reason
Like sweet bells jangled, out of tune and harsh,
That unmatched form and feature of blown youth
Blasted with ecstasy. O, woe is me
T' have seen what I have seen, see what I see!

Enter KING *and* POLONIUS.

KING
170 Love? His affections do not that way tend,
Nor what he spake, though it lacked form a little,
Was not like madness. There's something in his soul
O'er which his **melancholy** sits on brood,
And I do doubt the hatch and the disclose
175 Will be some danger; which for to prevent,
I have in quick determination
Thus set it down: he shall with speed to England
For the demand of our neglected tribute.
Haply the seas, and countries different,
180 With variable objects, shall expel
This something-settled matter in his heart,
Whereon his brains still beating puts him thus
From fashion of himself. What think you on 't?

POLONIUS
It shall do well. But yet do I believe
185 The origin and commencement of his grief
Sprung from neglected love. How now, Ophelia?
You need not tell us what Lord Hamlet said;
We heard it all. My lord, do as you please,
But if you hold it fit, after the play,
190 Let his queen mother all alone entreat him
To show his grief. Let her be round with him,
And I'll be placed, so please you, in the ear

the model for proper style and behavior;
the center of the court's attention; all this has been destroyed
　　completely!
And I, the most miserable and wretched of ladies,
who drank the honey of his musical vows,
now see that noble and powerful mind   165
become, like sweet bells jangled together, all harsh and out of
　　rhythm;
now see his unequaled shape and elegance blighted with
　　madness
in the bloom of youth. Oh, how sorrowful I am,
to see the man I once saw, so greatly changed.

　　　　　The KING *and* POLONIUS *come out of hiding.*

KING

Love? His inclinations do not tend that way.   170
And even though what he spoke made little sense,
it didn't sound like madness. There's something in his soul
that his sadness sits on, like a bird on its eggs;
and I fear that some danger
will hatch and break out. To prevent this,
I have quickly arrived   175
at this decision: He will speedily go to England
to demand a payment owed to us by the English king.
Perhaps the sea, different countries,
and unusual sights will drive   180
from his heart this fixed obsession
which keeps hammering in his head, causing him to behave
so unlike himself. What do you think of this idea?

POLONIUS

It should work well. But I still believe
that the origin and beginning of his troubles   185
sprang from unrequited love.—What is it, Ophelia?
You don't need to tell us what Lord Hamlet said;
We heard it all.—My lord, do as you please.
But if you think it suitable, after the play
let his mother the queen beg him to share his sorrows   190
alone with her. Let her be frank with him;
and if it pleases you, I'll be hidden within earshot

Of all their conference. If she find him not,
To England send him, or confine him where
195 Your wisdom best shall think.

KING

                    It shall be so.
Madness in great ones must not unwatched go.

Exeunt.

of their entire conversation. If she doesn't learn his secret,
then send him to England, or lock him up
wherever, in your wisdom, you think best.   195

KING
This will be done.
Madness in powerful people must not go ignored.

They exit.

ACT III, SCENE II

[*The castle.*] *Enter* HAMLET *and three of the* PLAYERS.

HAMLET

Speak the speech, I pray you, as I pronounced it to you,
trippingly on the tongue. But if you mouth it, as many of
our players do, I had as lief the town crier spoke my lines.
Nor do not saw the air too much with your hand, thus,
but use all gently, for in the very torrent, tempest, and (as
I may say) whirlwind of your passion, you must acquire
and beget a **temperance** that may give it smoothness. O, it
offends me to the soul to hear a robustious periwig-pated
fellow tear a passion to tatters, to very rags, to split the
ears of the groundlings,* who for the most part are
capable of nothing but inexplicable dumb shows and
noise. I would have such a fellow whipped for o'erdoing
Termagant.* It out-Herods Herod.* Pray you avoid it.

PLAYER

I warrant your honor.

HAMLET

Be not too tame neither, but let your own discretion be
your tutor. Suit the action to the word, the word to the
action, with this special observance, that you o'erstep not
the modesty of nature. For anything so o'erdone is from
the purpose of playing, whose end, both at the first and
now, was and is, to hold, as 'twere, the mirror up to
nature; to show virtue her own feature, scorn her own
image, and the very age and body of the time his form
and pressure. Now, this overdone, or come tardy off,
though it makes the unskillful laugh, cannot but make the
judicious grieve, the censure of the which one must in
your allowance o'erweigh a whole theater of others. O,
there be players that I have seen play, and heard others
praise, and that highly (not to speak it **profanely**), that

---

10   *groundlings* those who paid the lowest admission price to the theater and stood
on the "ground" or in the pit of the playhouse, the area we now call the
"orchestra"

13   *Termagant* the name given in medieval drama to a deity, supposedly worshipped
by the Moslems, who was violent and overbearing

ACT 3, SCENE 2

The castle. HAMLET *and three of the* PLAYERS *enter.*

HAMLET
I beg you to speak the speech just as I spoke it to you—
flowing off the tongue. If you overact it, as many players do, I'd
just as soon the town crier spoke my lines. And do not wave
your hand through the air too much, like this, but do everything with moderation. For in the midst, so to speak, of the   5
downpour, storm, and whirlwind of your emotions, you must
assume and convey a calmness that gives it all smoothness.
Oh, it disgusts me to the soul to hear a boisterous, wig-wearing
fellow tear a passionate speech to tatters and rags, splitting
the ears of the groundlings, who for the most part appreciate   10
nothing but nonsensical dumb shows and noise. I'd like to have
such a fellow whipped for overacting Termagant. It's too violent
even for the part of Herod. I ask you, please avoid it.

PLAYER
I promise we will, your Honor.

HAMLET
Don't be too tame, either, but let your own discretion be your   15
guide. Suit the action to the word, the word to the action,
taking special care not to go beyond natural moderation. For
any overacting strays from the purpose of performing plays—
which is and has always been, so to speak, to hold a mirror up   20
to the world; to show virtue its own features; to show folly its
own appearance; and to show the present age its very own
shape and image. Now if this is overdone, or not done
adequately, it might make the unsophisticated laugh, but it
will also cause the discerning to grieve; and one discerning   25
audience member's judgment must be valued above that of
everyone else in a theater. Oh, there are players whom I've seen
perform, and heard others praise—and highly. And yet they

---

13   *Herod* The Jewish king who sought to kill the infant Jesus was represented in
       medieval drama as an extravagant and blustering tyrant.

neither having th' accent of Christians, nor the gait of
30 Christian, pagan, nor man, have so strutted and bellowed
that I have thought some of Nature's journeymen had
made men, and not made them well, they imitated
humanity so abominably.

PLAYER
I hope we have reformed that indifferently with us, sir.

HAMLET
35 O, reform it altogether! And let those that play your
clowns speak no more than is set down for them, for there
be of them that will themselves laugh, to set on some
quantity of barren spectators to laugh too, though in the
meantime some necessary question of the play be then to
40 be considered. That's villainous and shows a most pitiful
ambition in the fool that uses it. Go make you ready.

Exit PLAYERS.

Enter POLONIUS, GUILDENSTERN, *and*
ROSENCRANTZ.

How now, my lord? Will the King hear this piece of work?

POLONIUS
And the Queen too, and that presently.

HAMLET
Bid the Players make haste.

Exit POLONIUS.

45 Will you two help to hasten them?

ROSENCRANTZ
Ay, my lord.

Exeunt they two.

HAMLET
What, ho, Horatio!

Enter HORATIO.

HORATIO
Here, sweet lord, at your service.

don't speak like Christians—nor do they walk like Christians,   30
pagans, or any kind of man. Not to speak irreligiously, but
they've strutted and bellowed so much that I thought some
of God's apprentices must have made such men—and not
made them well, they imitated humanity so abominably.

PLAYER

I hope we have reformed that pretty well among ourselves, sir.

HAMLET

Oh, reform it completely. And make sure that those who play   35
the comic parts speak only what is written down for them. For
there are some of them who will laugh at themselves in order
to get a few stupid spectators to laugh, too; even though in
the meantime, some important issue in the play ought to be
considered. That's villainous, and shows a truly pathetic   40
ambition in the comedian that acts that way. Go and make
yourselves ready.

> *The* PLAYERS *exit;* POLONIUS, GUILDENSTERN, *and*
> ROSENCRANTZ *enter.*

Well, now, my lord—will the King attend the performance of this
play?

POLONIUS

And the Queen, too—and right away.

HAMLET

Tell the Players to hurry.

> POLONIUS *exits.*

Will you two help them get ready quickly?   45

ROSENCRANTZ

Yes, my lord.

> ROSENCRANTZ *and* GUILDENSTERN *exit.*

HAMLET

Hello, there! Horatio!

> HORATIO *enters.*

HORATIO

Here I am, my good lord—at your service.

HAMLET

Horatio, thou art e'en as just a man
50 As e'er my conversation coped withal.

HORATIO

O, my dear lord—

HAMLET

Nay, do not think I flatter.
For what advancement may I hope from thee,
That no revenue hast but thy good spirits
55 To feed and clothe thee? Why should the poor be
         flattered?
No, let the candied tongue lick absurd pomp,
And crook the pregnant hinges of the knee
Where thrift may follow fawning. Dost thou hear?
60 Since my dear soul was mistress of her choice
And could of men distinguish her election,
Hath sealed thee for herself, for thou hast been
As one, in suff'ring all, that suffers nothing,
A man that Fortune's **buffets** and rewards
65 Hast ta'en with equal thanks; and blest are those
Whose blood and judgment are so well commeddled
That they are not a pipe for Fortune's finger
To sound what stop she please. Give me that man
That is not passion's slave, and I will wear him
70 In my heart's core, ay, in my heart of heart,
As I do thee.—Something too much of this—
There is a play tonight before the King.
One scene of it comes near the circumstance
Which I have told thee, of my father's death.
75 I prithee, when thou seest that act afoot,
Even with the very comment of thy soul
Observe my uncle. If his occulted guilt
Do not itself unkennel in one speech,
It is a damned ghost that we have seen,
80 And my imaginations are as foul
As Vulcan's stithy.* Give him heedful note,
For I mine eyes will rivet to his face,

---

81 *Vulcan's stithy* Vulcan is the god of fire, the metalworker and artisan of the gods, who presides over a large forge.

HAMLET

Horatio, you are as honest a man
as my dealings have ever brought me into contact with.   50

HORATIO

Oh, my dear lord—

HAMLET

No, don't think I'm flattering you.
For what favors can I hope to receive from you,
since you have no property but your good spirits
to feed and clothe yourself? Why should the poor be flattered?   55
No, let flattering tongues lick those with outrageous power,
and let the readily flexible knee curtsey
where profit can be gained from flattery. Are you listening?
Ever since my priceless soul was able to choose for itself,
and learned to distinguish between men, it has chosen   60
you for its friend. For no matter how you've suffered,
you've shown no outward signs of suffering;
you are a man who accepts Fortune's blows and rewards
with equal thanks. Blessed is a man   65
whose passion and reason are so well-mixed
that he is not like a flute on which Fortune's fingers
can play whatever notes she pleases. Give me a man
who is not a slave to his emotions, and I will hold him
in the center of my heart—indeed, in the heart of my heart,   70
just as I do you. But I'm going on too much like this.
A play will be performed tonight for the King.
One scene of it comes very close to the circumstances
of my father's death, which I have told you about.
I ask you, when you see that action unfold,   75
observe my uncle with the deepest wisdom
of your soul. If his hidden guilt
doesn't reveal itself during one particular speech,
it is an evil ghost that we have seen,
and my suspicions are as filthy   80
as Vulcan's forge. Pay close attention to him,
for I will also fix my eyes on his face;

And after we will both our judgments join
In censure of his seeming.

HORATIO

Well, my lord.
If 'a steal aught the whilst this play is playing,
And 'scape detecting, I will play the theft.

> *Enter Trumpets and Kettledrums,* KING, QUEEN,
> POLONIUS, OPHELIA, ROSENCRANTZ,
> GUILDENSTERN, *and other* LORDS *attendant with
> his* GUARD *carrying torches. Danish March. Sound
> a flourish.*

HAMLET

They are coming to the play. I must be idle.
Get you a place.

KING

How fares our cousin Hamlet?

HAMLET

Excellent, i' faith, of the chameleon's dish.*
I eat the air, promise-crammed; you cannot feed capons so.

KING

I have nothing with this answer, Hamlet; these words are
not mine.

HAMLET

No, nor mine now. [*to* POLONIUS] My lord, you played
once i' th' university, you say?

POLONIUS

That did I, my lord, and was accounted a good actor.

HAMLET

What did you enact?

---

91   *chameleon's dish* Hamlet deliberately misinterprets the King's "fares" to mean
     "what sort of food do you eat?" Chameleons were thought to feed on air, and
     Hamlet claims ironically that he lives on the King's promise that he will succeed
     to the throne.

afterwards, we will compare our observations
and judge his reaction.

HORATIO

Fine, my lord.
If he conceals anything while the play is being performed
and it escapes detection, I'll repay the loss.

> MUSICIANS *enter playing trumpets and kettledrums; also the*
> KING *and* QUEEN, POLONIUS, OPHELIA, ROSENCRANTZ,
> GUILDENSTERN, *and other attendant* LORDS; *the King's*
> GUARDS *carry torches. A fanfare is heard.*

HAMLET

They are coming to the play. I must play the fool.
Find yourself a seat.

KING

How is my nephew Hamlet? 90

HAMLET

Very well, indeed—and dining on the chameleon's food. I eat
the air, which is crammed with promises. You cannot stuff
poultry that way.

KING

I can make no sense of this answer, Hamlet. These words have
nothing to do with me.

HAMLET

Nor with me, either, now that they've left my mouth. *(to* 95
POLONIUS*)* My lord, didn't you say that you once acted at
the university?

POLONIUS

That I did, my lord—and was considered a good actor.

HAMLET

What part did you play?

POLONIUS

I did enact Julius Caesar. I was killed i' th' Capitol.*

100 Brutus killed me.

HAMLET

It was a brute part of him to kill so capital a calf there.
Be the Players ready?

ROSENCRANTZ

Ay, my lord. They stay upon your patience.

QUEEN

Come hither, my dear Hamlet, sit by me.

HAMLET

105 No, good mother. Here's metal more attractive.

POLONIUS [to the KING]

O ho! Do you mark that?

HAMLET

Lady, shall I lie in your lap?

[He lies at OPHELIA's feet.]

OPHELIA

No, my lord.

HAMLET

I mean, my head upon your lap?

OPHELIA

110 Ay, my lord.

HAMLET

Do you think I meant country matters?

OPHELIA

I think nothing, my lord.

HAMLET

That's a fair thought to lie between maids' legs.

---

99 *Capitol* the great temple of Jupiter in Rome, but generally taken to be the Senate
House. Hamlet puns in his reply: "capital/Capitol".

POLONIUS

I played Julius Caesar. I was killed in the Capitol. Brutus
killed me.   100

HAMLET

That was brutal of him, to kill so fine a fool there. Are the
Players ready?

ROSENCRANTZ

Yes, my lord. They're waiting for your permission to begin.

QUEEN

Come here, my dear Hamlet—sit beside me.

HAMLET

No, good mother. *(indicating* OPHELIA*) This* metal draws me
like a magnet.   105

> HAMLET *goes to* OPHELIA.

POLONIUS

(to the KING*)* Oh, listen! Did you hear that?

HAMLET

Lady, shall I lie in your lap?

> *He lies at* OPHELIA's *feet.*

OPHELIA

No, my lord.

HAMLET

I mean, with my head upon your lap?

OPHELIA

Yes, my lord.   110

HAMLET

Do you think I meant something indecent?

OPHELIA

I think nothing, my lord.

HAMLET

That's a lovely thought to find lying between a young lady's legs.

OPHELIA
What is, my lord?

HAMLET
115   Nothing.

OPHELIA
You are merry, my lord.

HAMLET
Who, I?

OPHELIA
Ay, my lord,

HAMLET
O God, your only jig-maker.* What should a man do but
120   be merry? For look you how cheerfully my mother looks,
and my father died within 's two hours.

OPHELIA
Nay, 'tis twice two months, my lord.

HAMLET
So long? Nay then, let the devil wear black, for I'll have a
suit of sables.* O heavens! Die two months ago, and not
125   forgotten yet? Then there's hope a great man's memory
may outlive his life half a year. But, by'r Lady, 'a must
build churches then, or else shall 'a suffer not thinking on,
with the hobby-horse, whose epitaph is "For O, for O, the
hobby-horse is forgot!"*

The trumpets sound. Dumb show follows:

*Enter a King and Queen very lovingly, the Queen
embracing him, and he her. She kneels and makes show
of protestation unto him. He takes her up and declines his
head upon her neck. He lies him down upon a bank of
flowers. She, seeing him asleep, leaves him. Anon come
in another man: takes off his crown, kisses it, pours
poison in the sleeper's ears, and leaves him. The Queen*

---

119   *jig-maker* A jig was a comic performance given at the end of a play or during an
      interval. A "jig-maker" is a comedian.

124   *sables* then as now, extremely expensive fur, but Hamlet plays on the other
      meaning of the word, "black"

OPHELIA

What is, my lord?

HAMLET

Nothing. 115

OPHELIA

You are merry, my lord.

HAMLET

Who, I?

OPHELIA

Yes, my lord.

HAMLET

Oh, God, I'm nothing more than your jester. What should a man
do but be merry? For look at how cheerful my mother looks, 120
and my father died less than two hours ago.

OPHELIA

No, it's been two months twice over, my lord.

HAMLET

That long? Well, then, the devil can wear black, for I'll have a
suit of dark fur. Oh, heavens, he died two months ago, and he's
not forgotten yet? Then there's hope that a great man's 125
memory may outlast his life by half a year. But, by the Virgin
Mary, he must build churches where he'll be prayed for, or
else he'll end up forgotten—along with the hobby-horse,
whose epitaph is, "For oh, for oh, the hobby-horse is forgotten."

The trumpets sound. A pantomime follows:

A PLAYER KING *and* PLAYER QUEEN *enter, embracing each
other very lovingly. She kneels, seeming to declare her love for
him. He lifts her up and leans his head upon her neck. He lies
down on a bed of flowers. Seeing that he's asleep, she leaves
him. Soon another* MAN *comes in, takes off the sleeping*
PLAYER KING's *crown, kisses it, pours poison in the*
PLAYER KING's *ear, and leaves him. The* PLAYER QUEEN

---

129   *hobby-horse is forgot*   The "hobby-horse" is a character dressed as a horse in
traditional country sports and skits like the Morris dance. The line Hamlet quotes
is from a popular ballad lamenting the suppression of such sports in
Shakespeare's day.

*returns, finds the King dead, makes passionate action.
The poisoner, with some three or four, come in again,
seem to condole with her. The dead body is carried away.
The poisoner woos the Queen with gifts; she seems harsh
awhile, but in the end accepts love.*

Exeunt.

OPHELIA

130   What means this, my lord?

HAMLET

Marry, this is miching mallecho; it means mischief.

OPHELIA

Belike this show imports the argument of the play.

Enter PROLOGUE.

HAMLET

We shall know by this fellow. The Players cannot keep
counsel; they'll tell all.

OPHELIA

135   Will 'a tell us what this show meant?

HAMLET

Ay, or any show that you will show him. Be not you
ashamed to show, he'll not shame to tell you what it
means.

OPHELIA

You are naught, you are naught; I'll mark the play.

PROLOGUE

140   *For us, and for our tragedy,
Here stooping to your clemency,
We beg your hearing patiently.*

[*Exits.*]

HAMLET

Is this a prologue or the posy of a ring?

OPHELIA

'Tis brief, my lord.

returns, finds the PLAYER KING *dead, and makes gestures of grief. The* POISONER *reenters with three or four other* MEN, *and seems to comfort her. The dead body is carried away. The* POISONER *courts the* PLAYER QUEEN *with gifts. She seems to reject him for a while, but in the end accepts his love.*

The PLAYERS *exit.*

OPHELIA

What does this mean, my lord? 130

HAMLET

Indeed, this is sneaking wickedness. It means that mischief's afoot.

OPHELIA

Perhaps this represents the plot of the play.

The PLAYER *who speaks the prologue enters.*

HAMLET

We'll find out from this fellow. The Players cannot keep secrets; they'll tell all.

OPHELIA

Will he tell us what the show we just saw meant? 135

HAMLET

Yes—or any show that *you* want to put on for him. If you're not ashamed to show yourself to him, he'll not be ashamed to tell you what it means.

OPHELIA

You're being crude, you're being crude. I'll listen to the play.

PROLOGUE

As we kneel for your mercy, 140
We beg you to listen patiently
to us and our tragedy.

The PLAYER *who speaks the prologue exits.*

HAMLET

Is this a prologue, or the motto carved inside a ring?

OPHELIA

It's short, my lord.

HAMLET

145   As woman's love.

Enter [two PLAYERS as] KING and QUEEN.

PLAYER KING

        Full thirty times hath Phoebus's cart gone round
        Neptune's salt wash and Tellus's orbed ground,
        And thirty dozen moons with borrowed sheen
        About the world have times twelve thirties been,
150   Since love our hearts, and Hymen did our hands,
        Unite commutual in most sacred bands.

PLAYER QUEEN

        So many journeys may the sun and moon
        Make us again count o'er ere love be done!
        But woe is me, you are so sick of late,
155   So far from cheer and from your former state,
        That I distrust you. Yet, though I distrust,
        Discomfort you, my lord, it nothing must.
        For women fear too much, even as they love,
        And women's fear and love hold quantity,
160   In neither aught, or in extremity.
        Now what my love is, proof hath made you know,
        And as my love is sized, my fear is so.
        Where love is great, the littlest doubts are fear;
        Where little fears grow great, great love grows there.

PLAYER KING

165   Faith, I must leave thee, love, and shortly too;
        My operant powers their functions leave to do:
        And thou shalt live in this fair world behind,
        Honored, beloved, and haply one as kind
        For husband shalt thou—

PLAYER QUEEN

170   O, confound the rest!
        Such love must needs be treason in my breast.
        In second husband let me be accurst!
        None wed the second but who killed the first.

HAMLET
Like a woman's love.   145

  The PLAYER KING *and* QUEEN *enter.*

PLAYER KING
A full thirty times, Phoebus's chariot has gone around
Neptune's sea and Tellus's round globe;
and three hundred and sixty moons, with borrowed light,
have made twelve times thirty circlings of the world
since love joined our hearts and Hymen joined our hands   150
in the sacred, mutual bond of marriage.

PLAYER QUEEN
May we count as many more journeys
of the sun and moon before our love is over!
But how sorrowful I am! You have been sick lately—
so far from cheerful, so unlike your old self   155
that I fear for you. But although I am afraid,
you mustn't let my fear discomfort you, my lord.
Women fear too much whenever they love too much;
for women's fear and love are always equal,
whether they feel too little or too much of both.   160
The size of my love has been proven to you,
and my fear is just as large as my love.
When love is great, the smallest worries turn into fear;
so when little fears become great, that is a sign of great love.

PLAYER KING
Indeed, my dear, I must leave this life and you—and shortly,
    too.   165
My health is failing more and more.
And you will live on in this splendid world after I die,
honored and beloved; and perhaps you'll find a husband
just as kind as—

PLAYER QUEEN
Oh, don't say the rest!   170
To love again would be treasonous in my heart.
Let me be cursed if I remarry.
No woman should marry a second husband who didn't kill the
    first.

HAMLET [*aside*]
That's wormwood.

PLAYER QUEEN
175   The instances that second marriage move
Are base respects of thrift, but none of love.
A second time I kill my husband dead
When second husband kisses me in bed.

PLAYER KING
I do believe you think what now you speak,
180   But what we do determine oft we break.
Purpose is but the slave to memory,
Of violent birth, but poor validity,
Which now like fruit unripe sticks on the tree,
But fall unshaken when they mellow be.
185   Most necessary 'tis that we forget
To pay ourselves what to ourselves is debt.
What to ourselves in passion we propose,
The passion ending, doth the purpose lose.
The violence of either grief or joy
190   Their own enactures with themselves destroy:
Where joy most revels, grief doth most lament;
Grief joys, joy grieves, on slender accident.
This world is not for aye, nor 'tis not strange
That even our loves should with our fortunes change,
195   For 'tis a question left us yet to prove,
Whether love lead fortune, or else fortune love.
The great man down, you mark his favorite flies;
The poor advanced makes friends of enemies;
And hitherto doth love on fortune tend,
200   For who not needs shall never lack a friend;
And who in want a hollow friend doth try,
Directly seasons him his enemy.
But, orderly to end where I begun,
Our wills and fates do so contrary run
205   That our devices still are overthrown;
Our thoughts are ours, their ends none of our own.

HAMLET (*aside*)
That will taste bitter!

PLAYER QUEEN
The causes that lead to a second marriage 175
are lowly concerns of wealth, not love.
Having a second husband kiss me in bed
would mean killing my first husband a second time.

PLAYER KING
I'm sure you believe what you now say,
but we often fail to do what we decide. 180
Your purpose can only be carried out if you remember it,
and it's been made in a passionate moment that cannot last;
now it's like an unripe fruit that clings to the tree,
but it will fall without being shaken once it grows ripe.
We inevitably neglect to carry out 185
the promises we make to ourselves.
What we propose to do in the heat of the moment
is forgotten when that moment cools.
The intensity of either grief or joy
destroys itself, along with its intended actions. 190
Whenever joy brings great celebration, grief will bring great
     weeping;
grief turns to joy, and joy turns to grief, for trivial reasons.
This world is not eternal, and it is not strange
that our affections should change along with our fortunes;
for experience will teach us 195
whether love guides fortune, or fortune guides love.
When a great man falls from power, notice how his best friend
     flees;
when a poor man gains power, his enemies become his friends.
So it would seem that love is always guided by fortune;
for a prosperous person will never lack a friend, 200
while if someone poor seeks help from a shallow friend,
he'll quickly turn him into an enemy.
But to end quite logically where I began:
Our wishes and our fates are in such conflict
that our plans for the future are always undone. 205
We may think whatever we like, but what our thoughts lead
     to is beyond our control.

So think thou wilt no second husband wed,
But die thy thoughts when thy first lord is dead.

PLAYER QUEEN

210 Nor earth to me give food, nor heaven light,
Sport and repose lock from me day and night,
To desperation turn my trust and hope,
And anchor's cheer in prison be my scope,
Each opposite that blanks the face of joy
215 Meet what I would have well, and it destroy:
Both here and hence pursue me lasting strife,
If, once a widow, ever I be wife!

HAMLET

If she should break it now!

PLAYER KING

'Tis deeply sworn. Sweet, leave me here awhile;
My spirits grow dull, and fain I would beguile
220 The tedious day with sleep.

     [He] sleeps.

PLAYER QUEEN

                     Sleep rock thy brain,
And never come mischance between us twain!

     Exit.

HAMLET

Madam, how like you this play?

QUEEN

The lady doth protest too much, methinks.

HAMLET

225 O, but she'll keep her word.

KING

Have you heard the argument? Is there no offense in 't?

HAMLET

No, no, they do but jest, poison in jest. No offense
i' th' world.

So although you think you'll not wed a second husband,
that thought will die when your first husband is dead.

PLAYER QUEEN

Let earth give me no food, nor heaven light;
let me be deprived of both recreation and sleep, both day   210
    and night;
let all my trust and hope turn into despair;
let a hermit's meager diet be all I have to look forward to;
let every obstacle that makes a happy face turn sad
thwart and destroy everything I wish for;
let everlasting strife pursue me in this life and the next   215
if I ever become a wife after I've been a widow.

HAMLET

If she should break this vow now!

PLAYER KING

This is a profound oath. Sweetheart, leave me here awhile.
My spirits fade, and I'd like to ease
the tedious day with sleep.   220

>   The PLAYER KING *sleeps.*

PLAYER QUEEN

May sleep soothe your brain,
and may no misfortune ever come between us two.

>   The PLAYER QUEEN *exits.*

HAMLET

Madam, how do you like this play?

QUEEN

The lady makes too many promises, I think.

HAMLET

Oh, but she'll keep her word.   225

KING

Do you know the plot? Is there nothing offensive it?

HAMLET

No, no, they're only pretending; it's a make-believe poisoning.
Nothing offensive at all.

KING

What do you call this play?

HAMLET

230 "The Mousetrap." Marry, how? Tropically.* This play is the
image of a murder done in Vienna: Gonzago is the Duke's
name; his wife, Baptista. You shall see anon. 'Tis a knavish
piece of work, but what of that? Your Majesty and we that
have free souls, it touches us not. Let the galled jade
235 winch; our withers are unwrung.

> *Enter* LUCIANUS.

This is one Lucianus, nephew to the King.

OPHELIA

You are as good as a chorus, my lord.

HAMLET

I could interpret between you and your love, if I could see
the puppets dallying.

OPHELIA

240 You are keen, my lord, you are keen.

HAMLET

It would cost you a groaning to take off mine edge.

OPHELIA

Still better and worse.

HAMLET

So you mistake your husbands.—Begin, murderer. Leave
thy damnable faces and begin. Come, the croaking raven
245 doth bellow for revenge.

LUCIANUS

Thoughts black, hands apt, drugs fit, and time agreeing,
Confederate season, else no creature seeing,
Thou mixture rank, of midnight weeds* collected,

---

230 *Tropically* wordplay on "tropically/trap"; the word is in fact spelled "trapically" in
the 1604 edition of the play. "Tropically" is from "trope," a figure of speech.

KING

> What do you call the play?

HAMLET

> "The Mousetrap." Why, you may ask? It's a figure of speech.   230
> This play recounts a murder committed in Vienna. Gonzago is
> the Duke's name; his wife is Baptista. You'll understand shortly.
> It's a wicked piece of work, but what does that matter? Your
> Majesty and the rest of us have clean consciences; it's got
> nothing to do us. Let the bruised horse squirm in its bridle;
> our shoulders are unhurt.   235

> > LUCIANUS *enters.*

> This is a certain Lucianus, nephew to the king.

OPHELIA

> You are as good as a chorus, my lord.

HAMLET

> I could narrate a puppet show showing you and your lover
> together.

OPHELIA

> You are sharp, my lord, you are sharp.   240

HAMLET

> You'd have to do some groaning to take the edge off my
> sharp lust.

OPHELIA

> That's even better—but also worse.

HAMLET

> "For better or worse"—that's how you women falsely take your
> husbands. *(to the* ACTOR *playing Lucianus)* But get started,
> murderer! Curse you, quit making those damned faces, and get
> on with it. Come on, the croaking raven is calling for revenge!   245

LUCIANUS

> Black thoughts, skillful hands, strong drugs, and a fitting time have
> > joined together;
> opportunity is on my side, and no other creature sees me.
> And so, you evil-smelling potion made from weeds gathered at
> > midnight,

---

248   *midnight weeds* According to popular beliefs about magic, weeds collected at
       midnight were especially effective for casting spells.

With Hecate's ban* thrice blasted, thrice infected,
250   Thy natural magic and dire property
On wholesome life usurps immediately.

Pours the poison in his ears.

HAMLET

'A poisons him i' th' garden for his estate. His name's
Gonzago. The story is extant and written in very choice
Italian. You shall see anon how the murderer gets the love
255   of Gonzago's wife.

OPHELIA

The King rises.

HAMLET

What, frighted with false fire?

QUEEN

How fares my lord?

POLONIUS

Give o'er the play.

KING

260   Give me some light. Away!

POLONIUS

Lights, lights, lights!

Exeunt all but HAMLET *and* HORATIO.

HAMLET

    "Why, let the strucken deer go weep,
        The hart ungalled play:
    For some must watch, while some must sleep;
265   Thus runs the world away."
Would not this, sir, and a forest of feathers—if the rest of
my fortunes turn Turk with me—with two Provincial roses
on my razed* shoes, get me a fellowship in a cry of players?

---

249   *Hecate's ban* Hecate was the Greek goddess of ghosts and magic, a protectress of
enchanters and witches.

blasted and infected three times with Hecate's curse,
use your inborn magic and dangerous powers   250
to steal his healthy life immediately.

> LUCIANUS *pours the poison in the* PLAYER KING'S *ears.*

HAMLET

He poisons him in the garden to get his throne. Gonzago is
the sleeping man's name. The story is well-known, and written
in very fine Italian. You'll soon see how the murderer wins the
love of Gonzago's wife.   255

> CLAUDIUS *rises.*

OPHELIA

The King rises.

HAMLET

What, frightened by blank cartridges?

QUEEN

How do you feel, my lord?

POLONIUS

Stop the play.

KING

Put on the lights. I must leave!   260

POLONIUS

Lights, lights, lights!

> *All but* HAMLET *and* HORATIO *exit.*

HAMLET

Why, let the wounded deer go weep,
  and the uninjured stag play.
For some must stay awake, while some must sleep;
  such is the way of the world.   265
Tell me, sir; if my luck should turn bad, wouldn't this play
(along with a bunch of plumes, and shoes decorated with
slashes and French rose patterns) get me a partnership in a
company of players?

266–268   *forest of feathers . . . razed* Hamlet describes an Elizabethan actor's trimmings:
  "feathers"—plumes worn by tragic actors; "Provincial roses"—ribbon rosettes
  designed to look like roses (of Provençe); and "razed shoes"—shoes
  decorated with slashes.

HORATIO
Half a share.

HAMLET
270 A whole one, I.
"For thou dost know, O Damon* dear,
This realm dismantled was
Of Jove himself; and now reigns here
A very, very—pajock."*

HORATIO
275 You might have rhymed.

HAMLET
O good Horatio, I'll take the Ghost's word for a thousand
pound. Didst perceive?

HORATIO
Very well, my lord.

HAMLET
Upon the talk of poisoning?

HORATIO
280 I did very well note him.

HAMLET
Ah ha! Come, some music! Come, the recorders!
[*Sings.*] "For if the King like not the comedy,
Why then, belike he likes it not, perdy."
Come, some music!

Enter ROSENCRANTZ *and* GUILDENSTERN.

GUILDENSTERN
285 Good my lord, vouchsafe me a word with you.

HAMLET
Sir, a whole history.

GUILDENSTERN
The King, sir—

---

271 *Damon* In the well-known story from Roman mythology, Damon and Pythias
were such devoted friends that Damon pledged his life as a hostage for the
condemned Pythias.

HORATIO
> It would get you half a share.

HAMLET
> I'd get a whole share, certainly.   270
> > *For you know, O dear Damon,*
> > > *this country was stripped bare*
> > *by Jove himself; and now the ruler here is*
> > > *a real—peacock.*

HORATIO
> You might have ended with a rhyme.   275

HAMLET
> Oh, good Horatio, I'll bet a thousand pounds that the ghost
> told the truth. Did you see the King?

HORATIO
> Very well, my lord.

HAMLET
> During the part about poisoning?

HORATIO
> I watched him very well.   280

HAMLET
> Aha! Come on, let's have come music. Come on, bring some
> flutes!
> *(song) For if the King does not like the play—*
> *well, then, he probably just doesn't like it, by God.*
> Come on, some music!

> > ROSENCRANTZ *and* GUILDENSTERN *enter.*

GUILDENSTERN
> My good lord, permit me to have a word with you.   285

HAMLET
> Sir, you can have a whole history with me.

GUILDENSTERN
> The King, sir—

---

274   *pajock* substitute for "ass," the word that would have rhymed. According to the
natural history of the time, the habits of the peacock were repulsive.

HAMLET

Ay, sir, what of him?

GUILDENSTERN

Is in his retirement marvelous distemper'd.

HAMLET

290 With drink, sir?

GUILDENSTERN

No, my lord, with choler.

HAMLET

Your wisdom should show itself more richer to signify this
to the doctor, for me to put him to his purgation would
perhaps plunge him into more choler.*

GUILDENSTERN

295 Good my lord, put your discourse into some frame, and
start not so wildly from my affair.

HAMLET

I am tame, sir. Pronounce.

GUILDENSTERN

The Queen, your mother, in most great affliction of spirit,
hath sent me to you.

HAMLET

300 You are welcome.

GUILDENSTERN

Nay, good my lord, this courtesy is not of the right breed.
If it shall please you to make me a wholesome answer, I
will do your mother's commandment: if not, your pardon
and my return shall be the end of my business.

HAMLET

305 Sir, I cannot.

ROSENCRANTZ

What, my lord?

---

294   *choler* Hamlet deliberately takes "choler" (anger) to mean that the King is
bilious, that is, suffering from an excess of bile. Bile was one of the four fluids of
the human body, according to the physiological theory of the time: blood,
phlegm, choler (or bile), and black bile.

HAMLET
Indeed, sir, what about him?

GUILDENSTERN
—has gone away very upset.

HAMLET
With drink, sir? 290

GUILDENSTERN
No, my lord—with anger.

HAMLET
You'd prove yourself more wise to tell a doctor about this; for if I were to try to cure him, it might make him more angry.

GUILDENSTERN
Good sir, try to make some sense, and don't leap so wildly 295 away from what I'm telling you.

HAMLET
I'll be tame, sir. Tell me.

GUILDENSTERN
The Queen your mother, in a most troubled spirit, has sent me to you.

HAMLET
Welcome, then. 300

GUILDENSTERN
No, my good lord; welcoming me is not the right sort of reply. If you'll be so kind as to give me a reasonable answer, I'll do as your mother commanded me. If not, your forgiveness and my return to her will bring an end to my business.

HAMLET
Sir, I cannot. 305

ROSENCRANTZ
What, my lord?

HAMLET

Make you a wholesome answer; my wit's diseased. But, sir, such answer as I can make, you shall command, or rather, as you say, my mother. Therefore no more, but to the matter. My mother, you say—

310

ROSENCRANTZ

Then thus she says: your behavior hath struck her into amazement and admiration.

HAMLET

O wonderful son, that can so 'stonish a mother! But is there no sequel at the heels of this mother's admiration? Impart.

315

ROSENCRANTZ

She desires to speak with you in her closet ere you go to bed.

HAMLET

We shall obey, were she ten times our mother. Have you any further trade with us?

ROSENCRANTZ

My lord, you once did love me.

HAMLET

And do still, by these pickers and stealers.*

320

ROSENCRANTZ

Good my lord, what is your cause of distemper? You do surely bar the door upon your own liberty if you deny your griefs to your friend.

HAMLET

Sir, I lack advancement.

ROSENCRANTZ

How can that be, when you have the voice of the King himself for your succession in Denmark?

325

Enter the PLAYERS *with recorders.*

---

320   *stealers* The catechism of the Church of England says that we must keep our hands from "picking and stealing."

HAMLET

Give you a reasonable answer. My sanity is diseased. But sir, you may command me to give whatever answer I can—or rather, as you say, my *mother* may command it. And so let's get right to the point. My mother, you say— 310

ROSENCRANTZ

This is what she says: your behavior has overwhelmed her with amazement and bewilderment.

HAMLET

Oh, what a wonderful son, who can astonish a mother so much! But have you anything more to tell me than of my mother's bewilderment? Speak up. 315

ROSENCRANTZ

She wishes to speak with you in her private chamber before you go to bed.

HAMLET

We shall obey, as if she were ten times our mother. Do you have any further business with us?

ROSENCRANTZ

My lord, you once loved me.

HAMLET

And swear by these thieving hands, I still do. 320

ROSENCRANTZ

My good lord, what is the cause of your madness? You'll shut the door on any cure if you refuse to tell your sorrows to your friend.

HAMLET

Sir, I lack promotion.

ROSENCRANTZ

How can that be, when the King himself has named you the 325 heir to Denmark's throne?

The PLAYERS enter with wooden flutes.

HAMLET

Ay, sir, but "while the grass grows"—the proverb* is something musty.

[*Enter the* PLAYERS *with recorders.*]

O, the recorders. Let me see one. To withdraw with you why do you go about to recover the wind of me as if you would drive me into a toil?

GUILDENSTERN

O my lord, if my duty be too bold, my love is too unmannerly.

HAMLET

I do not well understand that. Will you play upon this pipe?

GUILDENSTERN

My lord, I cannot.

HAMLET

I pray you.

GUILDENSTERN

Believe me, I cannot.

HAMLET

I pray you.

GUILDENSTERN

Believe me, I cannot.

HAMLET

I do beseech you.

GUILDENSTERN

I know no touch of it, my lord.

HAMLET

It is as easy as lying. Govern these ventages with your fingers and thumb, give it breath with your mouth, and it will discourse most eloquent music. Look you, these are the stops.

GUILDENSTERN

But these cannot I command to any utt'rance of harmony; I have not the skill.

---

327   *proverb* "While the grass grows, the horse starves."

HAMLET

Indeed, sir, but "While the grass grows"—that proverb is too old to quote.

The PLAYERS enter with recorders.

Oh, the flutes! Let me see one! *(to GUILDENSTERN)* Let's speak privately. Why are you trying to get downwind of me, as if you were driving me into a trap? 330

GUILDENSTERN

Oh, my lord, if I pursue my duty too boldly, it's because I love you too much to worry about proper manners.

HAMLET

I don't understand that well. Will you play upon this flute?

GUILDENSTERN

My lord, I cannot. 335

HAMLET

I beg you.

GUILDENSTERN

Believe me, I cannot.

HAMLET

I implore you.

GUILDENSTERN

I don't know how to play it, my lord.

HAMLET

Please, I want you to play. 340

GUILDENSTERN

I have no skill to play it, my lord.

HAMLET

It's as easy as lying. Cover these openings with your fingers and thumb, breathe into it with your mouth, and it will let forth the most eloquent music. Look, these are the holes. 345

GUILDENSTERN

But I have no mastery of this instrument to make it sing. I don't have the skill.

HAMLET
Why, look you now, how unworthy a thing you make of
me! You would play upon me, you would seem to know
350   my stops, you would pluck out the heart of my mystery,
you would sound me from my lowest note to the top of
my compass, and there is much music, excellent voice, in
this little organ, yet cannot you make it speak. 'Sblood, do
you think I am easier to be played on than a pipe? Call
355   me what instrument you will, though you can fret* me,
you cannot play upon me.

       Enter POLONIUS.

God bless you, sir!

POLONIUS
My lord, the Queen would speak with you, and presently.

HAMLET
Do you see yonder cloud that's almost in shape of a camel?

POLONIUS
360   By th' mass and 'tis, like a camel indeed.

HAMLET
Methinks it is like a weasel.

POLONIUS
It is backed like a weasel.

HAMLET
Or like a whale.

POLONIUS
Very like a whale.

HAMLET
365   Then I will come to my mother by and by.
[*aside*] They fool me to the top of my bent.—I will come
by and by.

POLONIUS
I will say so.

       Exit.

---

355   *fret* wordplay on "fret," meaning "annoy," and the "frets" or ridges that guide the
fingers on stringed instruments

HAMLET

Well, then, consider what a poor thing you suppose me to be!
You want to play me, you think you understand my openings,
you want to pluck the heart out of my mystery, you want to   350
make music on me from my lowest note to the highest pitch
of my range. *(indicating the flute)* There is much music and a
fine voice in this little instrument, and yet you cannot play it.
By God's blood, do you think that I am easier to play than a
flute? Call me whatever instrument you like—no matter how   355
much you vex me, you cannot play me.

     POLONIUS *enters.*

God bless you, sir.

POLONIUS

My lord, the Queen wishes to speak with you, and soon.

HAMLET

Do you see that cloud yonder that's shaped almost like a camel?

POLONIUS

By heaven, it looks like a camel, indeed.   360

HAMLET

I think it is a weasel.

POLONIUS

It has a back like a weasel's.

HAMLET

Or like a whale.

POLONIUS

Much like a whale.

HAMLET

Then I will come to my mother at once. *(aside)* They make me   365
play the fool to the limits of my ability. *(to POLONIUS)* I will
come at once.

POLONIUS

I will tell her so.

     POLONIUS *exits.*

HAMLET

"By and by" is easily said. Leave me, friends.

[*Exeunt all but* HAMLET.]

370 'Tis now the very witching time of night,
When churchyards yawn, and hell itself breathes out
Contagion to this world. Now could I drink hot blood
And do such business as the bitter day
Would quake to look on. Soft, now to my mother.
375 O heart, lose not thy nature; let not ever
The soul of Nero* enter this firm bosom.
Let me be cruel, not unnatural;
I will speak daggers to her, but use none.
My tongue and soul in this be hypocrites:
380 How in my words somever she be shent,
To give them seals never, my soul, consent!

Exit.

---

376   *Nero* The Roman emperor Nero (37–68 A.D.) accused his mother, Agrippina, of
poisoning her husband and had her executed.

HAMLET

Yes—for it's easy to say "at once." Leave me alone, friends.

All but HAMLET *exit.*

It's now the time of night when spells are cast,
when churchyards open their graves, and hell itself breathes
diseases into this world. Now I could drink hot blood,
and do such horrible deeds that the day itself
would shudder to witness them. Well, then—now I'll go to my
    mother.
Oh, my heart, don't lose all your natural feeling; don't ever let   375
the soul of Nero enter this devoted breast.
Let me be cruel, but not unnatural.
The words I say to her will be like daggers, but I won't use real
    daggers.
And so my tongue and soul will not really mean what they say.
Oh, my soul, however harshly she may be   380
rebuked by my words, do not put them into murderous
    action!

He exits.

ACT III, SCENE III

[*The castle.*] *Enter* KING, ROSENCRANTZ, *and*
GUILDENSTERN.

KING
 I like him not, nor stands it safe with us
 To let his madness range. Therefore prepare you.
 I your commission will forthwith dispatch,
 And he to England shall along with you.
5 The terms of our estate may not endure
 Hazard so near 's as doth hourly grow
 Out of his brows.

GUILDENSTERN
                            We will ourselves provide.
 Most holy and religious fear it is
10 To keep those many many bodies safe
 That live and feed upon your Majesty.

ROSENCRANTZ
 The single and peculiar life is bound
 With all the strength and armor of the mind
 To keep itself from noyance, but much more
15 That spirit upon whose weal depends and rests
 The lives of many. The cess of majesty
 Dies not alone, but like a gulf doth draw
 What's near it with it; or it is a massy wheel
 Fixed on the summit of the highest mount,
20 To whose huge spokes ten thousand lesser things
 Are mortised and adjoined, which when it falls,
 Each small annexment, petty consequence,
 Attends the boist'rous ruin. Never alone
 Did the King sigh, but with a general groan.

KING
25 Arm you, I pray you, to this speedy voyage,
 For we will fetters put about this fear,
 Which now goes too free-footed.

ACT 3, SCENE 3

The castle. The KING, ROSENCRANTZ, *and* GUILDENSTERN
enter.

KING
I don't like his behavior, nor is it safe for us
to let him run free in his madness. So get yourselves ready.
I'll put your orders in writing immediately,
and he will go along with you to England.
Our position as king might not survive   5
this danger which is so near to us—and growing hourly
with his every impudent action.

GUILDENSTERN
We will act prudently.
It is a most holy and sacred duty
to keep safe the great number of people   10
who depend upon your Majesty for their lives.

ROSENCRANTZ
The life of a private individual requires
all the strength and armor of the mind
to protect it from harm; but the life of a man
upon whose welfare the lives of many depend   15
must be even better protected. The death of a king
is not a single death, but pulls down all the lives around him
like a whirlpool. Or else it's like a massive wheel
placed on the summit of the highest mountain;
its huge spokes are fitted together   20
from ten thousand lesser parts; when the wheel falls,
each small attachment and unimportant piece
is destroyed in the tumultuous collapse. The King has never
sighed alone; his subjects have always groaned along with him.

KING
I ask you to prepare for this speedy voyage,   25
for we will put shackles on this fear
which now roams about too freely.

ROSENCRANTZ

                        We will haste us.

Exeunt GENTLEMEN.

Enter POLONIUS.

POLONIUS

My lord, he's going to his mother's closet.
30   Behind the arras I'll convey myself
To hear the process. I'll warrant she'll tax him home,
And, as you said—and wisely was it said—
'Tis meet that some more audience than a mother,
Since nature makes them partial, should o'erhear
35   The speech of vantage. Fare you well, my liege.
I'll call upon you ere you go to bed
And tell you what I know.

KING

                   Thanks, dear my lord.

Exit POLONIUS.

O, my offense is rank, it smells to heaven;
40   It hath the primal eldest curse upon 't,
A brother's murder. Pray can I not,
Though inclination be as sharp as will.
My stronger guilt defeats my strong intent,
And like a man to double business bound
45   I stand in pause where I shall first begin,
And both neglect. What if this cursed hand
Were thicker than itself with brother's blood,
Is there not rain enough in the sweet heavens
To wash it white as snow? Whereto serves mercy
50   But to confront the visage of offense?
And what's in prayer but this twofold force,
To be forestalled ere we come to fall,
Or pardon being down? Then I'll look up.
My fault is past. But, O, what form of prayer
55   Can serve my turn? "Forgive me my foul murder"?
This cannot be, since I am still possessed

ROSENCRANTZ

We will hurry.

> ROSENCRANTZ *and* GUILDENSTERN *exit;* POLONIUS *enters.*

POLONIUS

My lord, he's going to his mother's private chamber.
I'll hide myself behind the hanging tapestry   30
to hear what happens. I'm sure that she'll scold him strongly;
and as you said—so wisely—
it's best that someone other than his mother
should hear what's spoken from an advantageous place,
since mothers are naturally partial to their sons. Farewell, my   35
  lord.
I'll call on you before you go to bed
and tell you what I know.

KING

Thanks, my dear lord.

> POLONIUS *exits.*

Oh, my crime smells bad; it stinks all the way up to heaven.
It is condemned by the world's oldest curse—   40
the curse on a brother's murderer. I cannot pray,
even though I sincerely wish to do so.
My strong desire is defeated by my guilt, which is even
  stronger;
and like a man committed to two different tasks,
I stand here and pause, trying to decide which to do first,   45
and fail to do either. What if this cursed hand
were covered with a layer of brother's blood thicker than itself?
Isn't there enough rain in the sweet heavens
to wash it as white as snow? What is mercy for,
except to meet sin face to face?   50
And what does prayer offer but this double power:
to come to our aid before we fall into sin,
or to pardon us after we've fallen? Then I'll look upward
  toward heaven.
My fault will be a thing of the past. But, oh, what sort of prayer
can serve my purpose? "Forgive me for my wicked murder"?   55
I cannot be forgiven, since I still possess

Of those effects for which I did the murder,
My crown, mine own ambition, and my queen.
May one be pardoned and retain th' offense?
60 In the corrupted currents of this world
Offense's gilded hand may shove by justice,
And oft 'tis seen the wicked prize itself
Buys out the law. But 'tis not so above.
There is no shuffling; there the action lies
65 In his true nature, and we ourselves compelled,
Even to the teeth and forehead of our faults,
To give in evidence. What then? What rests?
Try what repentance can. What can it not?
Yet what can it when one cannot repent?
70 O wretched state! O bosom black as death!
O limed* soul, that struggling to be free
Art more engaged! Help, angels! Make assay.
Bow, stubborn knees, and, heart with strings of steel,
Be soft as sinews of the newborn babe.
75 All may be well.

     [*He kneels.*]

     Enter HAMLET.

HAMLET
Now might I do it pat, now 'a is a-praying,
And now I'll do't.

     [*He draws his sword.*]

            And so 'a goes to heaven,
And so am I revenged. That would be scanned.
80 A villain kills my father, and for that
I, his sole son, do this same villain send
To heaven.
Why, this is hire and salary, not revenge.
'A took my father grossly, full of bread,
85 With all his crimes broad blown, as flush as May;
And how his audit stands, who knows save heaven?
But in our circumstance and course of thought,
'Tis heavy with him; and am I then revenged,

---

71 *limed* caught, as in bird lime, a sticky substance used for trapping birds

the benefits for which I committed the murder:
my crown, the realization of my ambitions, and my queen.
May one be pardoned while keeping the rewards of the crime?
In the corrupt ways of this world,   60
a criminal's hand may shove justice aside with ill-gotten wealth,
and it often happens that the prize of the crime
buys exemption from lawful punishment. But this is not so in
    heaven;
there, one cannot evade justice; there, the deed is exposed
for what it is; we are even forced   65
to testify against ourselves, and brought face to face
with all our sins. What then? What's left for me to do?
I'll find out what repentance can do. And what *can't* it do?
And yet, what *can* it do, when one cannot sincerely repent?
Oh, my wretched condition! Oh, my heart, as black as death!   70
And, oh, my soul! Like a bird caught in lime, the more you
    struggle to get free,
the more you are ensnared! Help, angels! Come to my aid!
Bow, my stubborn knees; and my heart, now as hard as steel,
become as soft as a newborn baby's muscles.
All may still be well.   75

> *He kneels;* HAMLET *enters.*

HAMLET
Now I could do it easily—now while he's praying;
I'll do it now.

> *He draws his sword.*

And so he'll go to heaven,
and so I'll get revenge. That needs to be thought over.
A villain kills my father, and for that,   80
I, my father's only son, send this same villain
to heaven.
Why, I'd be doing him a favor, not getting revenge.
He killed my father when he was grossly unprepared—when
    his worldly appetites were satisfied,
and all his sins were in full bloom, like flowers in May.   85
Who but heaven knows how his final account stands?
As well as we on earth can determine,
the state of his soul is dire. So can I get revenge

To take him in the **purging** of his soul,
90 When he is fit and seasoned for his passage?
No.
Up, sword, and know thou a more horrid hent.

[*He sheathes his sword.*]

When he is drunk asleep, or in his rage,
Or in th' incestuous pleasure of his bed,
95 At game a-swearing, or about some act
That has no relish of salvation in 't—
Then trip him that his heels may kick at heaven,
And that his soul may be as damned and black
As hell, whereto it goes. My mother stays.
100 This physic but prolongs thy sickly days.

Exit.

KING [*rises*]
My words fly up, my thoughts remain below;
Words without thoughts never to heaven go.

Exit.

by killing the King while he's repenting with all his soul,
and is fit and prepared for his passage to the next world?   90
No.
Away, my sword, and wait for a more horrible occasion.

He sheathes his sword.

When he is passed out drunk, or raging,
or in the incestuous pleasure of his bed,
cursing at a card game, or doing some deed   95
that has no flavor of salvation about it—
then I'll trip him, so that his heels fly up toward heaven as he
    falls headfirst,
and so that his soul may be as damned and black
as hell, where it will go. My mother awaits me.
This prayer only prolongs your days of spiritual sickness.   100

    HAMLET *exits.*

KING (*The* KING *rises.*)
My words fly upward, but my thoughts remain with the world;
words without holy thoughts never go to heaven.

He exits.

ACT III, SCENE IV

[*The* QUEEN's *closet.*] *Enter* [QUEEN] GERTRUDE
and POLONIUS.

POLONIUS
'A will come straight. Look you lay home to him.
Tell him his pranks have been too broad to bear with,
And that your Grace hath screened and stood between
Much heat and him. I'll silence me even here.
5   Pray you be round with him.

HAMLET (*within*)
Mother, Mother, Mother!

QUEEN
I'll warrant you; fear me not. Withdraw; I hear him
coming.

[POLONIUS *hides behind the arras.*]

Enter HAMLET.

HAMLET
Now, Mother, what's the matter?

QUEEN
10   Hamlet, thou hast thy father much offended.

HAMLET
Mother, you have my father much offended.

QUEEN
Come, come, you answer with an idle tongue.

HAMLET
Go, go, you question with a wicked tongue.

QUEEN
Why, how now, Hamlet?

HAMLET
15   What's the matter now?

QUEEN
Have you forgot me?

ACT 3, SCENE 4

The QUEEN'*s private chamber.* GERTRUDE *and* POLONIUS *enter.*

POLONIUS
He'll come right away. Be sure to rebuke him thoroughly.
Tell him that his antics have been too reckless to put up with,
and that your Grace has protected him, and has stood between
him and the King's anger. I'll keep silent right here.
I beg you to be blunt with him.   5

HAMLET (*offstage*)
Mother, Mother, Mother!

QUEEN
I promise to do it; don't doubt me.
Hide, I hear him coming.

    POLONIUS *hides behind a hanging tapestry.*

    HAMLET *enters.*

HAMLET
Now, Mother, what's the matter?

QUEEN
Hamlet, you have greatly offended your father.   10

HAMLET
Mother, *you* have greatly offended my father.

QUEEN
Come, come, you answer me with a foolish tongue.

HAMLET
Go, go, you question me with a wicked tongue.

QUEEN
Why, what do you mean, Hamlet?

HAMLET
What's the matter now?   15

QUEEN
Have you forgotten who I am?

HAMLET
No, by the rood, not so!
You are the Queen, your husband's brother's wife,
And, would it were not so, you are my mother.

QUEEN
20   Nay, then I'll set those to you that can speak.

HAMLET
Come, come, and sit you down. You shall not budge.
You go not till I set you up a glass
Where you may see the inmost part of you!

QUEEN
What wilt thou do? Thou wilt not murder me? Help, ho!

POLONIUS [*behind*]
25   What, ho! Help!

HAMLET [*Draws.*]
How now? A rat? Dead for a ducat, dead!

[*Makes a pass through the arras and*] *kills* POLONIUS.

POLONIUS [*behind*]
O, I am slain!

QUEEN
O me, what hast thou done?

HAMLET
Nay, I know not. Is it the King?

QUEEN
30   O, what a rash and bloody deed is this!

HAMLET
A bloody deed—almost as bad, good Mother,
As kill a king, and marry with his brother.

QUEEN
As kill a king?

HAMLET
Ay, lady, it was my word.

HAMLET
No, by the cross, I haven't.
You are the Queen, your husband's brother's wife;
and although I wish it were not so, you are my mother.

QUEEN
(trying to leave) Well, I'll send for someone whom you'll listen to. 20

HAMLET
Come, come, and sit yourself down; you will not budge.
You may not go till I have shown you a mirror
where you may see into the depths of your soul.

QUEEN
What are you going to do? Are you going to murder me?
Help, help!

POLONIUS *(behind the tapestry)*
Somebody, help! 25

HAMLET *(Draws his sword.)*
What's this—do I hear a rat? I'll bet a dollar that I kill it.

> *He thrusts his sword through the tapestry, killing* POLONIUS.

POLONIUS *(behind the tapestry)*
Oh, I've been killed!

QUEEN
Oh, no—what have you done?

HAMLET
Indeed, I don't know. Is it the King?

> *He pulls back the tapestry and discovers the dead* POLONIUS.

QUEEN
Oh, what a rash and bloody deed this is! 30

HAMLET
A bloody deed—almost as bad, good mother,
as killing a king and marrying his brother.

QUEEN
As killing a king?

HAMLET
Yes, lady, that's what I said.

[*Lifts up the arras and sees* POLONIUS.]

35 Thou wretched, rash, intruding fool, farewell!
I took thee for thy better. Take thy fortune.
Thou find'st to be too busy is some danger.—
Leave wringing of your hands. Peace, sit you down
And let me wring your heart, for so I shall
40 If it be made of penetrable stuff,
If damned custom have not brazed it so
That it be proof and bulwark against sense.

QUEEN

What have I done that thou dar'st wag thy tongue
In noise so rude against me?

HAMLET

45   Such an act
That blurs the grace and blush of modesty,
Calls virtue hypocrite, takes off the rose
From the fair forehead of an innocent love,
And sets a blister* there, makes marriage vows
50 As false as dicers' oaths. O, such a deed
As from the body of contraction plucks
The very soul, and sweet religion makes
A rhapsody of words! Heaven's face does glow,
Yea this solidity and compound mass
55 With heated visage, as against the doom
Is thoughtsick at the act.

QUEEN

         Ay me, what act,
That roars so loud and thunders in the index?

HAMLET

Look here upon this picture, and on this,
60 The counterfeit presentment of two brothers.
See what a grace was seated on this brow:
Hyperion's curls, the front of Jove himself,
An eye like Mars, to threaten and command,
A station like the herald Mercury*

---

49 *blister* the result of branding. Prostitutes were branded on the forehead as a
punishment for sin.

(to POLONIUS's body)

You pathetic, rash, intruding fool, farewell.   35
I took you for someone more important. Accept your bad luck.
You've learned that it's somewhat dangerous to be a busybody.
(to the QUEEN) Stop wringing your hands. Quiet, sit down,
and let me wring your heart; for that's what I'll do,
if it's made of any vulnerable stuff,   40
and if habitual wickedness hasn't turned it to brass,
armoring and walling it up against feeling.

QUEEN

What have I done, that you should dare rave
so noisily and rudely against me?

HAMLET

Such an act   45
that smudges the precious blush of modesty;
makes all virtue seem only a pretence; snatches the rosy hue
from the tender forehead of an innocent lover
and burns the brand of a harlot there; makes marriage vows
as false as the curses of dice players. Oh, such a deed   50
that plucks the very soul
out of the solemn marriage contract, and turns sweet religion
into a senseless string of words! Heaven's face blushes
over this great, solid world—
blushes with sadness, as if the Day of Judgment were near;   55
it has grown sick with horror at your deed.

QUEEN

Oh—what action
will follow this roaring, thundering introduction?

HAMLET

Look at this picture here, and at this one—
the artistic representations of two brothers.   60
Look at what elegance rested on my father's face—
Hyperion's curling hair; the forehead of Jove himself;
an eye like that of Mars, to threaten and command;
a stance like that of the messenger Mercury

62–64 *Hyperion . . . Mercury* Hyperion, the sun god and a model of male beauty;
Jove, the chief of the gods; Mars, the god of war; and Mercury, the messenger
of the gods

65 New lighted on a heaven-kissing hill—
A combination and a form indeed
Where every god did seem to set his seal
To give the world assurance of a man.
This was your husband. Look you now what follows.
70 Here is your husband, like a mildewed ear
Blasting his wholesome brother. Have you eyes?
Could you on this fair mountain leave to feed,
And batten on this moor? Ha! Have you eyes?
You cannot call it love, for at your age
75 The heyday in the blood is tame, it's humble,
And waits upon the judgment, and what judgment
Would step from this to this? Sense sure you have,
Else could you not have emotion, but sure that sense
Is apoplexed, for madness would not err,
80 Nor sense to ecstasy was ne'er so thrilled
But it reserved some quantity of choice
To serve in such a difference. What devil was 't
That thus hath cozened you at hoodman-blind?
Eyes without feeling, feeling without sight,
85 Ears without hands or eyes, smelling sans all,
Or but a sickly part of one true sense
Could not so mope.
O shame, where is thy blush? Rebellious hell,
If thou canst mutine in a matron's bones,
90 To flaming youth let virtue be as wax
And melt in her own fire. Proclaim no shame
When the compulsive ardor gives the charge,
Since frost itself as actively doth burn,
And reason **panders** will.

QUEEN
95 O Hamlet, speak no more.
Thou turn'st mine eyes into my very soul,
And there I see such black and grainèd spots
As will not leave their tint.

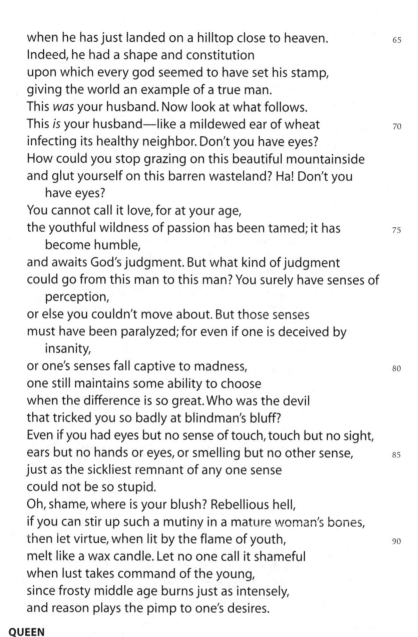

when he has just landed on a hilltop close to heaven. 65
Indeed, he had a shape and constitution
upon which every god seemed to have set his stamp,
giving the world an example of a true man.
This *was* your husband. Now look at what follows.
This *is* your husband—like a mildewed ear of wheat 70
infecting its healthy neighbor. Don't you have eyes?
How could you stop grazing on this beautiful mountainside
and glut yourself on this barren wasteland? Ha! Don't you
    have eyes?
You cannot call it love, for at your age,
the youthful wildness of passion has been tamed; it has 75
    become humble,
and awaits God's judgment. But what kind of judgment
could go from this man to this man? You surely have senses of
    perception,
or else you couldn't move about. But those senses
must have been paralyzed; for even if one is deceived by
    insanity,
or one's senses fall captive to madness, 80
one still maintains some ability to choose
when the difference is so great. Who was the devil
that tricked you so badly at blindman's bluff?
Even if you had eyes but no sense of touch, touch but no sight,
ears but no hands or eyes, or smelling but no other sense, 85
just as the sickliest remnant of any one sense
could not be so stupid.
Oh, shame, where is your blush? Rebellious hell,
if you can stir up such a mutiny in a mature woman's bones,
then let virtue, when lit by the flame of youth, 90
melt like a wax candle. Let no one call it shameful
when lust takes command of the young,
since frosty middle age burns just as intensely,
and reason plays the pimp to one's desires.

QUEEN
Oh, Hamlet, say no more! 95
You've turned my eyes into my very soul,
and there I see spots so black and indelible
that they cannot be washed out.

HAMLET

                              Nay, but to live
100   In the rank sweat of an enseamed bed,
Stewed in corruption, honeying and making love
Over the nasty sty!

QUEEN

O, speak to me no more.
These words like daggers enter in my ears.
105   No more, sweet Hamlet!

HAMLET

                      A murderer and a villain,
A slave that is not twentieth part the tithe
Of your precedent lord, a vice* of kings,
A cutpurse of the empire and the rule,
110   That from a shelf the precious diadem stole
And put it in his pocket—

QUEEN

No more!

       Enter GHOST.

HAMLET

A king of shreds and patches*—
Save me and hover o'er me with your wings,
115   You heavenly guards!—What would your gracious figure?

QUEEN

Alas, he's mad.

HAMLET

Do you not come your tardy son to chide,
That, lapsed in time and passion, lets go by
Th' important acting of your dread command?
120   O, say!

GHOST

Do not forget. This visitation
Is but to whet thy almost blunted purpose.

---

108   *vice* a clown in the so-called "morality" plays of the Middle Ages

HAMLET
Indeed, to live
in the filthy sweat of a greasy bed,   100
soaked with corruption, caressing and making love
in a nasty pigsty.

QUEEN
Oh, do not speak to me anymore!
These words enter my ears like daggers.
No more, sweet Hamlet!   105

HAMLET
A murderer and a villain;
a scoundrel who is not worth the twentieth of a tenth part
of your previous husband; a buffoon of a king,
a thief who robs the entire kingdom,
who stole the precious crown from a shelf   110
and put it in his pocket—

QUEEN
No more.

       The GHOST *enters.*

HAMLET
A king dressed in clownish patches—
Save me and hover over me with your wings,
you guardian angels! *(to the* GHOST*)* What does your Majesty   115
    want?

QUEEN
Alas, he's mad.

HAMLET
Haven't you come to scold your tardy son,
who lets the time go by and his passion cool, putting off
the urgent acting of your stern command?
Oh, tell me!   120

GHOST
Do not forget. This visit
is only to sharpen your almost blunted purpose.

---

113   *patches* Hamlet may refer to the "motley" costume worn by a jester or a clown,
      or to the makeshift and patched up kind of king he accuses Claudius of being.

But look, amazement on thy mother sits.
O, step between her and her fighting soul!
125 Conceit in weakest bodies strongest works.
Speak to her, Hamlet.

HAMLET
How is it with you, lady?

QUEEN
Alas, how is 't with you,
That you do bend your eye on vacancy,
130 And with th' incorporal air do hold discourse?
Forth at your eyes your spirits wildly peep,
And as the sleeping soldiers in th' alarm
Your bedded hair like life in excrements
Start up and stand on end. O gentle son,
135 Upon the heat and flame of thy distemper
Sprinkle cool patience. Whereon do you look?

HAMLET
On him, on him! Look you, how pale he glares!
His form and cause conjoined, preaching to stones,
Would make them capable. [*to the* GHOST] Do not look
140   upon me,
Lest with this piteous action you convert
My stern effects. Then what I have to do
Will want true color; tears perchance for blood.

QUEEN
To whom do you speak this?

HAMLET
145 Do you see nothing there?

QUEEN
Nothing at all; yet all that is I see.

HAMLET
Nor did you nothing hear?

QUEEN
No, nothing but ourselves.

But look—your mother is stunned and bewildered.
Oh, step between her and her agonized mind.
Imagination works most strongly on the weakest bodies.   125
Speak to her, Hamlet.

HAMLET
How are you, lady?

QUEEN
Alas, how are *you*,
that you should stare where there is nothing
and carry on a conversation with the empty air?   130
Your eyes look wildly astonished,
and like sleeping soldiers wakened by a call to arms,
your combed-down hairs start up and stand on end,
as if those lifeless strands had come to life. Oh, noble son,
sprinkle some cool patience on the flaming heat   135
of your distress. What are you looking at?

HAMLET
At him, at him! Look at how pale he is, how he glares.
With his appearance and his cause joined together, even
     stones would listen
if he preached to them. *(to the* GHOST*)* Do not look at me,   140
or else you'll inspire me to pity and divert me
from my stern intentions. Then what I have to do
will lack its proper shade of red; I'll shed tears instead of blood.

QUEEN
To whom are you saying this?

HAMLET
Don't you see anything there?   145

QUEEN
Nothing at all; and yet I see everything there is to see.

HAMLET
Nor do you hear anything?

QUEEN
No, nothing but ourselves.

HAMLET

Why, look you there! Look how it steals away!
150 My father, in his habit as he lived!
Look where he goes even now out at the portal!

Exit GHOST.

QUEEN

This is the very coinage of your brain.
This bodiless creation ecstasy
Is very cunning in.

HAMLET

155 Ecstasy?
My pulse as yours doth temperately keep time
And makes as healthful music. It is not madness
That I have uttered. Bring me to the test,
And I the matter will reword, which madness
160 Would gambol from. Mother, for love of grace,
Lay not that flattering unction to your soul,
That not your trespass but my madness speaks.
It will but skin and film the ulcerous place
Whiles rank corruption, mining all within,
165 Infects unseen. Confess yourself to heaven,
Repent what's past, avoid what is to come,
And do not spread the compost on the weeds
To make them ranker. Forgive me this my virtue.
For in the fatness of these pursy times
170 Virtue itself of vice must pardon beg,
Yea, curb and woo for leave to do him good.

QUEEN

O Hamlet, thou hast cleft my heart in twain.

HAMLET

O, throw away the worser part of it,
And live the purer with the other half.
175 Good night—but go not to my uncle's bed.
Assume a virtue, if you have it not.

HAMLET

Why, look over there, look how it is creeping away!
It is my father, dressed as he was in life! 150
Look at how he's going directly out the door!

The GHOST *exits.*

QUEEN

This is simply an invention of your brain.
Madness is very cunning at creating
such bodiless phantoms.

HAMLET

Madness? 155
My pulse rate is as moderate as yours,
and keeps as healthy a rhythm. It is not madness
that I have spoken. Put me to the test,
and I'll speak again in rational words that madness
would flee from. Mother, for your own salvation, 160
do not put soothing ointment on your soul,
flattering yourself that it's my madness talking, not your own
   sins.
Such ointment will only thinly cover up the festering wound,
while filthy corruption creeps underneath it,
causing an unseen infection. Make a confession to heaven, 165
repent your past sins, avoid future sins,
and do not spread more compost on the weeds
to make them more abundant. Forgive my virtuous talk,
for in the grossness of these lax times,
virtue itself must beg pardon of vice— 170
indeed, must bow and ask for permission to do vice some
   good.

QUEEN

Oh, Hamlet, you have torn my loyalties down the middle!

HAMLET

Oh, then throw away the worse half of your loyalty,
and live a purer life with the other half!
Good night. But do not go to my uncle's bed. 175
Practice virtue, even if you lack it in your heart.

That monster custom, who all sense doth eat,
Of habits devil, is angel yet in this,
That to the use of actions fair and good
180 He likewise gives a frock or livery
That aptly is put on. Refrain tonight,
And that shall lend a kind of easiness
To the next abstinence; the next more easy;
For use almost can change the stamp of nature,
185 And either [master] the devil, or throw him out
With wondrous potency. Once more, good night,
And when you are desirous to be blest,
I'll blessing beg of you.—For this same lord,
I do repent; but heaven hath pleased it so,
190 To punish me with this, and this with me,
That I must be their scourge and minister.
I will bestow him and will answer well
The death I gave him. So again, good night.
I must be cruel only to be kind.
195 Thus bad begins, and worse remains behind.
One word more, good lady.

QUEEN

What shall I do?

HAMLET
Not this, by no means, that I bid you do:
Let the bloat King tempt you again to bed,
200 Pinch wanton on your cheek, call you his mouse,
And let him, for a pair of reechy kisses,
Or paddling in your neck with his damned fingers,
Make you to ravel all this matter out,
That I essentially am not in madness,
205 But mad in craft. 'Twere good you let him know,
For who that's but a queen, fair, sober, wise,
Would from a paddock, from a bat, a gib,

Custom, that monster which hardens one's sensibilities
to evil habits, is still an angel in this sense:
when one practices good and moral behavior,
custom easily puts on the appropriate   180
dress or uniform. Refrain from sin tonight,
and that will make your next abstinence
somewhat easier—and the abstinence after that easier still.
For by changing habits, one can almost change one's inborn
    personality,
and either control the devil or throw him out   185
with amazing force. Once more, good night—
and when you wish to repent and be blessed,
I will come to you myself and beg for your blessing.

     Indicating POLONIUS.

As for this lord,
I repent what I've done. But it has pleased heaven
to punish both him and me with this deed;   190
for I must be heaven's punishing lash, and also the man who
    wields it.
I will put him away somewhere, and will pay dearly
for having killed him. So again, good night.
I must be cruel only to be kind.
This is just the beginning of trouble; the worst remains ahead.   195
One more word, good lady.

QUEEN
What shall I do?

HAMLET
By no means do what I suggest to you now:
Let the bloated king tempt you again to bed,
pinch your cheek indecently, call you his darling mouse;   200
and for a pair of vile kisses,
or for caressing your neck with his damned fingers,
let him persuade you to tell him the truth—
that I am essentially not mad at all,
but only pretending. (*sarcastically*) Oh, it would be fine for   205
    you to let him know—
for would a queen who is lovely, clear-headed, and wise

Such dear concernings hide? Who would do so?
No, in despite of sense and secrecy,
210 Unpeg the basket on the house's top,
Let the birds fly, and like the famous ape,
To try conclusions, in the basket creep
And break your own neck down.*

QUEEN
Be thou assured, if words be made of breath,
215 And breath of life, I have no life to breathe
What thou hast said to me.

HAMLET
I must to England; you know that.

QUEEN
Alack,
I had forgot. 'Tis so concluded on.

HAMLET
220 There's letters sealed, and my two schoolfellows,
Whom I will trust as I will adders fanged,
They bear the **mandate**; they must sweep my way
And marshal me to knavery. Let it work;
For 'tis the sport to have the engineer
225 Hoist with his own petard, and 't shall go hard
But I will delve one yard below their mines
And blow them at the moon. O, 'tis most sweet
When in one line two crafts directly meet.
This man shall set me packing:*
230 I'll lug the guts into the neighbor room.
Mother, good night. Indeed, this counselor
Is now most still, most secret, and most grave,

209–213 *No, in despite . . . neck down* Hamlet is referring to a story in which an ape
opens a bird cage and watches the birds fly away. The ape then tries to
imitate the birds and falls to his death.

hide such an important matter
from even a toad, a bat, or a tomcat? Who *would* keep such a secret?
No, despite all your inclinations toward secrecy,
open the wicker cage on the roof of the house,   210
let the birds fly out, and like the famous ape,
attempt an experiment by getting into the basket
and trying to fly out of it like the birds—only to break your
    neck when you fall.

QUEEN
Be assured, if words are made out of breath,
and if breath comes from life, there is no living part of me   215
    that will breathe
what you have said to me.

HAMLET
I must go to England; you know that.

QUEEN
Alas,
I had forgotten! It's been decided.

HAMLET
The orders are written and sealed; and my two school friends,   220
whom I will trust as if they were venomous snakes,
will carry out the command. They're supposed to lead me on
    my way
toward some kind of trap. Let them try,
for it's good sport to see a maker of bombs
blown up by his own explosives; and with any luck,   225
I'll dig a yard below their land mines
and blast them all the way to the moon. Oh, it's very sweet
when two crafty plots collide with one another.
Because of this man I've killed, I'll be sent off in a hurry.
I'll lug these guts into the room next door.   230
Mother, good night indeed. This counselor
is now very quiet, secretive, and serious,

---

229   *packing* wordplay on contriving or plotting/leaving in a hurry ("sent packing").
It may also be a pun on "packing" in the sense of taking on a load because
Hamlet has to pick up the body.

Who was in life a foolish prating knave.
Come, sir, to draw toward an end with you.
235 Good night, Mother.

> [*Exit the* QUEEN. *Then*] *exit* HAMLET, *tugging in*
> POLONIUS.

while in life he was a foolish, babbling rascal.
(to POLONIUS*'s body)* Come on, sir, and I'll finish my business
    with you.
Good night, Mother.

235

They exit, HAMLET *dragging away* POLONIUS.

Act III Review

Discussion Questions

1. Why does Claudius suspect that Hamlet "puts on this confusion"—pretends to act mad?

2. What major ideas does Hamlet express in his soliloquy in Scene i, lines 63–95?

3. Why is Hamlet so brutal to Ophelia in Scene i?

4. What does Hamlet's advice to the Players, in Scene ii, tell you about Shakespeare's own ideas about his craft?

5. Do you think Hamlet's manipulation of the performance to evoke Claudius's guilt is necessary? Explain why or why not.

6. What action does Claudius take against Hamlet in Act III, Scene iii?

7. How does Hamlet try to appeal to his mother in Scene iv?

8. What is the importance of Polonius's death in the last scene?

Literary Elements

1. By now you know that a **soliloquy** is a longer speech that a character shares with the audience. Reread Hamlet's famous soliloquy in Scene i. What are some things you learn about the Prince's inner state of mind from this speech? Note any particularly striking lines or images.

2. **Motivation** refers to the reasons why a character behaves as he or she does. In Act III, Scene i, Hamlet tells Ophelia "I did love you once" and "I loved you not" in the space of a few short lines. Why might he contradict himself and play with her feelings? Explain his possible motivation.

3. **Irony** is when appearances are at odds with reality. At the end of Scene ii, Hamlet says, "Now could I drink hot blood / And do such bitter business as the day / Would quake to look on (lines 372–374)." Discuss the irony of these lines.

4. A **theme** is the underlying meaning, or message, of a work of literature. What themes in the play are touched on in Claudius's soliloquy in Act III, Scene iii, lines 39–75? Cite lines from this speech to support your opinion.

5. In this same passage in Scene iii, there are at least five examples of **personification**. Find them and explain how they contribute to this scene.

Writing Prompts

1. A painting by Daniel Maclise called "The Play Scene in Hamlet" strongly influenced several famous actors. Find out about the theatrical tradition called "Hamlet's crawl" and write about it. You might consult stage histories of *Hamlet* or look for illustrations of Edmund Kean, William Charles Macready, Edwin Booth, and Sir Henry Irving. Resources available on the Internet include the Folger Shakespeare Library Web site: www.folger.edu and the Emory University Web site: http://shakespeare.cc.emory.edu/.

2. Hamlet justifies his harsh treatment of his mother Gertrude with these words: "I must be cruel only to be kind." Does this sound sincere or dishonest to you? Write about times when you might use this saying to justify your own behavior.

3. Choose a quotation from one of the scenes in Act III that you feel best characterizes that scene. In a paragraph, discuss why you think this quotation is significant and effective at conveying the events or emotions of this scene.

HAMLET
ACT IV

The army of Fortinbras, Kozintsev's *Hamlet*, 1964 film

"ONE WOE DOTH TREAD UPON ANOTHER'S
HEEL. SO FAST THEY FOLLOW."

✠ ✠ ✠

Before You Read

1. What do you expect Ophelia to do when she learns of the death of her father?

2. At this point in the story, what is your opinion of King Claudius and his actions?

3. Do you really expect Hamlet to go to England in Act IV? Explain why or why not.

4. Be on the lookout for images in Act IV that appeal to the senses. Sensory language carries a powerful emotional impact.

Literary Elements

1. A **simile** is a comparison of two unlike things using *like* or *as*. Hamlet tells Ophelia that it doesn't matter if she is "chaste as ice, as pure as snow," she will not escape other people's slander.

2. As explained earlier, a **metaphor** makes a direct comparison between two unlike things. In Act I, Scene iii, Laertes makes several direct comparisons between Hamlet's love for Ophelia and items that do not last: a "violet," "fashion," and "the perfume . . . of a minute."

3. *Hamlet* is filled with **imagery**—word pictures that appeal to the five senses and add emotion and power to the writing. When Hamlet decides to confront his mother in Act III, Scene ii, he promises, "I will speak daggers to her but use none."

4. An **inference** is a reasonable conclusion that the reader can draw based upon clues given in a work of literature. We can infer from Hamlet's constant self-questioning that he is seeking his own identity and the meaning of what he sees and feels.

5. A **symbol** is a person, object, action, or place that stands for something beyond its obvious meaning. In Act III, Scene iv, Hamlet refers to the "rood," or holy cross of Christ. For Christians, this cross symbolizes Christ's suffering.

Words to Know

The following vocabulary words appear in Act IV in the original text of Shakespeare's play. However, they are words that are still used today. Read the definitions here and pay attention to the words as you read the play (they will be in boldfaced type).

conjectures	guesses; speculations
countenance	tolerate; approve
divulging	revealing; making known
exhort	urge on; demand
exploit	scheme; plot
imminent	upcoming; at hand
impetuous	reckless; impulsive
incensed	angry; enraged
inter	bury; entomb
oblivion	forgetfulness; unconsciousness
obscure	concealed; hidden
peruse	study; examine
remiss	thoughtless; careless
spendthrift	wasteful; squandered
superfluous	extra; excessive

Act Summary

Gertrude tells Claudius that Hamlet has killed Polonius. Claudius fears that he might be blamed for Polonius's death. He claims that everyone would be better off if Hamlet were sent away immediately.

Hamlet goes with Rosencrantz and Guildenstern to see Claudius. The Prince taunts Claudius with images of death before revealing where Polonius's corpse is. Claudius informs Hamlet that he is being sent to England for his own safety. Alone, Claudius reveals that his letters to the English crown threaten war if Hamlet is not executed as soon as he arrives.

Fortinbras is making his way to Poland to fight for land and needs permission to pass through Danish territory. Hamlet compares Fortinbras's

Sir John Everett Millais' painting *Ophelia*, 1852

strength of purpose to his own delay in avenging his father's murder. His encounter with Fortinbras renews his determination to act soon.

Gertrude hears that Ophelia has gone mad and is alarmed. Ophelia sings of death, seduction, and deception. After she has gone, Claudius remarks that sorrows come in groups: Polonius is murdered, Hamlet exiled, Ophelia gone mad, and now the citizens of Denmark in an uproar. He is interrupted by news that Laertes has arrived with a mob shouting, "Laertes shall be king!"

Laertes demands to know the cause of Polonius's death. Claudius urges him to decide who is a friend, and who is a foe. Ophelia returns, singing strange songs and handing out herbs and flowers. Claudius tells Laertes that he will do everything in his power to help Laertes seek out Polonius's real murderer.

Via a letter, Hamlet lets Horatio know that he has managed to make his way back from England to Denmark. Horatio goes to meet him.

Claudius tells Laertes that Hamlet can't be punished directly because of his popularity and the Queen's love for him. A messenger announces Hamlet's return to Denmark. Claudius and Laertes plot to kill him in a fencing match. Gertrude enters and announces Ophelia's death by drowning. Laertes collapses in grief.

ACT IV, SCENE I

[*The castle.*] *Enter* KING *and* QUEEN, *with*
ROSENCRANTZ *and* GUILDENSTERN.

KING

There's matter in these sighs. These profound heaves
You must translate; 'tis fit we understand them.
Where is your son?

QUEEN

Bestow this place on us a little while.

[*Exeunt* ROSENCRANTZ *and* GUILDENSTERN.]

5   Ah, mine own lord, what have I seen tonight!

KING

What, Gertrude? How does Hamlet?

QUEEN

Mad as the sea and wind when both contend
Which is the mightier. In his lawless fit,
Behind the arras hearing something stir,
10   Whips out his rapier, cries, "A rat, a rat!"
And in this brainish apprehension kills
The unseen good old man.

KING

                              O heavy deed!
It had been so with us, had we been there.
15   His liberty is full of threats to us all—
To you yourself, to us, to everyone.
Alas, how shall this bloody deed be answered?
It will be laid to us, whose providence
Should have kept short, restrained, and out of haunt
20   This mad young man. But so much was our love
We would not understand what was most fit,
But, like the owner of a foul disease,

ACT 4, SCENE 1

The castle. The KING *and* QUEEN *enter, with* ROSENCRANTZ *and* GUILDENSTERN.

KING

(*to* ROSENCRANTZ *and* GUILDENSTERN) There's significance in
  these sighs; you must interpret
his deep groans; it's proper that I understand them.
(*to* GERTRUDE) Where is your son?

QUEEN

(*to* ROSENCRANTZ *and* GUILDENSTERN) Leave us alone here for a
  little while.

    ROSENCRANTZ *and* GUILDENSTERN *exit.*

Ah, my lord, what I have seen tonight!   5

KING

What's the matter, Gertrude? How is Hamlet?

QUEEN

As mad as the sea and wind when they fight each other
to prove which is mightier. He heard something
stirring behind the tapestry; and in a fit of wildness,
he whipped out his sword, crying, "A rat, a rat!"   10
And in this crazed moment of delusion, he killed
the unseen, good old man.

KING

Oh, what a dreadful deed!
I would have been killed if I had been there.
While he's at liberty, he's a threat to all—   15
to you yourself, to me, and everyone else.
Alas, how shall I explain this bloody deed?
It will be blamed on me, whose foresight
should have kept this mad young man on a short leash—
restrained, away from others. But I loved him so much   20
that I failed to understand what needed to be done;
I was like someone with a serious disease,

To keep it from **divulging**, let it feed
Even on the pith of life. Where is he gone?

QUEEN

25 To draw apart the body he hath killed;
O'er whom his very madness, like some ore
Among a mineral of metals base,
Shows itself pure. 'A weeps for what is done.

KING

O Gertrude, come away!
30 The sun no sooner shall the mountains touch
But we will ship him hence, and this vile deed
We must with all our majesty and skill
Both **countenance** and excuse.—Ho, Guildenstern!

Enter ROSENCRANTZ *and* GUILDENSTERN.

Friends both, go join you with some further aid:
35 Hamlet in madness hath Polonius slain,
And from his mother's closet hath he dragged him.
Go seek him out; speak fair, and bring the body
Into the chapel. I pray you haste in this.

[*Exeunt* ROSENCRANTZ *and* GUILDENSTERN.]

Come, Gertrude, we'll call up our wisest friends
40 And let them know both what we mean to do
And what's untimely done. [So haply slander],
Whose whisper o'er the world's diameter,
As level as the canon to his blank
Transports his poisoned shot, may miss our name
45 And hit the woundless air. O, come away!
My soul is full of discord and dismay.

Exeunt.

fearful that it should be discovered, letting it eat away
at the core of life itself. Where has he gone?

QUEEN

To take away the body of the man he killed—   25
over which his madness, like a vein of gold
in a mine full of worthless metals,
shows itself to be pure. He weeps for what he has done.

KING

Oh, Gertrude, come away!
No sooner will the sun rise over the mountaintops   30
than I shall ship him off; and I must fully explain
and excuse this vile deed
with all my royal power and shrewdness.—Come, Guildenstern!

ROSENCRANTZ *and* GUILDENSTERN *enter.*

You two friends, find other people to help you.
In his madness, Hamlet has killed Polonius,   35
and has dragged the body away from his mother's private
    chamber.
Go find him, speak to him gently, and bring the body
into the chapel. I implore you, hurry in doing this.

ROSENCRANTZ *and* GUILDENSTERN *exit.*

Come, Gertrude. I'll meet with my wisest advisors
and let them know what has suddenly happened,   40
and also what I mean to do about it. Perhaps slander,
whose slightest whisper sends its poisoned dart
across the width of the world as directly
as a cannon aims at its target, might miss our reputation
and pass through the invulnerable air. Oh, come away!   45
My soul is full of worry and dismay.

They exit.

ACT IV, SCENE II

[*The castle.*] *Enter* HAMLET.

HAMLET
Safely stowed.

GENTLEMEN (*within*)
Hamlet, Lord Hamlet!

HAMLET
But soft, what noise? Who calls on Hamlet?
O, here they come.

Enter ROSENCRANTZ *and* GUILDENSTERN.

ROSENCRANTZ
5   What have you done, my lord, with the dead body?

HAMLET
Compounded it with dust, whereto 'tis kin.

ROSENCRANTZ
Tell us where 'tis, that we may take it thence
And bear it to the chapel.

HAMLET
Do not believe it.

ROSENCRANTZ
10   Believe what?

HAMLET
That I can keep your counsel and not mine own. Besides,
to be demanded of a sponge, what replication should be
made by the son of a king?

ROSENCRANTZ
Take you me for a sponge, my lord?

HAMLET
15   Ay, sir, that soaks up the King's countenance, his rewards,
his authorities. But such officers do the King best service
in the end. He keeps them, like an ape an apple, in the
corner of his jaw, first mouthed, to be last swallowed.

ACT 4, SCENE 2

The castle. HAMLET *enters.*

HAMLET
The body's safely hidden.

GENTLEMEN (*offstage*)
Hamlet! Lord Hamlet!

HAMLET
But wait—what's that noise? Who's calling for Hamlet?
Oh, here they come.

    ROSENCRANTZ, GUILDENSTERN, *and* OTHERS *enter.*

ROSENCRANTZ
My lord, what have you done with the dead body? 5

HAMLET
I've combined it with dust, to which it is related.

ROSENCRANTZ
Tell us where it is, so we can take it away from there
and carry it to the chapel.

HAMLET
Do not believe it.

ROSENCRANTZ
Believe what? 10

HAMLET
That I can keep your secrets, but not my own. Besides, what
kind of reply should a king's son make when he's being
questioned by a sponge?

ROSENCRANTZ
Do you take me for a sponge, my lord?

HAMLET
Indeed, sir—a sponge that soaks up the King's favors, his 15
rewards, and the powers he grants you. But in the end, such
followers do the King the best service. As if he were an ape, he
holds them in his cheek like an apple; after keeping them in his

When he needs what you have gleaned, it is but squeezing
20 you and, sponge, you shall be dry again.

ROSENCRANTZ
I understand you not, my lord.

HAMLET
I am glad of it: a knavish speech sleeps in a foolish ear.

ROSENCRANTZ
My lord, you must tell us where the body is and go with
us to the King.

HAMLET
25 The body is with the King, but the King is not with the
body.* The King is a thing—

GUILDENSTERN
A "thing," my lord?

HAMLET
Of nothing. Bring me to him. Hide fox, and all after!*

Exeunt.

---

26 *body* Hamlet may merely be speaking nonsense; but like all of his crazy speeches,
these lines suggest various meanings: The King is only a body, the mere external
appearance of kingship; the real King is dead; or the King is guilty of this death.

28 *Hide fox, and all after* probably a cry from a game resembling hide-and-seek

mouth awhile, he swallows them. When you have learned what
he needs to know, all he has to do is squeeze you. And sponge   20
that you are, you will be dry again.

ROSENCRANTZ

I don't understand you, my lord.

HAMLET

I am glad of it. A shrewd remark is not understood by a
foolish ear.

ROSENCRANTZ

My lord, you must tell us where the body is and go with us
to the King.

HAMLET

The body is right here in the palace with the King; but the   25
King is not, like the body, dead. The King is a thing—

GUILDENSTERN

A "thing," my lord?

HAMLET

—of no importance. Take me to him. I'll hide like a fox, and
you come looking for me!

　　　　HAMLET rushes offstage; the OTHERS hurry after him.

ACT IV, SCENE III

[*The castle.*] *Enter* KING *and two or three* ATTENDANTS.

KING
I have sent to seek him and to find the body.
How dangerous is it that this man goes loose!
Yet must not we put the strong law on him:
He's loved of the distracted multitude,
5 Who like not in their judgment, but their eyes,
And where 'tis so, th' offender's scourge is weighed,
But never the offense. To bear all smooth and even,
This sudden sending him away must seem
Deliberate pause. Diseases desperate grown
10 By desperate appliance are relieved,
Or not at all.

Enter ROSENCRANTZ.

How now? What hath befall'n?

ROSENCRANTZ
Where the dead body is bestowed, my lord,
We cannot get from him.

KING
15 But where is he?

ROSENCRANTZ
Without, my lord; guarded, to know your pleasure.

KING
Bring him before us.

ROSENCRANTZ
Ho! Bring in the lord.

Enter HAMLET *and* GUILDENSTERN.

KING
Now, Hamlet, where's Polonius?

HAMLET
20 At supper.

KING
At supper? Where?

ACT 4, SCENE 3

The castle. The KING *and two or three* OTHERS *enter.*

KING
    I have sent people searching for him, and also to find the body.
    How dangerous it is that this man is on the loose!
    Yet I must not enforce the law too strongly against him.
    He's loved by the irrational commoners,
    who base their likings on appearances, not sound judgment;   5
    and when this is so, the offender's punishment is always
    considered too harsh for his crime. To manage everything
        smoothly and skillfully,
    my suddenly sending him away must seem
    the result of careful planning. Desperate diseases
    must be cured by desperate remedies—   10
    or not at all.

        ROSENCRANTZ *and* GUILDENSTERN *enter.*

    What now? What has happened?

ROSENCRANTZ
    He will not tell us where the dead body
    is hidden, my lord.

KING
    But where is he?   15

ROSENCRANTZ
    Outside, my lord: under guard while we await your orders.

KING
    Bring him to me.

ROSENCRANTZ
    Come! Bring in the lord.

        HAMLET *and* GUILDENSTERN *enter.*

KING
    Now, Hamlet, where's Polonius?

HAMLET
    At supper.   20

KING
    At supper where?

HAMLET

Not where he eats, but where 'a is eaten. A certain
convocation of politic worms are e'en at him. Your worm
is your only emperor for diet. We fat all creatures else to
25   fat us, and we fat ourselves for maggots. Your fat king and
your lean beggar is but variable service—two dishes, but to
one table. That's the end.*

KING

Alas, alas!

HAMLET

A man may fish with the worm that hath eat of a king,
30   and eat of the fish that hath fed of that worm.

KING

What dost thou mean by this?

HAMLET

Nothing but to show you how a king may go a progress
through the guts of a beggar.

KING

Where is Polonius?

HAMLET

35   In heaven. Send thither to see. If your messengers find
him not there, seek him i' th' other place yourself. But if
indeed you find him not within this month, you shall
nose him as you go up the stairs into the lobby.

KING [*to* ATTENDANTS]
Go seek him there.

HAMLET

40   'A will stay till you come.

[*Exeunt* ATTENDANTS.]

KING

Hamlet, this deed, for thine especial safety,
Which we do tender as we dearly grieve
For that which thou hast done, must send thee hence
With fiery quickness. Therefore prepare thyself.

---

27   *end* wordplay: the end of my story and the end of every human (i.e., death)

HAMLET

Not where he eats, but where he is eaten. A certain council of statesmanlike worms is munching on him. The worm is the only absolute ruler over what's eaten. We fatten all other creatures in order to fatten ourselves, and we fatten ourselves in order to feed maggots. The fat king and the skinny beggar are but different dinner courses—two dishes served at the same table. That's how things end.

25

KING

Alas, alas!

HAMLET

A man may fish with a worm that has eaten off a king, then eat the fish that has eaten that worm.

30

KING

What do you mean by this?

HAMLET

Nothing, except to show you how a king may pass on a royal procession through the guts of a beggar.

KING

Where is Polonius?

HAMLET

In heaven. Send someone there to look for him. If your messenger doesn't find him there, seek him in the other place yourself. But indeed, if you don't find him within this month, you will smell him as you go up the stairs into the lobby.

35

KING (*to* SERVANTS)

Go, look for him there.

HAMLET

He will wait till you come.

40

SERVANTS *exit.*

KING

Hamlet, because of this deed, and for your personal safety—
which I value as greatly as I grieve
what you have done—you must be sent away
extremely quickly. So prepare yourself.

45 The bark is ready and the wind at help,
Th' associates tend, and everything is bent
For England.

HAMLET
For England?

KING
Ay, Hamlet.

HAMLET
50 Good.

KING
So is it, if thou knew'st our purposes.

HAMLET
I see a cherub that sees them. But come, for England!
Farewell, dear Mother.

KING
                              Thy loving father, Hamlet.

HAMLET
55 My mother. Father and mother is man and wife, man and
wife is one flesh, and so, my mother.—Come, for England!

        Exit.

KING
Follow him at foot; tempt him with speed aboard.
Delay it not; I'll have him hence tonight.
Away! For everything is sealed and done
60 That else leans on th' affair. Pray you make haste.

        [*Exeunt all but the* KING.]

And, England, if my love thou hold'st at aught—
As my great power thereof may give thee sense,
Since yet thy cicatrice looks raw and red
After the Danish sword, and thy free awe
65 Pays homage to us—thou mayst not coldly set
Our sovereign process, which imports at full
By letters congruing to that effect

The ship is ready, and the winds favorable, 45
your companions await you, and everything else is set
for you to go to England.

HAMLET
To England?

KING
Yes, Hamlet.

HAMLET
Good. 50

KING
It is, indeed—especially if you knew my intentions.

HAMLET
A little angel sees your intentions for me. But let's go—to
    England!
Farewell, dear Mother.

KING
I'm your loving *father,* Hamlet.

HAMLET
I say farewell to my mother. Father and mother are man and 55
wife, and man and wife are one flesh; and so I say farewell
to my mother. But let's go—to England!

>   HAMLET *exits.*

KING
Follow him at his heels; urge him to board the ship speedily.
Don't let him delay. I want him gone tonight.
Get going, for all the documents that this business depends on
are signed and sealed. I implore you, hurry. 60

>   *All but the* KING *exit.*

Well, King of England, I hope you value my regard for you;
you should do so, out of consideration for my great power
    over you,
since your wounds are still raw and red
after your last war with Denmark, and you openly pledge
your allegiance to us. You don't dare take lightly 65
my royal command—which explicitly orders,
in letters pertaining to the matter,

The present death of Hamlet. Do it, England,
For like the hectic in my blood he rages,
70 And thou must cure me. Till I know 'tis done,
Howe'er my haps, my joys were ne'er begun.

Exit.

the immediate death of Hamlet. Do it, King of England,
for he rages through my blood like a fever,
and you must cure me. I'll begin to feel no joy   70
until I know that this has been done, no matter how fortunate I
  may be.

  He exits.

ACT IV, SCENE IV

> [*A plain in Denmark.*] *Enter* FORTINBRAS *with his* ARMY *over the stage.*

FORTINBRAS
> Go, Captain, from me greet the Danish king.
> Tell him that by his license Fortinbras
> Craves the conveyance of a promised march
> Over his kingdom. You know the rendezvous.
5   If that his Majesty would aught with us,
> We shall express our duty in his eye;
> And let him know so.

CAPTAIN
> I will do 't, my lord.

FORTINBRAS
> Go softly on.

> [*Exeunt all but the* CAPTAIN.]

> *Enter* HAMLET, ROSENCRANTZ, *etc.*

HAMLET
10   Good sir, whose powers are these?

CAPTAIN
> They are of Norway, sir.

HAMLET
> How purposed, sir, I pray you?

CAPTAIN
> Against some part of Poland.

HAMLET
> Who commands them, sir?

CAPTAIN
15   The nephew of old Norway, Fortinbras.

HAMLET
> Goes it against the main of Poland, sir,
> Or for some frontier?

ACT 4, SCENE 4

A plain in Denmark. FORTINBRAS *and his* ARMY *enter.*

FORTINBRAS
Go, Captain, and greet the Danish king for me.
Tell him that Fortinbras wishes to be granted
an escort during our march (which has already been agreed to)
across his kingdom. You know where we're supposed to meet.
If his Majesty wants anything with us,   5
we'll show our respect for him in his presence;
tell him so.

CAPTAIN
I will do it, my lord.

FORTINBRAS
(to his ARMY*)* March slowly on.

> *All but the* CAPTAIN *exit;* HAMLET, ROSENCRANTZ,
> GUILDENSTERN, *and* ATTENDANTS *enter.*

HAMLET
Good sir, whose army is this?   10

CAPTAIN
The King of Norway's, sir.

HAMLET
Would you tell me where it's going?

CAPTAIN
To attack some part of Poland, sir.

HAMLET
Who commands it, sir?

CAPTAIN
Fortinbras, the nephew of the old King of Norway.   15

HAMLET
Are you going to attack the main part of Poland, sir,
or just some frontier fortress?

CAPTAIN
    Truly to speak, and with no addition,
    We go to gain a little patch of ground
20   That hath in it no profit but the name.
    To pay five ducats, five, I would not farm it,
    Nor will it yield to Norway or the Pole
    A ranker rate, should it be sold in fee.

HAMLET
    Why, then the Polack never will defend it.

CAPTAIN
25   Yes, it is already garrisoned.

HAMLET
    Two thousand souls and twenty thousand ducats
    Will not debate the question of this straw.
    This is th' impostume of much wealth and peace,
    That inward breaks, and shows no cause without
30   Why the man dies.—I humbly thank you, sir.

CAPTAIN
    God be wi' you, sir.

        [He exits.]

ROSENCRANTZ
    Will 't please you go, my lord?

HAMLET
    I'll be with you straight. Go a little before.

        [Exeunt all but HAMLET.]

    How all occasions do inform against me
35   And spur my dull revenge! What is a man,
    If his chief good and market of his time
    Be but to sleep and feed? A beast, no more.
    Sure He that made us with such large discourse,
    Looking before and after, gave us not
40   That capability and godlike reason
    To fust in us unused. Now, whether it be
    Bestial **oblivion**, or some craven scruple

CAPTAIN

To tell you the truth without going into details,
we hope to win a little patch of ground
that has no value at all, except to be able to say that we   20
    conquered it.
I wouldn't rent it as a farm for five ducats—not even five.
Nor would it bring Norway or Poland
a higher price if it were sold outright.

HAMLET

Why, then, the Polish will never defend it.

CAPTAIN

Yes, it is already well armed.   25

HAMLET

Two thousand lives and twenty thousand ducats
won't be enough to settle this trivial quarrel.
Times of wealth and peace often lead to such an abscess,
which breaks beneath the skin, showing no outward cause
for the man's death. I humbly thank you, sir.   30

CAPTAIN

God be with you, sir.

> *He exits.*

ROSENCRANTZ

Are you ready to go, my lord?

HAMLET

I'll be with you right away. Go on a little ahead of me.

> *All but* HAMLET *exit.*

How everything that happens accuses me,
and urges me on to my delayed revenge! What is a man,   35
if the best profit he can gain from life
is only to sleep and eat? A beast, nothing more.
Surely God, who made us with such great intelligence
and the power to consider both the past and future, did not
    give us
such abilities and godlike reason   40
to mold away in us unused. Whether I've delayed
from beastlike forgetfulness, or from cowardly hesitation

Of thinking too precisely on th' event—
A thought which, quartered, hath but one part wisdom
45 And ever three parts coward—I do not know
Why yet I live to say, "This thing's to do,"
Sith I have cause, and will, and strength, and means
To do 't. Examples gross as earth **exhort** me.
Witness this army of such mass and charge,
50 Led by a delicate and tender prince,
Whose spirit, with divine ambition puffed,
Makes mouths at the invisible event,
Exposing what is mortal and unsure
To all that fortune, death, and danger dare,
55 Even for an eggshell. Rightly to be great
Is not to stir without great argument,
But greatly to find quarrel in a straw
When honor's at the stake. How stand I then,
That have a father killed, a mother stained,
60 Excitements of my reason and my blood,
And let all sleep, while to my shame I see
The **imminent** death of twenty thousand men
That for a fantasy and trick of fame
Go to their graves like beds, fight for a plot
65 Whereon the numbers cannot try the cause,
Which is not tomb enough and continent
To hide the slain? O, from this time forth,
My thoughts be bloody, or be nothing worth!

     Exit.

that comes from thinking too much about the outcome—
for when a thought is cut into fourths, it leaves only one part
    wisdom
and three parts cowardice—I do not know   45
why I continue to live and say, "This thing remains to be done,"
since I have the cause, the will, the strength, and means
to do it. Examples as solid as the earth provoke me:
Consider this army of such size and expense,
led by an inexperienced and youthful prince,   50
whose spirit is swollen with divine ambition,
and who looks scornfully at the unknowable outcome,
exposing everything that is mortal and vulnerable
to all the hazards of luck, death, and danger—
and for nothing more than an eggshell. To be truly great   55
does *not* mean not to act without a great cause,
but to show one's greatness by taking up a quarrel over a
    triviality
when honor is at stake. So how should I judge myself,
with my father killed, my mother dishonored,
and other spurs to both my reasons and passions—   60
and yet I sleep through it all? And now to my shame, I see
the impending deaths of twenty thousand men
who, for the illusion and whim of fame,
go to their graves as if they were beds, fighting for a plot of
    land
where there's not enough room for all of them to fight the   65
    battle,
and which is not big enough to serve as a tomb
to bury all the slain. Oh, from this time on,
let my thoughts be merciless, or be considered worthless!

    He exits.

ACT IV, SCENE V

[The castle.] Enter HORATIO, [QUEEN] GERTRUDE,
and a GENTLEMAN.

QUEEN

I will not speak with her.

GENTLEMAN

She is importunate,
Indeed distract. Her mood will needs be pitied.

QUEEN

What would she have?

GENTLEMAN

5   She speaks much of her father, says she hears
There's tricks i' th' world, and hems, and beats her heart,
Spurns enviously at straws, speaks things in doubt
That carry but half sense. Her speech is nothing,
Yet the unshaped use of it doth move
10   The hearers to collection; they yawn at it,
And botch the words up fit to their own thoughts,
Which, as her winks and nods and gestures yield them,
Indeed would make one think there might be thought,
Though nothing sure, yet much unhappily.

HORATIO

15   'Twere good she were spoken with, for she may stew
Dangerous **conjectures** in ill-breeding minds.

QUEEN

Let her come in.

[Exit GENTLEMAN.*]*

[aside] To my sick soul (as sin's true nature is)
Each toy seems prologue to some great amiss;
20   So full of artless jealousy is guilt
It spills itself in fearing to be spilt.

Enter OPHELIA *[distracted.]*

ACT 4, SCENE 5

The castle. HORATIO, QUEEN GERTRUDE, *and a* GENTLEMAN *enter.*

QUEEN
I will not speak with her.

GENTLEMAN
She is persistent—
her mental state is truly to be pitied.

QUEEN
What does she want?

GENTLEMAN
She speaks much about her father, says that she hears   5
that there are plots in the world, says "hmm," beats her breast,
becomes angry over trifles, and says strange things
that only half make sense. Her speech is pointless,
and yet its very pointlessness prompts those who hear her
to find some meaning in it. They guess at it,   10
and patch her words together to fit their guesses;
her winks, nods, and gestures, along with her words,
would make one think she might mean something—
and although her meaning is uncertain, it seems sinister.

HORATIO
It would be best if she were spoken to, for she might spread   15
dangerous guesses among those inclined to mischievous
   thoughts.

QUEEN
Let her come in.

     The GENTLEMAN *exits.*

(aside) To my sick soul (for one's soul is truly sick when one
   has sinned),
each trifle seems to predict some great disaster.
A guilty mind is so full of foolish suspicion,   20
it destroys itself out of fear of being destroyed.

     OPHELIA *enters, mad.*

OPHELIA

Where is the beauteous Majesty of Denmark?

QUEEN

How now, Ophelia?

OPHELIA [*Sings.*[

    "How should I your true love know
25   From another one?
    By his cockle hat* and staff
         And his sandal shoon."

QUEEN

Alas, sweet lady, what imports this song?

OPHELIA

Say you? Nay, pray you mark. [*Sings.*]
30   "He is dead and gone, lady,
         He is dead and gone;
    At his head a grass-green turf,
         At his heels a stone."
    O, ho!

QUEEN

35   Nay, but Ophelia—

OPHELIA

Pray you mark.
[*Sings.*] "White his shroud as the mountain snow—"

       Enter KING.

QUEEN

Alas, look here, my lord.

OPHELIA [*Sings.*]

    "Larded all with sweet flowers
40   Which bewept to the grave did not go
    With true-love showers."

KING

How do you, pretty lady?

---

26   *cockle hat* Pilgrims returning from the famous shrine of St. James of Compostela in Spain wore a cockle shell in their hat to mark their visit there.

270   *Hamlet*

OPHELIA
Where is her beautiful Majesty of Denmark?

QUEEN
What is it, Ophelia?

OPHELIA (*singing*)
> How should I know your true lover
> from someone else?
> By the cockle shell on his hat, and his staff,
> and his sandal shoes.

25

QUEEN
Alas, sweet lady, what does this song mean?

OPHELIA
What do you say? Indeed, I beg you to listen.
(*singing*)
> He is dead and gone, lady;
> he is dead and gone.
> Above his head is green, grassy soil;
> above his heels is a stone.

30

QUEEN
Indeed, but Ophelia—

35

OPHELIA
I beg you, listen.
(*singing*) *His shroud was as white as the mountain snow—*

The KING *enters.*

QUEEN
Alas, look at this, my lord.

OPHELIA (*singing*)
> *—all decorated with sweet flowers;*
> *they were not taken sorrowfully to his grave*
> *with showers of a true lover's tears.*

40

KING
How are you, pretty lady?

OPHELIA

Well, God dild you! They say the owl was a baker's
daughter.* Lord, we know what we are, but know not
45   what we may be. God be at your table!

KING

Conceit upon her father.

OPHELIA

Pray let's have no words of this, but when they ask you
what it means, say you this:
        "Tomorrow is Saint Valentine's day.*
50   All in the morning betime,
And I a maid at your window,
        To be your Valentine.
Then up he rose and donned his clothes
        And dupped the chamber door,
55   Let in the maid, that out a maid
        Never departed more."

KING

Pretty Ophelia.

OPHELIA

Indeed, la, without an oath, I'll make an end on 't:
[*Sings.*] "By Gis and by Saint Charity,
60   Alack, and fie for shame!
Young men will do 't if they come to 't,
        By Cock,* they are to blame.
Quoth she, "Before you tumbled me,
        You promised me to wed."
65   He answers:
        "So would I 'a done, by yonder sun,
                An thou hadst not come to my bed."

---

44   *baker's daughter* refers to the legend of a baker's daughter whom Jesus turned
into an owl because she would not give him bread

49   *Saint Valentine's day* The tradition was that a man would love the first girl he saw
on St. Valentine's day.

OPHELIA

I'm well, may God reward you. They say that the owl was once a baker's daughter. Lord, we know what we are right now, but we do not know what we might become. May God be at your dinner table! 45

KING

She's brooding about her father.

OPHELIA

I beg you, let's talk no more about this; but if anyone should ask you what it means, say this:

(singing)

> *Tomorrow is Saint Valentine's day,*
> > *early in the morning;* 50
> *and I, a virgin, have come to your window,*
> > *to be your Valentine.*
> *Then he rose from bed and put on his clothes,*
> > *and opened his bedroom door;*
> *he let in the virgin, who was no longer a virgin* 55
> > *when she left there.*

KING

Pretty Ophelia—

OPHELIA

Indeed, without further fuss, I'll finish the song.

(singing)

> *By Jesus and Saint Charity,*
> > *alas, how bad, for shame!* 60
> *Young men will have their way with girls if they get a chance;*
> > *by God, they are to blame.*
> *She said, "Before you bedded me,*
> > *you promised to marry me."*

(speaking)

He answers: 65

(singing)

> *"And I swear by yonder sun I would have done so*
> > *if you hadn't come to my bed."*

---

62   *By Cock* a corruption of "by God," but also, in context, an obscene reference

KING

How long hath she been thus?

OPHELIA

I hope all will be well. We must be patient, but I cannot
70   choose but weep to think they would lay him i' th' cold
ground. My brother shall know of it; and so I thank you
for your good counsel. Come, my coach! Good night,
ladies, good night. Sweet ladies, good night, good night.

       Exit.

KING

Follow her close; give her good watch, I pray you.

       [*Exit* HORATIO.]

75   O, this is the poison of deep grief; it springs
All from her father's death—and now behold!
O Gertrude, Gertrude,
When sorrows come, they come not single spies,
But in battalions: first, her father slain;
80   Next, your son gone, and he most violent author
Of his own just remove; the people muddied,
Thick and unwholesome in their thoughts and whispers
For good Polonius's death, and we have done but greenly
In huggermugger to **inter** him; poor Ophelia
85   Divided from herself and her fair judgment,
Without the which we are pictures or mere beasts;
Last, and as much containing as all these,
Her brother is in secret come from France,
Feeds on his wonder, keeps himself in clouds,
90   And wants not buzzers to infect his ear
With pestilent speeches of his father's death,
Wherein necessity, of matter beggared,
Will nothing stick our person to arraign
In ear and ear. O my dear Gertrude, this,
95   Like to a murd'ring piece, in many places
Gives me **superfluous** death.

       A noise within.

KING

How long has she been like this?

OPHELIA

I hope all will be well. We must be patient, but I cannot help
but weep to think that they would bury him in the cold   70
ground. My brother will learn of it. And so I thank you for your
good advice. Come, my coach! Good night, ladies, good night,
sweet ladies, good night, good night.

She exits.

KING

Follow her closely; watch her well, I implore you.

> HORATIO *exits.*

Oh, this madness is the poison of her deep grief. It all   75
springs from her father's death. And now see what is happening!
Oh, Gertrude, Gertrude,
when sorrows come, they don't arrive singly, like spies,
but in battalions. First, her father was slain;
next, your son was gone—and he the cause of his own   80
  departure,
by an act of violence. The people are confused,
full of unhealthy ideas and rumors
about good Polonius's death; and in our inexperience, we
  foolishly
buried him in secret haste. Poor Ophelia
is no longer herself and has lost her power of reason,   85
without which we are soulless—nothing more than pictures
  or beasts.
Last, and as dangerous as all these other threats,
her brother has secretly returned from France,
nurses his suspicions, ignores all facts,
and has plenty of rumormongers to fill his ear   90
with wicked talk about his father's death;
and lacking true information, he feels compelled to make guesses,
and thinks nothing of making accusations against us
to one person after another. Oh, my dear Gertrude, all this,
like a scattershot cannon, kills me again and again   95
with many wounds.

A noise offstage.

Enter a MESSENGER.

QUEEN
Alack, what noise is this?

KING
Attend, where are my Switzers? Let them guard the door.
What is the matter?

MESSENGER
100   Save yourself, my lord.
The ocean, overpeering of his list,
Eats not the flats with more **impetuous** haste
Than young Laertes, in a riotous head,
O'erbears your officers. The rabble call him lord,
105 And, as the world were now but to begin,
Antiquity forgot, custom not known,
The ratifiers and props of every word,
They cry, "Choose we! Laertes shall be king!"
Caps, hands, and tongues applaud it to the clouds,
110 "Laertes shall be king! Laertes king!"

      A noise within.

QUEEN
How cheerfully on the false trail they cry!
O, this is counter, you false Danish dogs!

     Enter LAERTES *with* OTHERS.

KING
The doors are broke.

LAERTES
Where is this King?—Sirs, stand you all without.

ALL
115 No, let's come in.

LAERTES
I pray you give me leave.

ALL
We will, we will.

LAERTES
I thank you. Keep the door. [*Exeunt his* FOLLOWERS.] O thou

A MESSENGER *enters.*

QUEEN
Listen!

KING
Where are my Swiss guards? Let them guard the door.
What is the matter?

MESSENGER
Save yourself, my lord.   100
The ocean, when overflowing its bounds,
does not sweep over the flatlands with more pitiless haste
than young Laertes, leading a rebellious force,
overcomes your officers. The rabble calls him "lord";
and as if civilization were just getting started,   105
and antiquity and tradition (those sanctions and supporters
of every pledge) were now forgotten and unknown,
they cry, "We choose! Laertes will be king!"
Throwing up their caps and clapping, they cheer to the clouds,
"Laertes will be king! Laertes king!"   110

    A noise offstage.

QUEEN
How cheerfully they go yelping along the wrong trail!
Oh, you follow a false scent, you treacherous Danish dogs!

    LAERTES *and his* FOLLOWERS *enter.*

KING
They've broken open the doors.

LAERTES
Where is this King? *(to his* FOLLOWERS*)* Sirs, all of you wait outside.

ALL
No, let us come in!   115

LAERTES
I implore you, leave me alone.

ALL
We will, we will.

LAERTES
Thank you. Guard the door.

    FOLLOWERS *exit.*

vile King,
120　Give me my father.

QUEEN
　　　　　　　　　　Calmly, good Laertes.

LAERTES
　　That drop of blood that's calm proclaims me bastard,
　　Cries cuckold to my father, brands the harlot
　　Even here between the chaste unsmirchèd brow
125　Of my true mother.

KING
　　　　　　　　　　What is the cause, Laertes,
　　That thy rebellion looks so giant-like?
　　Let him go, Gertrude. Do not fear our person.
　　There's such divinity doth hedge a king
130　That treason can but peep to what it would,
　　Acts little of his will.—Tell me, Laertes,
　　Why thou art thus **incensed**.—Let him go, Gertrude.
　　Speak, man.

LAERTES
　　Where is my father?

KING
135　Dead.

QUEEN
　　But not by him.

KING
　　　　　　　　　　Let him demand his fill.

LAERTES
　　How came he dead? I'll not be juggled with.
　　To hell allegiance, vows to the blackest devil,
140　Conscience and grace to the profoundest pit!
　　I dare damnation. To this point I stand,
　　That both the worlds I give to negligence,
　　Let come what comes, only I'll be revenged
　　Most throughly for my father.

Hamlet

Oh, you wicked King,
give me my father!   120

QUEEN

Be calm, good Laertes.

LAERTES

The drop of my blood that's calm declares me a bastard;
says that my father was betrayed by his wife; and marks the
    chaste, unstained forehead
of my faithful mother right here *(pointing to his forehead)*
with the brand of a whore.   125

KING

What is the reason, Laertes,
that your rebellion has grown so great?—
Let him go, Gertrude. Do not fear for my safety.
A king is under such divine protection
that a traitor can only peek at what he wishes to do,   130
and carries out little of what he intends.—Tell me, Laertes,
why you are so angry.—Let him go, Gertrude.—
Speak, man.

LAERTES

Where is my father?

KING

Dead.   135

QUEEN

But not killed by him.

KING

Let him ask all his questions.

LAERTES

How was he killed? I'll not be deceived.
To hell with my allegiance to you! May all my vows of loyalty
    go to the blackest devil,
my scruples and God's grace go to the deepest pit of hell!   140
I dare to be damned. Now that I've come this far,
I care nothing about this life or the next;
no matter what happens, I'll get full revenge
for my father.

KING

145   Who shall stay you?

LAERTES

My will, not all the world's.
And for my means, I'll husband them so well
They shall go far with little.

KING

                                   Good Laertes,

150   If you desire to know the certainty
Of your dear father, is 't writ in your revenge
That swoopstake you will draw both friend and foe,
Winner and loser?

LAERTES

None but his enemies.

KING

155   Will you know them then?

LAERTES

To his good friends thus wide I'll ope my arms
And like the kind life-rend'ring pelican*
Repast them with my blood.

KING

                                  Why, now you speak

160   Like a good child and a true gentleman.
That I am guiltless of your father's death,
And am most sensibly in grief for it,
It shall as level to your judgment 'pear
As day does to your eye.

      A noise within: "Let her come in."

LAERTES

165   How now? What noise is that?

      Enter OPHELIA.

O heat, dry up my brains; tears seven times salt
Burn out the sense and virtue of mine eye!

---

157   *pelican* The female pelican was thought to feed her young with her own blood.

KING

What can stop you? 145

LAERTES

My own decision, nothing else in the world.
As for my resources, I'll use them so frugally that they
will accomplish much, although they are small.

KING

Good Laertes,
if you really want to know the truth 150
about your dear father, does it make sense to avenge
yourself like a rash gambler, claiming all the stakes of both
    winners and losers,
destroying both friends and foes?

LAERTES

I'll harm no one but his enemies.

KING

And will you know who they are? 155

LAERTES

To his good friends, I'll open my arms wide, like this;
and like the kind, life-giving pelican,
I'll feed them with my blood.

KING

Why, now you speak
like a good son and a true gentleman. 160
That I am guiltless of your father's death,
and grieve for him most deeply,
will soon appear as clearly to your judgment
as daylight does to your eyesight.

    Voices offstage cry, "Let her come in."

LAERTES

What is it? What is that noise? 165

    OPHELIA *enters.*

Oh, heat, dry up my brains! Tears, may your salt burn out
the sense and power of my eyes seven times over!

By heaven, thy madness shall be paid with weight
Till our scale turn the beam. O rose of May,
170   Dear maid, kind sister, sweet Ophelia!
O heavens, is 't possible a young maid's wits
Should be as mortal as an old man's life?
Nature is fine in love, and where 'tis fine,
It sends some precious instance of itself
175   After the thing it loves.

OPHELIA [*Sings.*]
    "They bore him barefaced on the bier
        Hey non nony, nony, hey nony
    And in his grave rained many a tear—"
Fare you well, my dove!

LAERTES
180   Hadst thou thy wits, and didst persuade revenge,
It could not move thus.

OPHELIA
You must sing "A-down a-down"—and you "Call him
a-down-a."—O, how the wheel becomes it! It is the false
steward that stole his master's daughter.

LAERTES
185   This nothing's more than matter.

OPHELIA
There's rosemary, that's for remembrance. Pray you, love,
remember. And there is pansies, that's for thoughts.

LAERTES
A document in madness, thoughts and remembrance
fitted.

OPHELIA
190   There's fennel for you, and columbines. There's rue for
you, and here's some for me. We may call it herb of grace
o' Sundays. O, you must wear your rue with a difference.
There's a daisy. I would give you some violets, but they

By heaven, Ophelia, I'll gain enough revenge
to outweigh your madness in the scales! Oh, rose of May!
Dear girl, kind sister, sweet Ophelia! 170
Oh, heavens, is it possible that a young girl's sanity
can be as easily destroyed as an old man's life?
Love makes a daughter delicate; and because she is delicate,
she sends some precious sample of herself
after her father when he is gone. 175

OPHELIA (*singing*)
> *They carried him on the bier, his face uncovered—*
>   *Hey non nonny, nonny, hey nonny—*
> *and many tears were rained on his grave.*
Farewell to you, my dove.

LAERTES
If you were sane and trying to persuade me toward revenge, 180
you couldn't move me like this.

OPHELIA
You must sing, "A-down a-down." And you, "Call him a-down-a."
Oh, how the refrain suits the song! It was the treacherous servant
who stole his master's daughter.

LAERTES
This nonsense has more to say than sensible speech. 185

OPHELIA
(*giving flowers to different characters*) Here's rosemary; that's
for memory. I beg you to remember me, my love. And here are
some pansies; that's for sad thoughts.

LAERTES
This is a lesson in madness. Sad thoughts and memories suit
each other well.

OPHELIA
Here's fennel for you, and columbines. Here's rue for you, and 190
also some for me; on Sundays, we call it an "herb of grace." You
must wear it for different reasons than I. Here's a daisy. I wish
I could give you some violets, but they all withered when my

withered all when my father died. They say 'a made a
good end.
[*Sings.*] "For bonny sweet Robin is all my joy."

LAERTES
Thought and affliction, passion, hell itself,
She turns to favor and to prettiness.

OPHELIA [*Sings.*]
    "And will 'a not come again?
    And will 'a not come again?
        No, no, he is dead,
        Go to thy deathbed,
    He never will come again.

    His beard was as white as snow,
    All flaxen was his poll.
        He is gone, he is gone,
        And we cast away moan.
    God 'a mercy on his soul!"

And of all Christian souls, I pray God. God be wi' you.

    Exit.

LAERTES
Do you see this, O God?

KING
Laertes, I must commune with your grief,
Or you deny me right. Go but apart,
Make choice of whom your wisest friends you will,
And they shall hear and judge 'twixt you and me.
If by direct or by collateral hand
They find us touched, we will our kingdom give,
Our crown, our life, and all that we call ours,
To you in satisfaction; but if not,
Be you content to lend your patience to us,
And we shall jointly labor with your soul

father died. They say he died a holy death. 195

(*singing*)
    For handsome sweet Robin is my only joy.

LAERTES
    Sadness, suffering, violent feelings, and hell itself—
    she turns them all into charming, pretty things.

OPHELIA (*singing*)
    And won't he come again?
    And won't he come again? 200
      No, no, he is dead.
      Go to your deathbed.
    He will never come again.

    His beard was as white as snow,
    his face was as pale as flax. 205
      He is gone, he is gone,
      and we waste our moans of grief.
    May God have mercy on his soul.
(*speaking*)
And I pray God to have mercy on all Christians' souls. God be
    with you.

      She exits.

LAERTES
    Do you see this, oh, God? 210

KING
    Laertes, you must let me share in your grief,
    or you'll deny me my right. Go off by yourself,
    choose whom you wish among your wisest friends,
    and they will listen and judge between you and me.
    If they find me guilty of this deed, either directly 215
    or by an accomplice, I will give you my kingdom,
    my crown, my life, and all that I call mine
    in repayment. But if not,
    be content to show me patience,
    and I shall labor along with you 220
    to give your soul comfort.

To give it due content.

LAERTES
                    Let this be so.
His means of death, his **obscure** funeral—
No trophy, sword, nor hatchment o'er his bones,
No noble rite nor formal ostentation—
Cry to be heard, as 'twere from heaven to earth,
That I must call 't in question.

KING
                              So you shall;
And where th' offense is, let the great ax fall.
I pray you go with me.

      Exeunt.

225

230

LAERTES
Let it be so.
The way he died, and his hidden funeral
(no trophy, sword, or coat of arms hung over his body,
nor any noble rite or formal ceremony)   225
demand to be explained—to both heaven and earth, so to
    speak;
and I must question you fully about it.

KING
So you shall.
And let the great axe fall upon the person at fault.
I beg you, come with me.   230

     They exit.

ACT IV, SCENE VI

> [*The castle.*] *Enter* HORATIO *and* OTHERS.

HORATIO
What are they that would speak with me?

GENTLEMAN
Seafaring men, sir. They say they have letters for you.

HORATIO
Let them come in.

> [*Exit* ATTENDANT.]

5   I do not know from what part of the world
I should be greeted, if not from Lord Hamlet.

> *Enter* SAILORS.

SAILOR
God bless you, sir.

HORATIO
Let Him bless thee too.

SAILOR
'A shall, sir, an 't please Him. There's a letter for you, sir—
it came from th' ambassador that was bound for England—
10   if your name be Horatio, as I am let to know it is.

HORATIO [*Reads the letter.*]
"Horatio, when thou shalt have overlooked this, give these
fellows some means to the King. They have letters for him.
Ere we were two days old at sea, a pirate of very warlike
appointment gave us chase. Finding ourselves too slow of
15   sail, we put on a compelled valor, and in the grapple I
boarded them. On the instant they got clear of our ship;
so I alone became their prisoner. They have dealt with me
like thieves of mercy, but they knew what they did: I am
to do a good turn for them. Let the King have the letters I
20   have sent, and repair thou to me with as much speed as
thou wouldest fly death. I have words to speak in thine
ear will make thee dumb; yet are they much too light for

ACT 4, SCENE 6

The castle. HORATIO *and a* SERVANT *enter.*

HORATIO
Who are these people that wish to speak with me?

SERVANT
Seafaring men, sir. They say that they have letters for you.

HORATIO
Let them come in.

>*The* SERVANT *exits.*

I don't know why I should hear from anyone
anywhere in the world—unless it's Lord Hamlet.   5

>SAILORS *enter.*

SAILOR
God bless you, sir.

HORATIO
Let Him bless you, too.

SAILOR
He will, sir, if it pleases Him. Here's a letter; it came from the
ambassador who was on his way to England. It's for you, sir—
if your name is Horatio, as I've been told it is.   10

>*He gives* HORATIO *the letter.*

HORATIO (*reading the letter*)
Horatio, once you have read this letter, see to it that these
fellows meet with the King. They have letters for him. Before
we had been at sea for two days, a very well-armed pirate ship
chased after us. Finding ourselves sailing too slowly to escape,
we put on a display of courage, and during the fight that   15
followed, I boarded their ship. At that very instant, they got
clear of our ship; so I alone became their prisoner. They have
dealt with me like merciful thieves, but they had good reason
for doing so; I'm expected to do a good turn for them. Let the King
have the letters I have sent, then come to me as quickly   20
as you would run away from death. I have words to speak in
your ear that will leave you speechless; and yet they cannot

the bore of the matter. These good fellows will bring thee
where I am. Rosencrantz and Guildenstern hold their
25   course for England. Of them I have much to tell thee.
Farewell.

                  He that thou knowest thine, HAMLET."
Come, I will give you way for these your letters,
And do 't the speedier that you may direct me
30   To him from whom you brought them.

       Exeunt.

begin to convey the enormity of the matter. These good
fellows will take you where I am. Rosencrantz and
Guildenstern are still on their way to England; of them, I have 25
much to tell you. Farewell.

                  He whom you know to be your friend, Hamlet.

    (to the SAILORS*)*

Come, I will help you deliver your letters—
and I'll do it all the more quickly, so that you can lead me
to the man from whom you brought them. 30

    They exit.

ACT IV, SCENE VII

[The castle.] Enter KING *and* LAERTES.

KING

    Now must your conscience my acquittance seal,
    And you must put me in your heart for a friend,
    Sith you have heard, and with a knowing ear,
    That he which hath your noble father slain
5   Pursued my life.

LAERTES

                It well appears. But tell me
    Why you proceeded not against these feats
    So criminal and so capital in nature,
    As by your safety, greatness, wisdom, all things else,
10   You mainly were stirred up.

KING

    O, for two special reasons,
    Which may to you perhaps seem much unsinewed,
    But yet to me they're strong. The Queen his mother
    Lives almost by his looks, and for myself—
15   My virtue or my plague, be it either which—
    She is so conjunctive to my life and soul,
    That, as the star moves not but in his sphere,*
    I could not but by her. The other motive
    Why to a public count I might not go
20   Is the great love the general gender bear him,
    Who, dipping all his faults in their affection,
    Would, like the spring that turneth wood to stone,*
    Convert his gyves to graces; so that my arrows,
    Too slightly timbered for so loud a wind,
25   Would have reverted to my bow again,
    And not where I had aimed them.

LAERTES

    And so have I a noble father lost,
    A sister driven into desp'rate terms,

---

17   *sphere* According to the astronomy of the time, the planets were thought to move within concentric, transparent, revolving globes that contained them.

ACT 4, SCENE 7

The castle. The KING *and* LAERTES *enter.*

KING

Now, in good conscience, you must acknowledge my
    innocence
and regard me in your heart as a friend,
since you have heard, and with an understanding ear,
that the man who killed your noble father
also wanted to kill me.   5

LAERTES

This appears to be true. But tell me
why you took no action against these crimes,
which are serious enough to be punishable by death;
you were surely greatly stirred to do so by political prudence,
concern for your power and safety, and all other things.   10

KING

Oh, I had two special reasons—
which to you, perhaps, might seem weak,
although to me they're strong. The Queen his mother
almost lives to look at him; and as for myself
(I don't know whether to call it my blessing or my curse),   15
she is so closely joined to my life and soul
that, just as a star moves only in its sphere,
I cannot part from her. The other reason
why I couldn't go to the public for judgment
is the great love that the common people hold for him;   20
they would dip all his faults in their affections,
acting like a spring that turns wood into stone,
and convert his punishment into martyrdom. The shafts
of my arrows would have been too light for so strong a wind;
they would have returned to my bow again   25
and not gone where I aimed them.

LAERTES

And so I have lost a noble father,
while my sister has been driven to a state of despair;

---

22   *wood to stone* There were several English springs whose waters were so charged
    with lime that they would petrify wood placed in them.

Whose worth, if praises may go back again,
30 Stood challenger on mount of all the age
For her perfections. But my revenge will come.

KING

Break not your sleeps for that. You must not think
That we are made of stuff so flat and dull
That we can let our beard be shook with danger,
35 And think it pastime. You shortly shall hear more.
I loved your father, and we love ourself,
And that, I hope, will teach you to imagine—

Enter a MESSENGER *with letters.*

How now? What news?

MESSENGER

Letters, my lord, from Hamlet:
40 These to your Majesty; this to the Queen.

KING

From Hamlet? Who brought them?

MESSENGER

Sailors, my lord, they say; I saw them not.
They were given me by Claudio; he received them
Of him that brought them.

KING

Laertes, you shall hear them.—
45 Leave us.

Exit MESSENGER.

[*Reads.*] "High and mighty, you shall know I am set naked
on your kingdom. Tomorrow shall I beg leave to see your
kingly eyes; when I shall (first asking your pardon
50 thereunto) recount the occasion of my sudden and more
strange return.

HAMLET."

What should this mean? Are all the rest come back?
Or is it some abuse, and no such thing?

LAERTES

55 Know you the hand?

if I may praise her for what she once was, her value
conspicuously challenged all competitors   30
of this age. But my revenge will come.

KING

Don't lose sleep over that. You must not suppose
that I am made of such dull, submissive stuff
that I can let my beard be shaken with danger
and take it lightly. You will hear more shortly.   35
I loved your father, and I love myself;
and because of that, I hope you can imagine—

    A MESSENGER *enters with letters.*

What now? What news?

MESSENGER

I have letters from Hamlet, my lord.
This is to your Majesty, this is to the Queen.   40

KING

From Hamlet? Who brought them?

MESSENGER

Some sailors, they say, my lord. I did not see them.
The letters were given to me by Claudio. He received them
from the man who brought them.

KING

Laertes, you shall hear this.   45
(to the MESSENGER*)* Leave us.

    The MESSENGER *exits.*

*(reading) High and mighty king, you should know that I have
returned, defenseless, to your kingdom. Tomorrow I shall beg
permission to see your kingly eyes; then (after first asking your
consent to do so) I shall tell you the cause of my sudden and*   50
extremely strange return.

                        Hamlet.

(to LAERTES*)* What does this mean? Have he and all his
    companions come back?
Or is this some deception, and not at all true?

LAERTES

Do you know the handwriting?   55

KING
'Tis Hamlet's character. "Naked"—
And in a postscript here, he says "alone."
Can you advise me?

LAERTES
I am lost in it, my lord. But let him come.
60   It warms the very sickness in my heart
That I shall live and tell him to his teeth,
"Thus did'st thou."

KING
                            If it be so, Laertes
(As how should it be so? How otherwise?),
65   Will you be ruled by me?

LAERTES
                                    Ay, my lord,
So you will not o'errule me to a peace.

KING
To thine own peace. If he be now returned,
As checking at his voyage, and that he means
70   No more to undertake it, I will work him
To an **exploit**, now ripe in my device,
Under the which he shall not choose but fall;
And for his death no wind of blame shall breathe,
But even his mother shall uncharge the practice
75   And call it accident.

LAERTES
My lord, I will be ruled;
The rather if you could devise it so
That I might be the organ.

KING
                                    It falls right.
80   You have been talked of since your travel much,
And that in Hamlet's hearing, for a quality
Wherein they say you shine. Your sum of parts
Did not together pluck such envy from him
As did that one, and that, in my regard,
85   Of the unworthiest siege.

KING

It's Hamlet's handwriting. "Defenseless"!
And in a postscript here, he says that he's alone.
Can you advise me?

LAERTES

I am puzzled by this, my lord. But let him come.
It comforts my heart in its sickness   60
to know I'll live to tell him to his face,
"Here's revenge for what you did."

KING

Laertes, if he's really returned
(which seems to be both impossible and certain),
will you follow my orders?   65

LAERTES

Indeed, my lord—
as long as you don't order me to make peace.

KING

Only to make peace with yourself. If he has now returned,
turning aside from his voyage and not intending
to undertake it again, I will urge him   70
toward an endeavor—now ripening in my scheming brain—
which cannot help but lead to his downfall.
As for his death, no one will breathe a word of blame,
and even his mother will find no treachery in it,
calling it an accident.   75

LAERTES

My lord, I will be ordered by you—
but I hope that you will plan his death
so I might carry it out.

KING

That's how it will be.
Since your travels, you have been much talked about   80
(and within Hamlet's hearing) for a skill
in which you are said to shine. All your other abilities
combined did not stir such envy in him
as that particular skill—which is, in my opinion,
the least important of all.   85

LAERTES
What part is that, my lord?

KING
A very riband in the cap of youth,
Yet needful too, for youth no less becomes
The light and careless livery that it wears
90   Than settled age his sables and his weeds,
Importing health and graveness. Two months since
Here was a gentleman of Normandy.
I have seen myself, and served against, the French,
And they can well on horseback, but this gallant
95   Had witchcraft in 't. He grew unto his seat,
And to such wondrous doing brought his horse
As had he been incorpsed and deminatured
With the brave beast. So far he topped my thought
That I, in forgery of shapes and tricks,
100   Come short of what he did.

LAERTES
                    A Norman was 't?

KING
A Norman.

LAERTES
Upon my life, Lamord.

KING
               The very same.

LAERTES
105   I know him well. He is the brooch indeed
And gem of all the nation.

KING
He made confession of you,
And gave you such a masterly report,
For art and exercise in your defense,
110   And for your rapier most especial,
That he cried out 'twould be a sight indeed
If one could match you. The scrimers of their nation

LAERTES

Which skill is that, my lord?

KING

A mere decoration in a young man's cap—
yet necessary, too; for light and frivolous clothes
are no less fitting for a youth
than sober attire is for someone old and settled, 90
showing him to be both prosperous and serious. Two months
    ago,
there was a gentleman here from Normandy.
I have observed the French and fought against them,
and they are very skilled on horseback; but this gentleman's
riding seemed like witchcraft. He grew into his saddle, 95
and made his horse do such wonderful things
that he actually appeared to share the same body
with the noble beast. He so greatly exceeded anything I could
    imagine, that
no matter how I might try to describe it in words,
I'd fall short of what he really did. 100

LAERTES

A Norman, was he?

KING

A Norman.

LAERTES

Upon my life, it was Lamord.

KING

That was the man.

LAERTES

I know him well. He is, indeed, the ornament 105
and jewel of all France.

KING

He talked about you,
and praised you so highly
for your skill and artfulness at fencing
(your use of the rapier most of all), 110
that he exclaimed it would be a remarkable thing to see
if you ever met your equal. He swore that the fencers

He swore had neither motion, guard, nor eye,
If you opposed them. Sir, this report of his
115 Did Hamlet so envenom with his envy
That he could nothing do but wish and beg
Your sudden coming o'er to play with you.
Now, out of this—

LAERTES

What out of this, my lord?

KING

120 Laertes, was your father dear to you?
Or are you like the painting of a sorrow,
A face without a heart?

LAERTES

Why ask you this?

KING

Not that I think you did not love your father,
125 But that I know love is begun by time,
And that I see, in passages of proof,
Time qualifies the spark and fire of it.
There lives within the very flame of love
A kind of wick or snuff that will abate it,
130 And nothing is at a like goodness still,
For goodness, growing to a pleurisy,
Dies in his own too-much. That we would do
We should do when we would, for this "would" changes,
And hath abatements and delays as many
135 As there are tongues, are hands, are accidents,
And then this "should" is like a **spendthrift** sigh,*
That hurts by easing. But to the quick of th' ulcer—
Hamlet comes back; what would you undertake
To show yourself in deed your father's son
140 More than in words?

LAERTES

To cut his throat i' th' church!

---

136 *spendthrift sigh* Sighs were thought to draw blood from the heart and thereby to
shorten life.

of his nation lacked the movement, guard, and eyesight
to take you on. Sir, Hamlet was so poisoned
with envy at this report of his,   115
that he could do nothing but wish and beg
for you to suddenly come back, so he could fence with you.
Now because of this—

LAERTES
Because of this, *what*, my lord?

KING
Laertes, was your father dear to you?   120
Or are you like a painting of a sorrowful son—
all appearance and no feeling?

LAERTES
Why do you ask this?

KING
It's not because I think you did not love your father;
but I know that circumstances lead to love;   125
and I've seen proven instances
of how further circumstances diminish love's spark and fire.
Inside the flame of love itself, part of the wick
burns down and weakens its heat.
Nothing can remain at the same level of goodness—   130
for goodness, when it grows too abundant,
dies from its own excess. Whatever we wish to do,
we should do it as soon as we wish it; for our wishes change,
and are delayed and diminished by as many things
as there are tongues to advise us, hands to help or hinder us,   135
    or simple accidents of life;
and soon our wish is like a wasted sigh
that harms us even while it comforts us. But let's get right to the
    heart of the matter.
Hamlet has come back. What would you endeavor
to show yourself, indeed, your father's son—
in more than just words?   140

LAERTES
I'd cut his throat in the church.

KING
No place indeed should murder sanctuarize;
Revenge should have no bounds. But, good Laertes,
Will you do this? Keep close within your chamber.

145 Hamlet returned shall know you are come home.
We'll put on those shall praise your excellence
And set a double varnish on the fame
The Frenchman gave you, bring you in fine together
And wager on your heads. He, being **remiss**,

150 Most generous, and free from all contriving,
Will not **peruse** the foils, so that with ease,
Or with a little shuffling, you may choose
A sword unbated, and, in a pass of practice,
Requite him for your father.

LAERTES

155   I will do 't.
And for that purpose I'll anoint my sword.
I bought an unction of a mountebank,
So mortal that, but dip a knife in it,
Where it draws blood, no cataplasm so rare,

160 Collected from all simples that have virtue
Under the moon, can save the thing from death
That is but scratched withal. I'll touch my point
With this contagion, that, if I gall him slightly,
It may be death.

KING

165   Let's further think of this,
Weigh what convenience both of time and means
May fit us to our shape. If this should fail,
And that our drift look through our bad performance,
'Twere better not assayed. Therefore this project

170 Should have a back or second, that might hold
If this did blast in proof. Soft, let me see.
We'll make a solemn wager on your cunnings—
I ha 't!
When in your motion you are hot and dry—

KING

> Indeed, no place should offer sanctuary to a murderer;
> revenge should have no bounds. But good Laertes,
> will you do as I say? Stay shut up in your room.
> Now that he's back, Hamlet will hear that you've come home,   145
>   too.
> We'll get some people to praise your excellence at fencing,
> and double the shining fame
> that the Frenchman gave you. Finally, we'll bring you together for
>   a match
> and take bets on each of you. Because he will be careless,
> noble-minded, and unaware of any treachery,   150
> he will not check the foils. So you can easily
> (perhaps by switching swords) choose
> one without a blunted tip; and with a treacherous thrust,
> you'll repay him for your father's death.

LAERTES

> I will do it—   155
> and to make sure of success, I'll poison my sword.
> I bought some ointment from a traveling drug-seller.
> It's so deadly, all one has to do is dip a knife in it,
> and when that knife draws blood, no poultice in the world
> (even if it's made from all the healing herbs
> that can be collected by moonlight) will save from death a   160
>   creature
> that's merely been scratched by it. I'll dip my point
> in this poison so that if I only graze him,
> he'll certainly die.

KING

> Let's think about this further,   165
> so that we can arrange both time and opportunity
> to best suit our purpose. If this scheme should fail,
> and our intention should reveal itself through our failure,
> it would be better not to try it at all. And so this project
> should have a backup that might succeed   170
> even if our first attempt goes wrong. Wait, let me see.
> I'll make serious wagers on both of your skills—
> I've got it!
> When you become hot and thirsty from your activity

175 As make your bouts more violent to that end—
And that he calls for drink, I'll have prepared him
A chalice for the nonce, whereon but sipping,
If he by chance escape your venomed stuck,
Our purpose may hold there.—But stay, what noise?

       Enter QUEEN.

QUEEN
180 One woe doth tread upon another's heel.
So fast they follow. Your sister's drowned, Laertes.

LAERTES
Drowned! O, where?

QUEEN
There is a willow grows askant the brook,
That shows his hoar leaves in the glassy stream:
185 Therewith fantastic garlands did she make
Of crowflowers, nettles, daisies, and long purples,
That liberal shepherds give a grosser name,
But our cold maids do dead men's fingers call them.
There on the pendent boughs her coronet weeds
190 Clamb'ring to hang, an envious sliver broke,
When down her weedy trophies and herself
Fell in the weeping brook. Her clothes spread wide,
And mermaid-like awhile they bore her up.
Which time she chanted snatches of old lauds,
195 As one incapable of her own distress,
Or like a creature native and endued
Unto that element. But long it could not be
Till that her garments, heavy with their drink,
Pulled the poor wretch from her melodious lay
200 To muddy death.

LAERTES
              Alas, then she is drowned.

QUEEN
Drowned, drowned.

(and keep your fighting vigorous so that you become thirsty),   175
he will ask for something to drink. I'll prepare him a cup
for the occasion; if he merely sips from it,
we'll succeed in our purpose—even if he should escape
your poisonous thrust by some chance. But listen—what's that
    noise?

> Cries from offstage. The QUEEN enters.

QUEEN
New sorrows follow on each others' heels,   180
they arrive so quickly. You're sister is drowned, Laertes.

LAERTES
Drowned! Oh, where?

QUEEN
There is a willow that grows out over the brook,
its silver-gray leaves reflecting in the glass-like stream.
From willow twigs, she made extravagant garlands   185
with buttercups, nettles, and daisies—and also purple orchids,
which plainspoken shepherds call by an obscene name,
but chaste virgins call "dead men's fingers."
She had climbed out on the outstretched boughs
to hang up her little plant-made crowns, when a treacherous   190
    branch broke,
and her weedy trophies and herself
tumbled down into the weeping brook. Her clothes spread wide,
and for a while they held her up as if she were a mermaid;
during this time, she sang snatches of old hymns,
as if she couldn't comprehend her own distress,   195
or as if she were like a creature born and well-suited
to live in water. But before long,
her garments became soaked and heavy
and pulled the poor wretch away from her melodious song
to a muddy death.   200

LAERTES
Alas, then she is drowned.

QUEEN
Drowned, drowned.

LAERTES

  Too much of water hast thou, poor Ophelia,
  And therefore I forbid my tears; but yet
205 It is our trick; nature her custom holds,
  Let shame say what it will: when these are gone,
  The woman will be out. Adieu, my lord.
  I have a speech o' fire, that fain would blaze,
  But that this folly drowns it.

    Exit.

KING

210   Let's follow, Gertrude.
  How much I had to do to calm his rage!
  Now fear I this will give it start again;
  Therefore let's follow.

    Exeunt.

LAERTES

You've already had too much water, poor Ophelia,
and so I forbid myself from shedding tears. And yet
it's only human; nature must have its way,   205
in spite of shame. When these tears of mine are gone,
I'll be rid of the womanly part of me.—Farewell, my lord.
I have words of fire that I wish I could let blaze freely,
but these foolish tears drown them.

He exits.

KING

Let's follow him, Gertrude.   210
How much I had to do to calm his rage!
Now I fear that this will start it up again.
And so, let's follow him.

They exit.

Act IV Review

Discussion Questions

1. How would you characterize the relationship between Claudius and Gertrude? Look at their conversation in Scene i of this act and refer to lines in the play to support your answer.

2. In what mood does Hamlet speak with Rosencrantz and Guildenstern in Scene ii?

3. How does Fortinbras compare with Hamlet?

4. Why do you think Gertrude is reluctant to meet with Ophelia in Scene v?

5. How is Ophelia's madness portrayed in Scene v?

6. In his anger, how does Laertes compare with Hamlet?

7. On the basis of Gertrude's description of Ophelia's death, in Scene vii, do you consider it a suicide? Explain.

8. How do the mounting troubles at court get reflected in the characters' actions and words?

Literary Elements

1. As you know, **similes** use the words *like* or *as* to make comparisons between unlike things. Find the simile that Gertrude uses at the beginning of Act IV to describe Hamlet's out-of-control behavior and explain whether or not you find it effective.

2. A **metaphor** is a direct comparison between two unlike things. Look for the comparison Hamlet draws of Rosencrantz in Scene ii. What message is he trying to send his old school friend?

3. How would you characterize the **imagery** used in the conversation between Hamlet and the King in Scene iii? Say which images you find especially striking.

4. An **inference** is a conclusion a reader draws from paying close attention to a text. Study Claudius's reaction upon hearing of Polonius's death. What do you think this reveals about his character and his plans?

5. A **symbol** is an object that stands for or represents a more abstract concept. Research the herbs and flowers that Ophelia distributes in Scene v to find out their symbolic meanings in Shakespeare's time. What significance do you think they have for the play?

Writing Prompts

1. In Scene ii, Hamlet compares Rosencrantz to a sponge. Come up with metaphors of your own that are appropriate for the other characters. Remember that a good metaphor doesn't usually require explanation; the reader will understand the sense of it right away.

2. Study Ophelia's songs in Act IV. Do they show a new side of her? Explain your opinion in writing, citing evidence from other acts as support.

3. Gertrude has had many painful experiences by the end of Act IV. Write a dialogue that might take place between her and a therapist.

4. Choose a scene and write a brief summary of its events in one sentence. You may choose to write it in standard English, contemporary slang or street talk, or the language of Shakespeare, Elizabethan English. Or write three summaries; use a different style for each one.

HAMLET
ACT V

Richard Burton as Hamlet, Old Vic, London, 1953

"ALAS, POOR YORICK! I KNEW HIM,
HORATIO—A FELLOW OF INFINITE JEST,
OF MOST EXCELLENT FANCY."

✠ ✠ ✠

Before You Read

1. Encountering Fortinbras's army has affected Hamlet deeply. Describe a situation in which you were similarly affected by somebody else's example.

2. Do your feelings about Hamlet change because of his role in the deaths of Rosencrantz and Guildenstern? Explain.

3. What effect do you expect Ophelia's death to have on Hamlet?

4. What outcome do you expect in the final act of this play?

5. As you read, try to determine whether Gertrude's death is an accident or planned.

Literary Elements

1. Shakespeare often adds humorous scenes and characters to an otherwise serious play. These additions are known as **comic relief**. Even in his most intense tragedies, such as *Romeo and Juliet* and *Macbeth*, there are humorous characters, scenes, and wordplay that offer a different perspective on the action and keep the plays from being unbearably tragic.

2. **Irony** occurs when appearances are at odds with reality. *Hamlet* is full of irony. For example, staging a comic scene in a graveyard—as in Act V, Scene i— is ironic because we don't expect humor to accompany Ophelia's burial.

3. **Dramatic irony** occurs when the audience has important knowledge that a main character lacks. In Act III, the audience knows all about Hamlet's plot to trick King Claudius into revealing his guilt by making him watch a play about a royal murder. Our awareness increases the tension as we see the play-within-the-play unfold.

4. As you know, a **symbol** is an object that stands for or represents a more abstract concept, such as a rose representing love. In Act IV, Ophelia distributes herbs and flowers that held symbolic meaning to people in the Elizabethan age. For example, fennel stood for flattery and deceit.

Words to Know

The following vocabulary words appear in Act V in the original text of Shakespeare's play. However, they are words that are still used today. Read the definitions here and pay attention to the words as you read the play (they will be in boldfaced type).

abhorred	disgusting; hateful
circumvent	go around; bypass
dearth	shortage; scarcity
diligence	attentiveness; thoroughness
edified	informed; educated
equivocation	lies; evasion
faction	splinter or partisan group; bloc
felicity	pleasure; happiness
germane	relevant; appropriate
gibes	mockery; taunting
indiscretion	poor judgment; mistakes
palpable	obvious; unmistakable
providence	destiny; divine plan
statutes	laws; legalities
vouchers	documents; references

Act Summary

Two gravediggers puzzle over how Ophelia can be given a Christian burial when she committed suicide. Hamlet and Horatio enter the graveyard and see skulls that have been turned out of the earth. Hamlet finds out that one of them belongs to Yorick, a court jester and companion to the young Prince.

Ophelia's funeral procession arrives. Distraught, Laertes leaps into his dead sister's grave. Hamlet comes forward when he finds out that Ophelia is being buried. Laertes, who blames Hamlet for his sister's death, tries to strangle him. Hamlet further enrages him by claiming he loved Ophelia far more than Laertes ever did. The fight is broken up, and Hamlet leaves in anger.

Hamlet tells Horatio how he searched the cabin of Rosencrantz and Guildenstern and found a letter from Claudius ordering his execution. For his name, he substituted the names of Rosencrantz and Guildenstern.

Osric, one of the King's courtiers, announces that Claudius has arranged for a duel between Laertes and Hamlet. Hamlet makes fun of Osric's affected language but sends him away with a promise to fight. He believes the time has come to take action.

With the King and Queen in attendance, Hamlet and Laertes begin their match. Hamlet makes two hits, and Claudius offers him the cup of poisoned wine but Hamlet declines. Instead, Gertrude drinks from it. Laertes wounds Hamlet, and in further scuffling they exchange rapiers, and Hamlet delivers a wound to Laertes. The Queen dies, and Laertes confesses the plot to Hamlet. Hamlet wounds Claudius and forces him to drink the poison. Claudius dies. Laertes forgives Hamlet before dying. Hamlet stops Horatio from drinking from the poisoned cup, saying someone should remain alive to tell the whole story.

Osric announces that Fortinbras is back from Poland. Before he dies, Hamlet declares that Fortinbras should be the next King of Denmark. Fortinbras claims the Danish throne and orders a ceremonial burial of Hamlet.

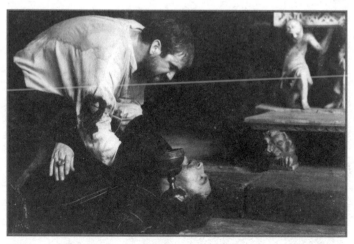

Mel Gibson as Hamlet and Alan Bates as Claudius, 1990 Franco Zeffirelli film

ACT V, SCENE I

[*A churchyard.*] *Enter two* CLOWNS.*

CLOWN

Is she to be buried in Christian burial* when she willfully
seeks her own salvation?

OTHER

I tell thee she is. Therefore make her grave straight. The
crowner hath sat on her, and finds it Christian burial.

CLOWN

5   How can that be, unless she drowned herself in her own
defense?

OTHER

Why, 'tis found so.

CLOWN

It must be *se offendendo*;* it cannot be else. For here lies
the point: if I drown myself wittingly, it argues an act, and
10   an act hath three branches—it is to act, to do, to perform.
Argal,* she drowned herself wittingly.

OTHER

Nay, but hear you, Goodman Delver.

CLOWN

Give me leave. Here lies the water—good. Here stands the
man—good. If the man go to this water and drown
15   himself, it is, will he nill he, he goes; mark you that. But if
the water come to him and drown him, he drowns not
himself. Argal, he that is not guilty of his own death,
shortens not his own life.

OTHER

But is this law?

---

s.d.   *CLOWNS* Actors who did comic roles.

1   *Christian burial* Church law denied Christian burial to suicides.

8   *se offendendo* the Gravedigger's blunder for *se defendendo*, "in self defense"

ACT 5, SCENE 1

A churchyard. A GRAVEDIGGER *and his* HELPER *enter.*

GRAVEDIGGER
Is she to be given a Christian burial even though she willfully
sought her own salvation?

HELPER
I tell you, she is. And so dig her grave right away. The coroner
has investigated her death, and finds that she deserves a
Christian burial.

GRAVEDIGGER
How can that be, unless she drowned herself in self-defense?   5

HELPER
Well, that's the coroner's decision.

GRAVEDIGGER
He must have decided it was *se offendendo;* there can't be
any other reason. For here's the point: If I drown myself
deliberately, it is clearly an act; and an act is divided into three
parts—to act, to do, and to perform. Argal, she drowned   10
herself deliberately.

HELPER
No, but wait a moment, Mr. Delver—

GRAVEDIGGER
Let me go on. Imagine that the water is here; good. Imagine
that the man stands here; good. If the man goes to the water
and drowns himself, it is *he* who goes, whether he wants to or   15
not. But if the water comes to him and drowns him, he does
not drown himself. Argal, he who is not guilty of his own
death and does not shorten his own life.

HELPER
But is this law?

---

11   *Argal* the Gravedigger's blunder for *ergo*, Latin for "therefore"

CLOWN

20   Ay, marry, is 't—crowner's quest law.

OTHER

Will you ha' the truth on 't? If this had not been a
gentlewoman, she should have been buried out o'
Christian burial.

CLOWN

Why, there thou say'st. And the more pity that great folk
25   should have count'nance in this world to drown or hang
themselves more than their even-Christian. Come, my
spade. There is no ancient gentlemen but gard'ners,
ditchers, and gravemakers. They hold up Adam's
profession.

OTHER

30   Was he a gentleman?

CLOWN

'A was the first that ever bore arms.

OTHER

Why, he had none.

CLOWN

What, art a heathen? How dost thou understand the
Scripture? The Scripture says Adam digged. Could he dig
35   without arms? I'll put another question to thee. If thou
answerest me not to the purpose, confess thyself—*

OTHER

Go to.

CLOWN

What is he that builds stronger than either the mason,
the shipwright, or the carpenter?

OTHER

40   The gallowsmaker, for that frame outlives a thousand
tenants.

---

36   *confess thyself* "Confess thyself and be hanged," a common proverb, is what the
Clown would have said if he had not been interrupted.

GRAVEDIGGER

Yes, indeed, it is—the law of a coroner's inquest.　　　20

HELPER

Do you want to hear the truth about it? If this had not been a noblewoman, she wouldn't be given a Christian burial.

GRAVEDIGGER

Why, you speak correctly. And more is the pity that noble folk in this world should have more of a right to drown or hang　　25 themselves than their fellow Christians. Well, I'll take up my shovel. Since ancient times, there have been no real gentlemen except gardeners, ditchdiggers, and gravediggers. They continue Adam's profession.

HELPER

Was he a gentleman?　　　30

GRAVEDIGGER

He was the first who ever bore arms.

HELPER

Why, he had no arms.

GRAVEDIGGER

What, aren't you a Christian? How do you interpret the Bible? The Bible says that Adam dug. Could he dig without arms? I'll put another question to you. If you can't answer it properly,　　35 you must confess yourself to be a fool.

HELPER

Get on with your question!

GRAVEDIGGER

Who builds things more strongly than a mason, a shipwright, or a carpenter?

HELPER

The gallows-builder; for his building outlasts a thousand　　40 tenants.

CLOWN

I like thy wit well, in good faith. The gallows does well.
But how does it well? It does well to those that do ill.
Now thou dost ill to say the gallows is built stronger than
the church. Argal, the gallows may do well to thee. To 't
again, come.

OTHER

Who builds stronger than a mason, a shipwright, or a
carpenter?

CLOWN

Ay, tell me that, and unyoke.

OTHER

Marry, now I can tell.

CLOWN

To 't.

OTHER

Mass, I cannot tell.

Enter HAMLET *and* HORATIO *afar off.*

CLOWN

Cudgel thy brains no more about it, for your dull ass will
not mend his pace with beating. And when you are asked
this question next, say "a gravemaker." The houses he
makes lasts till doomsday. Go, get thee in to Yaughan, and
fetch me a stoup of liquor.

[*Exit other* CLOWN.]

[*Sings.*] "In youth when I did love, did love,
            Methought it was very sweet
        To contract—O—the time for—a—my behove,
            O, methought there—a—was nothing
            a—meet."

HAMLET

Has this fellow no feeling of his business? 'A sings in
gravemaking.

HORATIO

Custom hath made it in him a property of easiness.

GRAVEDIGGER

I like your cleverness, my friend. The gallows does well. But
how does it do well? It does well to those who do ill. Now, *you*
do ill to say that a gallows is built more strongly than a church.
Argal, the gallows might do well for *you*. Come on, try again.   45

HELPER

Who builds things more strongly than a mason, a shipwright, or a
carpenter?

GRAVEDIGGER

Yes, tell me that, then take the rest of the day off.

HELPER

Indeed, now I can tell you.   50

GRAVEDIGGER

Do it.

HELPER

By the Mass, I cannot tell you.

> HAMLET *and* HORATIO *enter some distance off.*

GRAVEDIGGER

Don't beat your brains about it anymore, for a stupid donkey
won't move any faster because he is beaten. The next time
you are asked this question, say "a gravedigger." The houses   55
he makes will last until Judgment Day. Go away now, and fetch
me a pitcher of liquor.

> *The* HELPER *exits; the* GRAVEDIGGER *digs and sings, grunting
> as he does so.*

> *When I was young and in love, in love,*
> *   I thought it was very sweet*
> *to pass (oh!) the time (oof!) to my advantage;*   60
> *   oh, I thought there (oof!) was nothing (oof!) proper.*

HAMLET

Doesn't this fellow have any feeling for the solemnity of his
work? He sings while he digs graves.

HORATIO

Habit has made it easy for him to take his work lightly.   65

HAMLET

'Tis e'en so. The hand of little employment hath the
daintier sense.

CLOWN [*Sings.*]
"But age with his stealing steps
Hath clawed me in his clutch,
70   And hath shipped me into the land,
As if I had never been such."

[*Throws up a skull.*]

HAMLET

That skull had a tongue in it, and could sing once. How
the knave jowls it to the ground, as it 'twere Cain's
jawbone, that did the first murder! This might be the
75   pate of a politician, which this ass now o'erreaches, one
that would **circumvent** God, might it not?

HORATIO

It might, my lord.

HAMLET

Or of a courtier, which could say "Good morrow, sweet
lord! How dost thou, sweet lord?" This might be my Lord
80   Such-a-one, that praised my Lord Such-a-one's horse when
'a meant to beg it, might it not?

HORATIO

Ay, my lord.

HAMLET

Why, e'en so, and now my Lady Worm's, chapless, and
knocked about the mazzard with a sexton's spade. Here's
85   fine revolution, an we had the trick to see 't. Did these
bones cost no more the breeding but to play at loggets*
with them? Mine ache to think on 't.

CLOWN [*Sings.*]
"A pickax and a spade, a spade,
For and a shrouding sheet;

---

86 *loggets* a game in which blocks of wood were thrown at a stake

HAMLET

That's certainly true. A hand that does little work is more sensitive.

GRAVEDIGGER (*singing*)

> But old age, with its quiet footsteps,
>   has caught me in its clutches,
> and has thrown me into the ground
>   as if I had never been young.

70

     (*Throws up a skull.*)

HAMLET

That jaw once had a tongue in it and could sing. How the rascal hurls it to the ground, as if it were the jawbone of Cain, the first murderer! The head that this fool has gotten the better of might have belonged to a crafty politician, one who could   75 outwit even God, don't you think?

HORATIO

It's possible, my lord.

HAMLET

Or it might have belonged to a courtier, who could say, "Good morning, sweet lord! How are you, sweet lord?" This might be a certain Lord Such-a-one who praised another Lord Such-a-   80 one's horse when he wanted to have it, don't you think?

HORATIO .

Yes, my lord.

HAMLET

Indeed, it might be. And now it belongs to my Lady Worm, lacking a jaw, and knocked across the head by a church employee's shovel. Here's a fine lesson in how time reverses all fortune, if only we had the knack to understand it. Did these   85 bones cost so little to grow, that they should now be thrown about for sport? My own bones ache to think about it.

GRAVEDIGGER (*singing*)

> A pickax and a shovel, a shovel,
>   and also a sheet for a shroud;

90   O, a pit of clay for to be made
        For such a guest is meet."

   [*Throws up another skull.*]

HAMLET
   There's another. Why may not that be the skull of a
   lawyer? Where be his quiddities now, his quillities, his
   cases, his tenures, and his tricks? Why does he suffer this
95   mad knave now to knock him about the sconce with a
   dirty shovel, and will not tell him of his action of batter?
   Hum! This fellow might be in 's time a great buyer of land,
   with his **statutes**, his recognizances, his fines, his double
   vouchers, his recoveries.* Is this the fine of his fines, and
100   the recovery of his recoveries, to have his fine pate full of
   fine dirt? Will his vouchers vouch him no more of his
   purchases, and double ones too, than the length and
   breadth of a pair of indentures? The very conveyances of
   his lands will scarcely lie in this box, and must th'
105   inheritor himself have no more, ha?

HORATIO
   Not a jot more, my lord.

HAMLET
   Is not parchment made of sheepskins?

HORATIO
   Ay, my lord, and of calveskins too.

HAMLET
   They are sheep and calves which seek out assurance in
110   that. I will speak to this fellow. Whose grave's this, sirrah?

CLOWN
   Mine, sir.
        [*Sings.*] "O, a pit of clay for to be made
               For such a guest is meet."

98-99   *statutes . . . recoveries* These are technical legal terms of the time: *statutes*—bonds
   by which a creditor collects from a debtor by attaching his land and goods;
   recognizances—bonds by which a debtor acknowledges his indebtedness to a
   creditor; *fines, recoveries*—procedures for converting an entailed estate (one

> *oh, for such a guest, it's fit*
> *to dig a pit of clay.* 90

> *He digs up another skull.*

HAMLET

There's another. Why mightn't this be the skull of a lawyer? Where are his subtle arguments now, his fine distinctions, his cases, his holdings of property, and all the tricks of his trade? Why does he allow this wild rascal to knock him across the 95 head with a dirty shovel and not bring action against him for battery? Hmm, in his time, this fellow might have been a great buyer of land, with documents acknowledging debts; with bonds turning debtors' land over to him, giving him full ownership; with pairs of witnesses to vouch for the recovery 100 of that land. Is this the last of his deals, his very final recovery, to have his fine head full of fine dirt? Will his witnesses (even in pairs) not vouch for him to have a plot of land any wider or longer than a pair of contracts? The deeds for his lands would scarcely fit in this box; so must the owner himself have no more space than that? 105

HORATIO

Not a bit more, my lord.

HAMLET

Isn't parchment made of sheepskins?

HORATIO

Yes, my lord—and of calves' skins, too.

HAMLET

One would have to be as foolish as a sheep or a calf to put one's trust in parchments. I will speak to this fellow. *(to the* GRAVEDIGGER*)* Whose grave is this, fellow? 110

GRAVEDIGGER

Mine, sir.
(singing)
> *Oh, for such a guest, it's fit*
> *to dig a pit of clay.*

---

limited in its transmission to a certain succession of heirs) to fee simple or unrestricted ownership; *double vouchers*—documents signed by two persons testifying to the ownership of land.

HAMLET

I think it be thine indeed, for thou liest* in 't.

CLOWN

115   You lie out on 't, sir, and therefore 'tis not yours. For my
part, I do not lie in 't, yet it is mine.

HAMLET

Thou dost lie in 't, to be in 't and say it is thine. 'Tis for the
dead, not for the quick; therefore thou liest.

CLOWN

'Tis a quick lie, sir; 'twill away again from me to you.

HAMLET

120   What man dost thou dig it for?

CLOWN

For no man, sir.

HAMLET

What woman then?

CLOWN

For none neither.

HAMLET

Who is to be buried in 't?

CLOWN

125   One that was a woman, sir; but, rest her soul, she's dead.

HAMLET [*to* HORATIO]

How absolute the knave is! We must speak by the card,*
or **equivocation** will undo us. By the Lord, Horatio, this
three years I have took note of it, the age is grown so
picked that the toe of the peasant comes so near the heel
130   of the courtier he galls his kibe. How long hast thou been
a gravemaker?

CLOWN

Of all the days i' the year, I came to 't that day that our
last King Hamlet overcame Fortinbras.

---

114   *liest* wordplay on lie (be situated) / lie (tell an untruth)

126   *by the card* by the points of the compass, marked exactly on a navigator's card

HAMLET
I think it is your grave, indeed—for you lie in it.

GRAVEDIGGER
You lie outside of it, sir, and so it is not yours. For my part, I do not lie in it, and yet it is mine. 115

HAMLET
You *do* lie in it, since you are in it and say it is yours. It is for the dead, not for the living; and so you lie.

GRAVEDIGGER
It's a fast-moving lie, sir; it will soon return from me to you.

HAMLET
What man are you digging it for? 120

GRAVEDIGGER
For no man, sir.

HAMLET
What woman, then?

GRAVEDIGGER
For no woman, either.

HAMLET
Who is to be buried in it?

GRAVEDIGGER
Someone who was once a woman, sir, but rest her soul, she's dead. 125

HAMLET (*to* HORATIO)
How precise this rascal is! We must choose our
words carefully, or we'll be defeated by ambiguity. By the Lord,
Horatio, for the last three years, I have noticed something:
Everyone in the world has become so refined, the peasant's
toe follows so closely behind the courtier's heel that it makes 130
blisters on it.—How long have you been a gravedigger?

GRAVEDIGGER
Of all the days in the year, I took this job on the day when our last King Hamlet defeated Fortinbras.

HAMLET

How long is that since?

CLOWN

135   Cannot you tell that? Every fool can tell that. It was that
very day that young Hamlet was born—he that is mad,
and sent into England.

HAMLET

Ay, marry, why was he sent into England?

CLOWN

Why, because 'a was mad. 'A shall recover his wits there;
140   or, if 'a do not, 'tis no great matter there.

HAMLET

Why?

CLOWN

'Twill not be seen in him there. There the men are as mad
as he.

HAMLET

How came he mad?

CLOWN

145   Very strangely, they say.

HAMLET

How strangely?

CLOWN

Faith, e'en with losing his wits.

HAMLET

Upon what ground?

CLOWN

Why, here in Denmark. I have been sexton here, man and
150   boy, thirty years.

HAMLET

How long will a man lie i' th' earth ere he rot?

CLOWN

Faith, if 'a be not rotten before 'a die (as we have many
pocky corses nowadays that will scarce hold the laying in),
'a will last you some eight year or nine year. A tanner will
155   last you nine year.

HAMLET

How long has it been since then?

GRAVEDIGGER

Don't you know that? Every fool knows that. It was the very   135
day when young Hamlet was born—he who went mad and
was sent to England.

HAMLET

Yes, indeed—but why was he sent to England?

GRAVEDIGGER

Why, because he was mad. He will recover his sanity there. Or
if he doesn't, it won't much matter there.   140

HAMLET

Why?

GRAVEDIGGER

It won't be noticed in him there. There, all men are as mad as he.

HAMLET

How did he go mad?

GRAVEDIGGER

Very strangely, they say.   145

HAMLET

What do you mean, "strangely"?

GRAVEDIGGER

Indeed, by losing his mind.

HAMLET

Upon what grounds did that happen?

GRAVEDIGGER

Why, right here in Denmark. I have been a church employee
here, man and boy, for thirty years.   150

HAMLET

How long will a man lie in the ground before he rots?

GRAVEDIGGER

Indeed, if he isn't rotten before he dies (and we get many
syphilitic corpses these days that fall apart almost as soon as
you pick them up), he will last some eight or nine years. A
tanner will last nine years.   155

HAMLET

Why he, more than another?

CLOWN

Why, sir, his hide is so tanned with his trade that 'a will
keep out water a great while, and your water is a sore
decayer of your whoreson dead body. Here's a skull now
160   hath lien you i' th' earth three and twenty years.

HAMLET

Whose was it?

CLOWN

A whoreson mad fellow's it was. Whose do you think it was?

HAMLET

Nay, I know not.

CLOWN

A pestilence on him for a mad rogue! 'A poured a flagon
165   of Rhenish on my head once. This same skull, sir, was, sir,
Yorick's skull, the King's jester.

HAMLET

This?

CLOWN

E'en that.

HAMLET

Let me see. [*Takes the skull.*] Alas, poor Yorick! I knew him,
170   Horatio—a fellow of infinite jest, of most excellent fancy.
He hath borne me on his back a thousand times. And
now how **abhorred** in my imagination it is! My gorge
rises at it. Here hung those lips that I have kissed I know
not how oft. Where be your **gibes** now? Your gambols,
175   your songs, your flashes of merriment that were wont to
set the table on a roar? Not one now to mock your own
grinning? Quite chapfall'n*? Now get you to my lady's
chamber, and tell her, let her paint an inch thick, to this
favor she must come. Make her laugh at that. Prithee,
180   Horatio, tell me one thing.

---

177   *chapfall'n* wordplay: lacking the lower jaw or chap/downcast, glum

HAMLET
Why will he last longer than another?

GRAVEDIGGER
Why, sir, his hide is so tanned by practicing his trade, he will keep out water a great while; and water is a serious cause of decay in a vile dead body. Here's a skull that has lain in the earth for twenty-three years. 160

HAMLET
Whose was it?

GRAVEDIGGER
It belonged to a mad, rascally fellow. Whose skull do you think it was?

HAMLET
Indeed, I don't know.

GRAVEDIGGER
A curse on him, the mad rogue! He poured a pitcher of Rhine wine on my head once. This same skull, sir, belonged to Yorick, 165 the King's jester.

HAMLET
This?

GRAVEDIGGER
That same skull.

HAMLET
Let me see. *(taking the skull)* Alas, poor Yorick! I knew him, Horatio—a fellow with infinite jokes and a wonderful 170 imagination. He carried me on his back a thousand times. And now, how I loathe to remember it! It makes my stomach turn. Here hung those lips that I kissed I don't know how often. Where are your taunts now? Your dances? Your songs? Your flashes of merriment that always set everybody at the table 175 roaring with laughter? Aren't you one to mock your own grinning? Are you quite down in the mouth? Now hurry along to my lady's room and tell her that, even if she wears makeup an inch thick, she'll look like you eventually. Make her laugh at that.—Horatio, please tell me one thing. 180

HORATIO

What's that, my lord?

HAMLET

Dost thou think Alexander looked o' this fashion i' th' earth?

HORATIO

E'en so.

HAMLET

And smelt so? Pah!

[*Puts down the skull.*]

HORATIO

185   E'en so, my lord.

HAMLET

To what base uses we may return, Horatio! Why may not
imagination trace the noble dust of Alexander till 'a find it
stopping a bunghole?

HORATIO

'Twere to consider too curiously, to consider so.

HAMLET

190   No, faith, not a jot, but to follow him thither with
modesty enough, and likelihood to lead it, as thus:
Alexander died, Alexander was buried, Alexander returneth
to dust; the dust is earth; of earth we make loam; and why
of that loam whereto he was converted might they not
195   stop a beer barrel?
Imperious Caesar, dead and turned to clay,
Might stop a hole to keep the wind away.
O, that that earth which kept the world in awe
Should patch a wall t' expel the winter's flaw!
200   But soft, but soft awhile! Here comes the King.

Enter KING, QUEEN, LAERTES, *and a coffin, with*
LORDS ATTENDANT *and a* PRIEST.

The Queen, the courtiers. Who is this they follow?
And with such maimed rites? This doth betoken
The corse they follow did with desp'rate hand
Fordo its own life. 'Twas of some estate.
205   Couch we awhile, and mark.

HORATIO

What's that, my lord?

HAMLET

Do you think Alexander the Great looked like this when he was in the ground?

HORATIO

Exactly so.

HAMLET

And smelled like this? Pah!

He puts the skull down.

HORATIO

Exactly so, my lord.   185

HAMLET

To what lowly uses our bodies might come to, Horatio! In our imaginations, couldn't we trace the noble dust of Alexander until we find it stopping up a hole in a barrel?

HORATIO

It would take extremely elaborate thinking to imagine that.

HAMLET

No, indeed—not the least bit elaborate. We can follow him all   190
the way, with plenty of plausibility and likelihood, like this:
Alexander died, Alexander was buried, Alexander returned to
dust; dust is earth, and of earth we make plaster; and once he
was turned into plaster, why shouldn't somebody use him to
stop up a beer barrel?   195
Emperor Caesar, dead and turned to clay,
might stop a hole to keep the wind away.
Oh, that that flesh which kept the world in awe
should patch a wall to keep out a gust of winter wind!
But wait—wait a moment. Here comes the King,   200

The KING *and* QUEEN, LAERTES, *attendant* LORDS, *and a*
PRIEST *enter, with a coffin carried by pall bearers.*

the Queen, and the courtiers. Whose is this body they follow?
And with such limited ceremony? This shows
that the corpse they follow took its own life
with a desperate hand. It was a person of high rank.
Let us hide, and listen.   205

[*Retires with Horatio.*]

LAERTES

What ceremony else?

HAMLET

That is Laertes,
a very noble youth. Mark.

LAERTES

What ceremony else?

PRIEST

210 Her obsequies have been as far enlarged
As we have warranty. Her death was doubtful,
And, but that great command o'ersways the order,
She should in ground unsanctified been lodged
Till the last trumpet. For charitable prayers,

215 Shards, flints, and pebbles should be thrown on her.
Yet here she is allowed her virgin crants,
Her maiden strewments, and the bringing home
Of bell and burial.

LAERTES

Must there no more be done?

PRIEST

220 No more be done.
We should profane the service of the dead
To sing a requiem and such rest to her
As to peace-parted souls.

LAERTES

Lay her i' th' earth,

225 And from her fair and unpolluted flesh
May violets spring! I tell thee, churlish priest,
A minist'ring angel shall my sister be
When thou liest howling!

HAMLET

What, the fair Ophelia?

QUEEN

230 Sweets to the sweet! Farewell.

They step aside.

LAERTES

Why isn't there more ceremony?

HAMLET

That is Laertes, a very noble young man. Listen.

LAERTES

Why isn't there more ceremony?

PRIEST

We have expanded her rites   210
as much as we are authorized to do. Her death was suspicious,
and if the King's commands hadn't overruled the church's laws,
she would have been buried in unsanctified ground
until the trumpet announces the Last Judgment. Instead of
    affectionate prayers,
broken pottery, pieces of flint, and pebbles would have been
    thrown on her.   215
Yet here she is, permitted the garlands
and flowers suitable to a virgin, with a tolling bell
to bring her home to a proper grave.

LAERTES

Must no more be done?

PRIEST

No more may be done.   220
We would profane the funeral service
to sing a requiem or pray for her eternal rest,
as we would for souls that die in peace.

LAERTES

Lay her in the ground,
and from her lovely, pure flesh   225
may violets grow! I tell you, you disrespectful priest,
that my sister will be an angel of mercy
when you lie howling in hell.

HAMLET

(to HORATIO*)* What—the lovely Ophelia?

QUEEN

Sweet flowers for the sweet girl—farewell!   230

[*Scatters flowers.*]

I hoped thou shouldst have been my Hamlet's wife.
I thought thy bride bed to have decked, sweet maid,
And not have strewed thy grave.

LAERTES

                        O, treble woe
235   Fall ten times treble on that cursed head
Whose wicked deed thy most ingenious sense
Deprived thee of! Hold off the earth awhile,
Till I have caught her once more in mine arms.

    Leaps in the grave.

Now pile your dust upon the quick and dead
240   Till of this flat a mountain you have made
T'o'ertop old Pelion or the skyish head
Of blue Olympus.*

HAMLET [*coming forward*]
                   What is he whose grief
Bears such an emphasis, whose phrase of sorrow
245   Conjures the wand'ring stars, and makes them stand
Like wonder-wounded hearers? This is I,
Hamlet the Dane.

LAERTES

               The devil take thy soul!

[*Grapples with him.*]

HAMLET

Thou pray'st not well.
250   I prithee take thy fingers from my throat,
For though I am not splenitive and rash,
Yet have I in me something dangerous,
Which let thy wisdom fear. Hold off thy hand.

241–242   *Pelion . . . Olympus* mountains in Greece. Laertes alludes to the legend of the
Titans, giants in classical mythology, who tried to reach heaven (the top of
Mt. Olympus) by piling Mt. Ossa on Mt. Pelion.

She scatters flowers on the coffin.

I hoped you would have been my Hamlet's wife;
I thought I would have covered your bridal bed with flowers,
   sweet virgin,
and not scattered them on your grave.

LAERTES

Oh, may triple misfortune
fall ten times triple on that accursed man   235
whose wicked deed robbed you of
your excellent mind!—Don't throw in earth just yet,
until I have taken her in my arms once more.

   He leaps into the grave.

Now pile your dirt on both the living and the dead
until, on this flat land, you've made a mountain   240
taller than ancient Pelion, or the sky-touching top
of blue Olympus.

HAMLET (*coming forward*)

Who is he whose grief
is so exaggerated, whose talk of sorrow
casts a spell on the revolving planets and makes them stand   245
   still,
like listeners stunned with awe? Here I am—
Hamlet, the rightful ruler of Denmark.

LAERTES

The devil take your soul!

   They fight.

HAMLET

You do not pray well.
I ask you to take your fingers away from my throat,   250
for though I am not quick-tempered and rash,
I still have dangerous tendencies
which you would be wise to fear. Take away your hand.

KING

Pluck them asunder.

QUEEN

255   Hamlet, Hamlet!

ALL

Gentlemen!

HORATIO

Good my lord, be quiet.

[ATTENDANTS *part them.*]

HAMLET

Why, I will fight with him upon this theme
Until my eyelids will no longer wag.

QUEEN

260   O my son, what theme?

HAMLET

I loved Ophelia. Forty thousand brothers
Could not with all their quantity of love
Make up my sum. What wilt thou do for her?

KING

O, he is mad, Laertes.

QUEEN

265   For love of God forbear him.

HAMLET

'Swounds, show me what thou 't do.
Woo't weep? Woo't fight? Woo't fast? Woo't tear thyself?
Woo't drink up eisel? Eat a crocodile?
I'll do 't. Dost thou come here to whine?
270   To outface me with leaping in her grave?
Be buried quick with her, and so will I.
And if thou prate of mountains, let them throw
Millions of acres on us, till our ground,
Singeing his pate against the burning zone,
275   Make Ossa like a wart! Nay, an thou'lt mouth,
I'll rant as well as thou.

KING

Pull them apart.

QUEEN

Hamlet! Hamlet! 255

ALL

Gentlemen!

HORATIO

My good lord, calm yourself.

> HAMLET *and* LAERTES *are separated.*

HAMLET

Why, I will fight with him about this matter
until my eyelids are shut forever.

QUEEN

Oh, my son, what matter do you mean? 260

HAMLET

I loved Ophelia. All the combined love
of forty thousand brothers could not equal
the sum of my love. What would you do for her?

KING

Oh, he is mad, Laertes.

QUEEN

For the love of God, be patient with him. 265

HAMLET

By God's wounds, tell me what you would do for her.
Would you weep, fight, fast, injure yourself?
Would you drink vinegar, eat a crocodile?
I'd do all that. Did you come here to whine?
To outdo me by leaping into her grave? 270
Be buried alive with her, and so will I.
And if you chatter about mountains, let these diggers throw
millions of acres of land on us, until the top
of our mound is scorched by being so near the sun,
making Ossa look like a wart. Indeed, if you'll rave, 275
I'll rant as well as you.

QUEEN

                    This is mere madness;
And thus a while the fit will work on him.
Anon, as patient as the female dove
When that her golden couplets are disclosed,
His silence will sit drooping.

HAMLET

                        Hear you, sir.
What is the reason that you use me thus?
I loved you ever. But it is no matter.
Let Hercules* himself do what he may,
The cat will mew, and dog will have his day.

       Exit HAMLET.

KING

I pray thee, good Horatio, wait upon him.

       Exit HORATIO.

[*to* LAERTES] Strengthen your patience in our last night's
      speech.
We'll put the matter to the present push.
Good Gertrude, set some watch over your son.
This grave shall have a living monument.
An hour of quiet shortly shall we see;
Till then in patience our proceeding be.

       Exeunt.

---

285   *Hercules* Hamlet may be comparing Laertes's exaggerated behavior and language
     to that of Hercules, who was sometimes depicted on stage as a boasting and
     ranting tyrant.

QUEEN
> This is pure madness,
> and the fit will work on him awhile like this.
> Soon, his silence will sit drooping, as patient
> as a female dove when her twins are newly hatched   280
> with their golden down.

HAMLET
> Listen, sir—
> what is the reason for you to treat me like this?
> I've always loved you. But it doesn't matter.
> Let Hercules himself do what he may,   285
> the cat will mew, and the dog will have his day.

> > *HAMLET exits.*

KING
> I beg you, good Horatio, to go look after him.

> > *HORATIO exits.*

> *(to* LAERTES*)* Strengthen your patience by remembering what we
> > said last night.
> We'll put our plan into action right away.—   290
> Gertrude, send someone to watch over your son.—
> This grave will have a lasting monument.
> Before long, we'll have an hour of peace;
> until then, let's proceed with patience.

> > *They exit.*

ACT V, SCENE II

[The castle.] Enter HAMLET *and* HORATIO.

HAMLET
So much for this, sir; now shall you see the other.
You do remember all the circumstance?

HORATIO
Remember it, my lord!

HAMLET
Sir, in my heart there was a kind of fighting
5   That would not let me sleep. Methought I lay
Worse than the mutines in the bilboes. Rashly—
And praised be rashness for it—let us know,
Our **indiscretion** sometime serves us well
When our deep plots do pall, and that should learn us
10   There's a divinity that shapes our ends,
Rough-hew them how we will.

HORATIO
                         That is most certain.

HAMLET
Up from my cabin,
My sea gown scarf about me, in the dark
15   Groped I to find out them, had my desire,
Fingered their packet, and in fine withdrew
To mine own room again, making so bold,
My fears forgetting manners, to unseal
Their grand commission; where I found, Horatio—
20   A royal knavery!—an exact command,
Larded with many several sorts of reasons,
Importing Denmark's health, and England's too,
With, ho, such bugs and goblins in my life,
That on the supervise, no leisure bated,
25   No, not to stay the grinding of the ax,
My head should be struck off.

ACT 5, SCENE 2

The castle. HAMLET *and* HORATIO *enter.*

HAMLET
So much for what you already know. Now I'll tell you the rest.
Do you remember the circumstances of my being sent to
England?

HORATIO
Remember it, my lord!

HAMLET
Sir, there was a kind of agitation in my heart
that would not let me sleep. I felt as if I were lying there   5
in worse shackles than a mutineer. Then I did something rash—
and let rashness be praised for it. We should keep in mind
that poor judgment sometimes serves us well
when our cleverest plots fail; that should teach us
that there's a divinity that guides our destinies,   10
no matter how we try to roughly shape them.

HORATIO
That is very certain.

HAMLET
I came out of my cabin,
my sea clothes wrapped around me, and groped   15
in the dark to find Rosencrantz and Guildenstern; I succeeded,
stole their packet of letters, and finally went back
to my own room again. My fears made me
forget my manners, and so I boldly opened
their letter with its great command. And there I found, Horatio,
a piece of royal mischief; it was a precise order,   20
justified with numerous reasons
pertaining to the health of both the kings of Denmark and
England;
and—oh!—it said there was much to fear if I should be
allowed to live;
and that as soon as the letter was read, without the least delay
(no, not even the time needed to sharpen the ax),   25
my head must be cut off.

HORATIO
Is 't possible?

HAMLET
Here's the commission; read it at more leisure.
But wilt thou hear now how I did proceed?

HORATIO
30 I beseech you.

HAMLET
Being thus benetted round with villains,
Or I could make a prologue to my brains,
They had begun the play. I sat me down,
Devised a new commission, wrote it fair.
35 I once did hold it, as our statists do,
A baseness to write fair, and labored much
How to forget that learning, but, sir, now
It did me yeoman's service. Wilt thou know
Th' effect of what I wrote?

HORATIO
40 Ay, good my lord.

HAMLET
An earnest conjuration from the King,
As England was his faithful tributary,
As love between them like the palm might flourish,
As peace should still her wheaten garland wear
45 And stand a comma 'tween their amities,
And many suchlike as's* of great charge,
That on the view and knowing of these contents,
Without debatement further, more or less,
He should those bearers put to sudden death,
50 Not shriving time allowed.

HORATIO
How was this sealed?

---

46 *as's* wordplay on the plural of "as" and "asses"

HORATIO

Is this possible?

HAMLET

Here's the command. Read it when you have time.

Handing him the letter.

But would you like to hear what I did then?

HORATIO

I beg you. 30

HAMLET

There I was, surrounded by villainous plots;
and before I could tell my brains to get to work,
they'd already come up with a plot of their own. I sat down
and wrote out a new command in fine handwriting.
Like many statesmen, I used to consider it 35
beneath myself to write clearly, like a clerk, and I tried hard
to forget how to do it; but at this moment, sir,
that skill served me extremely well. Do you want to know
the substance of what I wrote?

HORATIO

Indeed, my good lord. 40

HAMLET

It was an earnest appeal from the King:
Because England so faithfully pays tribute to Denmark,
and in hopes that love between the two nations might flourish
    like a palm tree,
and in hopes that peace should always wear her garlands of
    wheat
linking Denmark and England in friendship, 45
and many similar "in hopes-es" of great weight,
the English King, as soon as he read and understood this letter,
without any further consideration one way or the other,
should put the carriers of the letter to sudden death,
not allowing them time to repent their sins. 50

HORATIO

How did you seal this letter?

HAMLET
Why, even in that was heaven ordinant.
I had my father's signet in my purse,
Which was the model of that Danish seal,
55 Folded the writ up in the form of th' other,
Subscribed it, gave 't th' impression, placed it safely,
The changeling never known. Now, the next day
Was our sea fight, and what to this was sequent
Thou knowest already.

HORATIO
60 So Guildenstern and Rosencrantz go to 't.

HAMLET
Why, man, they did make love to this employment.
They are not near my conscience; their defeat
Does by their own insinuation grow.
'Tis dangerous when the baser nature comes
65 Between the pass and fell incensed points
Of mighty opposites.

HORATIO
Why, what a king is this!

HAMLET
Does it not, think thee, stand me now upon—
He that hath killed my king and whored my mother,
70 Popped in between th' election and my hopes,
Thrown out his angle for my proper life,
And with such coz'nage—is 't not perfect conscience
To quit him with this arm? And is 't not to be damned
To let this canker of our nature come
75 In further evil?

HORATIO
It must be shortly known to him from England
What is the issue of the business there.

HAMLET

Why, even in that, heaven took charge.
I had my father's signet ring in my purse,
which was a perfect copy of the Danish seal;
I folded the letter up exactly like the other, 55
signed it, sealed it with wax, and put it safely where the other
    had been,
so that the switch would never be noticed. Now, the next day
was our sea fight; and you already know
what happened after that.

HORATIO

So Guildenstern and Rosencrantz go to their deaths. 60

HAMLET

Why, man, they relished their role in all these schemes.
Their deaths are not on my conscience. They were
destroyed by their own meddling.
It's dangerous for inferior people to come
between the thrusting, fiercely angry sword points 65
of two mighty opponents.

HORATIO

Why, what a king this is!

HAMLET

Don't you think my duty is now clear?
He has killed my king and made a whore of my mother,
popped in between the election of the next king and my own
    hope to rule, 70
thrown out his fish hook for my very life,
and with great trickery. May I not, with a clear conscience,
punish him with this arm of mine? And wouldn't it be sinful
to let this cancer grow among us
into something even more evil? 75

HORATIO

He will shortly hear from England
what has become of matters there.

HAMLET
    It will be short; the interim's mine,
    And a man's life's no more than to say "one."*
80   But I am very sorry, good Horatio,
    That to Laertes I forgot myself,
    For by the image of my cause I see
    The portraiture of his. I'll court his favors.
    But sure the bravery of his grief did put me
85   Into a tow'ring passion.

HORATIO
                            Peace, who comes here?

    Enter young OSRIC, *a courtier.*

OSRIC
    Your lordship is right welcome back to Denmark.

HAMLET
    I humbly thank you, sir. [*aside to Horatio*] Dost know this
        waterfly?

HORATIO [*aside to* HAMLET]
90   No, my good lord.

HAMLET [*to* HORATIO]
    Thy state is the more gracious, for 'tis a vice to know him.
    He hath much land, and fertile. Let a beast be lord of
    beasts, and his crib shall stand at the king's mess. 'Tis a
    chough, but, as I say, spacious in the possession of dirt.

OSRIC
95   Sweet lord, if your lordship were at leisure, I should
    impart a thing to you from his Majesty.

HAMLET
    I will receive it, sir, with all **diligence** of spirit. Put your
    bonnet to his right use. 'Tis for the head.

OSRIC
    I thank your lordship, it is very hot.

---

79 *"one"* Hamlet may mean that a man can be killed in no more time than it takes
to deliver one sword thrust.

HAMLET

There's little time. Meanwhile, I've got the advantage,
and a man's life may be ended by a single sword thrust.
But good Horatio, I am very sorry 80
that I lost my temper at Laertes,
for when I look at my own cause, I see
a portrait of his cause as well. I shall seek his friendship.
But truly, his brazen display of grief threw me
into an overwhelming rage. 85

HORATIO

Quiet—who comes here?

> OSRIC, *a young courtier, enters.*

OSRIC (*with an elaborate bow and flourish*)

You are very welcome back to Denmark.

HAMLET

I humbly thank you, sir. *(aside to* HORATIO*)* Do you know this vain
and overdressed insect?

HORATIO (*aside to* HAMLET)

No, my good lord. 90

HAMLET (*to* HORATIO)

You should consider yourself lucky, because it's wicked to
know him. He has much fertile land. Even a beastly sort of
man will be allowed to eat at the king's table if he owns
enough flocks and herds. This man is only a chatterer, but he
has many acres of land.

OSRIC (*taking off his hat to* HAMLET)

Sweet lord, if your lordship has a moment, I would convey a 95
message to you from his Majesty.

HAMLET

I will receive it, sir, with diligent attention. But put your hat to its
proper use. It's for the head.

OSRIC

I thank your lordship, but it's very hot.

HAMLET

No, believe me, 'tis very cold; the wind is northerly.

OSRIC

It is indifferent cold, my lord, indeed.

HAMLET

But yet methinks it is very sultry and hot for my
complexion.

OSRIC

Exceedingly, my lord; it is very sultry, as 'twere—I cannot
tell how. But, my lord, his Majesty bade me signify to you
that 'a has laid a great wager on your head. Sir, this is the
matter—

HAMLET

I beseech you remember.

[HAMLET *moves him to put on his hat.*]

OSRIC

Nay, good my lord; for my ease, in good faith. Sir, here is
newly come to court Laertes—believe me, an absolute
gentleman, full of most excellent differences, of very soft
society and great showing. Indeed, to speak feelingly of
him, he is the card or calendar of gentry; for you shall find
in him the continent of what part a gentleman would see.

HAMLET

Sir, his definement* suffers no perdition in you, though, I
know, to divide him inventorially would dozy th'
arithmetic of memory, and yet but yaw neither in respect
of his quick sail. But, in the verity of extolment, I take him
to be a soul of great article, and his infusion of such
dearth and rareness as, to make true diction of him, his
semblage is his mirror, and who else would trace him, his
umbrage, nothing more.

OSRIC

Your lordship speaks most infallibly of him.

---

115 *definement* . . . By imitating it, Hamlet is making fun of Osric's extravagant
and affected way of talking.

HAMLET

No, believe me, it's very cold, and the wind is from the north.   100

OSRIC

It is somewhat cold, my lord, indeed.

HAMLET

And yet I find it very sultry and hot for someone of my temperament.

OSRIC

Exceedingly, my lord; it is very sultry, as if it were—well, I cannot say. My lord, his Majesty asked me to inform you that he has   105
made a great wager on you. Sir, the business is this—

HAMLET

I beg you to remember.

> HAMLET *makes a gesture for* OSRIC *to put on his hat.*

OSRIC

No, my good lord, I keep it off for my comfort, I really do. Sir, Laertes has recently come to court—a perfect gentleman,   110
believe me, full of many distinguishing qualities, of a very sociable disposition and an impressive appearance. Indeed, to speak justly of him, he is the guide or directory of gentlemanliness, for you will find in him the embodiment of every characteristic a gentleman would like to see in another.

HAMLET

Sir, you've omitted nothing in your description of him—   115
although I know that, if his qualities were to be listed one by one, memory would be baffled by the sheer numbers, and would lurch along unsteadily while trying to keep pace with him. But to praise him honestly, I take him to be a soul of great importance, and his mixture of fine qualities is so precious and rare that, to speak truthfully about him, only his mirror can   120
show his true appearance. Anyone who tries to follow in his footsteps can be nothing more than his shadow.

OSRIC

Your lordship speaks of him most accurately.

HAMLET

The concernancy, sir? Why do we wrap the gentleman in
125   our more rawer breath?

OSRIC

Sir?

HORATIO

Is 't not possible to understand in another tongue? You
will to 't, sir, really.

HAMLET

What imports the nomination of this gentleman?

OSRIC

130   Of Laertes?

HORATIO [*aside to* HAMLET]

His purse is empty already. All 's golden words are spent.

HAMLET

Of him, sir.

OSRIC

I know you are not ignorant—

HAMLET

I would you did, sir; yet, in faith, if you did, it would not
135   much approve me. Well, sir?

OSRIC

You are not ignorant of what excellence Laertes is—

HAMLET

I dare not confess that, lest I should compare with him in
excellence; but to know a man well were to know himself.

OSRIC

I mean, sir, for his weapon; but in the imputation laid on
140   him by them, in his meed he's unfellowed.

HAMLET

What's his weapon?

OSRIC

Rapier and dagger.

HAMLET

That's two of his weapons—but well.

HAMLET

What is your purpose in all this, sir? Why do we wrap the
gentleman up in such unworthy words? 125

OSRIC

Sir?

HORATIO (*aside to* HAMLET)

Isn't it possible to make yourselves understood in plainer
language? Sir, I'm sure you could if you tried.

HAMLET (*to* OSRIC)

What is your reason for mentioning the name of this gentleman?

OSRIC

Of Laertes? 130

HORATIO (*aside to* HAMLET)

His purse is empty already; all his golden words have been spent.

HAMLET

Yes, of Laertes, sir.

OSRIC

I know you are not ignorant—

HAMLET

I wish you did, sir. And yet, by my faith, if you did know it, it
wouldn't do me much credit. Well, sir? 135

OSRIC

You are not ignorant of Laertes's excellence—

HAMLET

I don't dare confess that, for fear of trying to rival him in
excellence. To know a man well, one must first know oneself.

OSRIC

I mean, sir, his excellence with his weapon. According to the
reputation he has achieved, he is unequaled in merit. 140

HAMLET

What's his weapon?

OSRIC

Rapier and dagger.

HAMLET

That's two of his weapons. But anyway—

OSRIC

145   The King, sir, hath wagered with him six Barbary horses, against the which he has impawned, as I take it, six French rapiers and poniards, with the assigns, as girdle, hangers, and so. Three of the carriages,* in faith, are very dear to fancy, very responsive to the hilts, most delicate carriages, and of very liberal conceit.

HAMLET

150   What call you the "carriages"?

HORATIO [*aside to* HAMLET]

I knew you must be **edified** by the margent ere you had done.

OSRIC

The carriages, sir, are the hangers.

HAMLET

155   The phrase would be more **germane** to the matter if we could carry a cannon by our sides. I would it might be "hangers" till then. But on! Six Barbary horses against six French swords, their assigns, and three liberal-conceited carriages—that's the French bet against the Danish. Why is all impawned, as you call it.

OSRIC

160   The King, sir, hath laid, sir, that in a dozen passes between yourself and him he shall not exceed you three hits; he hath laid on twelve for nine, and it would come to immediate trial if your lordship would vouchsafe the answer.

HAMLET

165   How if I answer no?

OSRIC

I mean, my lord, the opposition of your person in trial.

HAMLET

Sir, I will walk here in the hall. If it please his Majesty, it is the breathing time of day with me. Let the foils be

---

147   *carriages* an affected synonym for "hangers." "Carriages" usually refer to guns or cannons.

OSRIC

The King, sir, has bet him six fine North African horses. Against
this, Laertes has wagered (as I understand it) six French rapiers   145
and daggers, with all their accessories—belt, straps, and so forth.
Three of the carriages, indeed, are lovely to behold, and go with
the hilts nicely. They are very fine carriages, of elaborate design.

HAMLET

What do you mean by "carriages"?   150

HORATIO (*aside to* HAMLET)

I knew you'd need to have something explained before you
were through.

OSRIC

The carriages, sir, are the straps.

HAMLET

The word "carriages" would be more appropriate to the
situation if Laertes and I both had cannons by our sides. I   155
would prefer to call them "straps" for now. But continue. Six
North African horses against six French swords, their
accessories, and three elaborately designed carriages—that's
the wager between the French and the Danish. Now tell me,
what is this wager about?

OSRIC

The King, sir, has bet, sir, that in a dozen rounds between   160
yourself and Laertes, he will not exceed your score by three
hits. Laertes expects to win at least twelve hits to your nine.
This will be put to the test immediately if you will kindly
give a reply.

HAMLET

What if my reply is no?   165

OSRIC

I mean, my lord, your acceptance of this challenge in person.

HAMLET

Sir, I will be walking here in the hall. If it pleases his Majesty,
this is the time of day when I take exercise. Let the foils be

brought, the gentleman willing, and the King hold his
170   purpose, I will win for him an I can; if not, I will gain
nothing but my shame and the odd hits.

OSRIC

Shall I deliver you e'en so?

HAMLET

To this effect, sir, after what flourish your nature will.

OSRIC

I commend my duty to your lordship.

HAMLET

175   Yours, yours. [*Exit* OSRIC.] He does well to commend it
himself; there are no tongues else for 's turn.

HORATIO

This lapwing* runs away with the shell on his head.

HAMLET

'A did comply, sir, with his dug before 'a sucked it. Thus
has he, and many more of the same breed that I know the
180   drossy age dotes on, only got the tune of the time and,
out of an habit of encounter, a kind of yeasty collection,
which carries them through and through the most fanned
and winnowed opinions; and do but blow them to their
trial, the bubbles are out.

> *Enter a* LORD.

LORD

185   My lord, his Majesty commended him to you by young
Osric, who brings back to him that you attend him in the
hall. He sends to know if your pleasure hold to play with
Laertes, or that you will take longer time.

HAMLET

I am constant to my purposes; they follow the King's
190   pleasure. If his fitness speaks, mine is ready; now or
whensoever, provided I be so able as now.

---

177   *lapwing* The newly hatched lapwing was thought to run from the nest with part
of the eggshell still over its head. Osric has apparently put on his hat at last.

brought. If the gentleman is willing, and the King stands by his wager, I'll win it for him if I can. If not, I will gain nothing but my shame and a few successful hits. 170

OSRIC

Shall I report what you have said?

HAMLET

Do so, sir—with whatever verbal decoration you find fit to add.

OSRIC

I offer my services to your lordship with praise.

HAMLET

Likewise.

    OSRIC exits.

He does well to praise his own services. Nobody else's tongue 175 will do it for him.

HORATIO

This lapwing runs away with the shell on his head.

HAMLET

Sir, he paid elaborate compliments to his mother's breast before he sucked it. He's like many others I know of the same type, whom this worthless age adores. They've learned the 180 fashionable manner of speech, and out of many social encounters, they've collected frothy phrases that make a favorable impression among refined people. But if you merely blow on these fellows to see if they have any real substance, they vanish like bubbles.

    A LORD enters.

LORD

My lord, his Majesty sent a message to you by young Osric, 185 who returned to him saying that you were awaiting him in the hall. He wishes to know if you still want to fence with Laertes, or if you'd rather wait until later.

HAMLET

I stand by my purpose, which is to do whatever pleases the King. If he is ready, so am I. I'll fence now or whenever he 190 wishes, as long as I'm as prepared as I am right now.

LORD

The King and Queen and all are coming down.

HAMLET

In happy time.

LORD

195   The Queen desires you to use some gentle entertainment
to Laertes before you fall to play.

HAMLET

She well instructs me.

[*Exit* LORD.]

HORATIO

You will lose this wager, my lord.

HAMLET

I do not think so. Since he went into France I have been in
continual practice. I shall win at the odds. But thou
200   wouldst not think how ill all's here about my heart. But it
is no matter.

HORATIO

Nay, good my lord—

HAMLET

It is but foolery, but it is such a kind of gain-giving as
would perhaps trouble a woman.

HORATIO

205   If your mind dislike anything, obey it. I will forestall their
repair hither and say you are not fit.

HAMLET

Not a whit, we defy augury. There is special **providence** in
the fall of a sparrow.* If it be now, 'tis not to come; if it be
not to come, it will be now; if it be not now, yet it will
210   come. The readiness is all. Since no man of aught he
leaves knows, what is 't to leave betimes? Let be.

---

208   *sparrow* an allusion to the well known passage: "Are not two sparrows sold for a
farthing? And one of them shall not fall on the ground without your father"
(Matthew 10:29).

LORD

The King and Queen and everyone are coming down.

HAMLET

Their timing is excellent.

LORD

The Queen wishes you to greet Laertes in a friendly way
before you begin to fence. 195

HAMLET

She advises me well.

The LORD *exits.*

HORATIO

You will lose this bet, my lord.

HAMLET

I do not think so. Since Laertes went to France, I have been
practicing continually. I will win on the terms that have been
set. And yet, you can't imagine the foreboding that I feel in 200
my heart. But it doesn't matter.

HORATIO

Indeed, my good lord—

HAMLET

It's only foolishness—the kind of misgiving that might worry
a woman.

HORATIO

If your mind suspects anything, take heed of it. I will delay 205
them from coming here and say you are not ready.

HAMLET

Don't think of it. We'll defy our forebodings. Heaven plays a
special part even in the fall of a sparrow. If my death comes
now, then it's not in the future; if it's not in the future, it will
come now; if it doesn't come now, it will still come. The most 210
important thing is to be ready for death. Since no man knows
what he is leaving behind, what does an early death matter?
Leave things as they are.

A table prepared. [Enter] TRUMPETS, DRUMS, *and*
OFFICERS *with cushions;* KING, QUEEN, [OSRIC,]
and all the STATE, *[with]* foils, daggers, *[and stoups of*
wine borne in]; and LAERTES.

KING

Come, Hamlet, come, and take this hand from me.

The KING *puts* LAERTES's *hand into* HAMLET's.]

HAMLET

Give me your pardon, sir. I have done you wrong,
But pardon 't, as you are a gentleman.
215 This presence knows, and you must needs have heard,
How I am punished with a sore distraction.
What I have done
That might your nature, honor, and exception
Roughly awake, I here proclaim was madness.
220 Was 't Hamlet wronged Laertes? Never Hamlet.
If Hamlet from himself be ta'en away,
And when he's not himself does wrong Laertes,
Then Hamlet does it not, Hamlet denies it.
Who does it then? His madness. If 't be so,
225 Hamlet is of the **faction** that is wronged;
His madness is poor Hamlet's enemy.
Sir, in this audience,
Let my disclaiming from a purposed evil
Free me so far in your most generous thoughts
230 That I have shot my arrow o'er the house
And hurt my brother.

LAERTES

I am satisfied in nature,
Whose motive in this case should stir me most
To my revenge. But in my terms of honor
235 I stand aloof, and will no reconcilement
Till by some elder master of known honor
I have a voice and precedent of peace
To keep my name ungored. But till that time
I do receive your offered love like love,
240 And will not wrong it.

A furnished table is brought in. MUSICIANS *with trumpets
and drums enter, along with* OFFICERS *carrying cushions.
The* KING *and* QUEEN, OSRIC, *all the* COURTIERS, *and* LAERTES
enter, with foils, daggers, and pitchers of wine.

KING

Come, Hamlet, come—and take this hand from me.

He puts LAERTES's *hand into* HAMLET's.

HAMLET (*to* LAERTES)

I beg your pardon, sir. I have done you wrong;
but since you are a gentleman, forgive me. Everyone in this
    royal assembly knows,
and you have surely heard, that I am afflicted   215
by serious insanity. Whatever I have done
to insult you personally, or rudely awaken your disapproval
and feelings of dishonor, I now declare was done out of madness.
Was it Hamlet who wronged Laertes? It was never Hamlet.   220
If Hamlet loses his mind
and wrongs Laertes when he is not himself,
then Hamlet does not do it; Hamlet denies it.
Who does it, then? His madness. If this is so,
Hamlet himself is among those who are wronged;   225
poor Hamlet's madness is his own enemy.
Sir, before all these people,
I hope that my denial of deliberate evil
will free me of guilt in your generous mind,
as if I had shot an arrow over a house   230
and accidentally hurt my brother.

LAERTES

You've satisfied my personal feelings,
which were my greatest motive for revenge
in this case. But regarding your offense to my honor,
I'll say nothing for now, and will make no reconciliation   235
until I have spoken with some elderly experts in such matters
who can tell me, based on precedent, how to make peace
    with you
and keep my reputation unharmed. Until that time,
I accept your offered love as sincere,
and will not reject it.   240

HAMLET
I embrace it freely,

And will this brother's wager frankly play.—
Give us the foils. Come on.

LAERTES
Come, one for me.

HAMLET

245 I'll be your foil,* Laertes. In mine ignorance
Your skill shall, like a star i' th' darkest night,
Stick fiery off indeed.

LAERTES
You mock me sir.

HAMLET
No, by this hand.

KING

250 Give them the foils, young Osric. Cousin Hamlet,
You know the wager?

HAMLET
Very well, my lord.

Your grace has laid the odds o' th' weaker side.

KING
I do not fear it, I have seen you both;

255 But since he is bettered, we have therefore odds.

LAERTES
This is too heavy; let me see another.

HAMLET
This likes me well. These foils have all a length?

Prepare to play.

OSRIC
Ay, my good lord.

---

245 *foil* wordplay: a fencing foil/a background, like dark velvet, which shows a jewel
to advantage

HAMLET
I openly welcome what you say,
and will fence earnestly in this brotherly wager.—
Give us the foils. Come on.

LAERTES
Come, a foil for me.

HAMLET
I'll make you look good, Laertes. Compared with my ignorance, 245
your skill will stand out brilliantly,
like a star in the darkest night.

LAERTES
You mock me, sir.

HAMLET
By my hand, I swear that I don't.

KING
Give them the foils, young Osric. My kinsman Hamlet, 250
do you know the wager?

HAMLET
Very well, my lord.
Your Grace has bet on the weaker player.

KING
I'm not worried about it; I have seen you both fence.
Since Laertes is thought to be better, we've given you three 255
    points.

LAERTES
(trying a foil) This is too heavy. Let me see another.

HAMLET
This one is fine for me. Are all these foils the same length?

> HAMLET *and* LAERTES *prepare to fence.*

OSRIC
Yes, my good lord.

KING
Set me the stoups of wine upon that table.
260   If Hamlet give the first or second hit,
Or quit in answer of the third exchange,
Let all the battlements their ordnance fire.
The King shall drink to Hamlet's better breath,
And in the cup an union* shall he throw
265   Richer than that which four successive kings
In Denmark's crown have worn. Give me the cups,
And let the kettle to the trumpet speak,
The trumpet to the cannoneer without,
The cannons to the heavens, the heaven to earth,
270   "Now the King drinks to Hamlet." Come, begin.

> *Trumpets the while.*

And you, the judges, bear a wary eye.

HAMLET
Come on, sir.

LAERTES
Come, my lord.

> *They play.*

HAMLET
One.

LAERTES
275   No.

HAMLET
Judgment?

OSRIC
A hit, a very **palpable** hit.

> *Drum, trumpets, and shot. Flourish; a piece goes off.*

LAERTES
Well, again.

---

264   *union* presumably a trick pearl, which has poison concealed in it

KING

Put the pitchers of wine on the table.
If Hamlet makes the first or second hit, 260
or repays Laertes's first two hits with a third of his own,
let the cannons in all the battlements be fired.
The King will drink to Hamlet's renewed energy,
and will toss a pearl in the cup
more precious than any worn in Denmark's crown 265
by four previous kings. Give me the cups;
let the kettledrum speak to the trumpet,
then the trumpet speak to the artillerymen outside,
then the cannons speak to the heavens, then the heavens speak
    to earth again—
all of them saying, "Now the King drinks to Hamlet." Come, 270
    let's begin.

> *Trumpets play.*

And you judges, watch the game closely.

HAMLET

Come on, sir.

LAERTES

Come on, my lord.

> *They fence.*

HAMLET

I made a hit.

LAERTES

No. 275

HAMLET

Let's have a judgment.

OSRIC

A hit—a very clear hit.

> *Drums, trumpets, and ceremonial shootings are heard.*
> *A flourish of trumpets; a cannon goes off.*

LAERTES

Well, let's go again.

KING
Stay, give me drink.—Hamlet, this pearl is thine.
280 Here's to thy health.

    [*He drinks and then drops the pearl in the cup.*]

    Drum, trumpets, and shot.

Give him the cup.

HAMLET
I'll play this bout first; set it by awhile.
Come. [*They play.*] Another hit. What say you?

LAERTES
A touch, a touch; I do confess 't.

KING
Our son shall win.

QUEEN
285   He's fat, and scant of breath.
Here, Hamlet, take my napkin, rub thy brows.
The Queen carouses to thy fortune, Hamlet.

HAMLET
Good madam!

KING
Gertrude, do not drink.

QUEEN
290 I will, my lord; I pray you pardon me.

    [*Drinks.*]

KING [*aside*]
It is the poisoned cup. It is too late.

HAMLET
I dare not drink yet, madam—by and by.

QUEEN
Come, let me wipe thy face.

LAERTES [*to* CLAUDIUS]
My lord, I'll hit him now.

KING
Wait, give me something to drink.—Hamlet, this pearl is for you.
Here's to your health.   280

He drinks, then drops the pearl in the cup. Drums and trumpets, followed by a cannon.

Give Hamlet the cup.

HAMLET
I'll play out this round first. Set it aside for now.
Come.

LAERTES *and* HAMLET *fence.*

Another hit. What do you think?

LAERTES
A touch, a touch. I admit it.

KING
Our son will win.

QUEEN
He's sweaty and out of breath.   285
Here, Hamlet—take my handkerchief; wipe your forehead.
The Queen drinks to your good luck, Hamlet.

HAMLET
Good madam!

KING
Gertrude, do not drink.

QUEEN
I will, my lord; I beg your pardon.   290

She drinks.

KING (*aside*)
It is the poisoned cup. It is too late.

HAMLET
I don't dare drink yet, madam—but I will soon.

QUEEN
Come here, let me wipe your face.

LAERTES (*to* CLAUDIUS)
My lord, I'll hit him now.

KING

295   I do not think 't.

LAERTES [*aside*]
And yet it is almost against my conscience.

HAMLET
Come for the third, Laertes. You do but dally.
I pray you pass with your best violence;
I am sure you make a wanton of me.

LAERTES
300   Say you so? Come on.

[*They play.*]

OSRIC
Nothing neither way.

LAERTES
Have at you now!

In scuffling they change rapiers, [and both are wounded.]

KING
Part them. They are incensed.

HAMLET
Nay, come—again!

[*The* QUEEN *falls.*]

OSRIC
305   Look to the Queen there, ho!

HORATIO
They bleed on both sides.—How is it, my lord?

OSRIC
How is 't, Laertes?

LAERTES
Why, as a woodcock* to mine own springe, Osric.
I am justly killed with mine own treachery.

HAMLET
310   How does the Queen?

---

308   *woodcock* proverbially a stupid bird

KING

I do not think so. 295

LAERTES *(aside)*

And yet it is almost against my conscience.

HAMLET

Come, let's have our third round, Laertes. You're only dawdling.
I beg you, come at me with your greatest vigor.
I am afraid that you're treating me like a child.

LAERTES

Is that what you think? Come on. 300

> *They fence.*

OSRIC

No hits on either side.

LAERTES

And now, take this!

> LAERTES *wounds* HAMLET. *Then they scuffle and switch
> rapiers;* HAMLET *wounds* LAERTES.

KING

Separate them. They are enraged.

HAMLET

No, come at me again.

> *The* QUEEN *falls.*

OSRIC

Look to the Queen there! Halt the duel! 305

HORATIO

Both players are bleeding. *(to* HAMLET*)* What is it, my lord?

OSRIC

What is it, Laertes?

LAERTES

Why, I'm like a stupid bird caught in my own trap, Osric.

> *He falls.*

I've been justly killed by my own treachery.

HAMLET

How is the Queen? 310

KING

                      She swoons to see them bleed.

QUEEN

No, no, the drink, the drink! O my dear Hamlet!
The drink, the drink! I am poisoned.

    [*Dies.*]

HAMLET

O villainy! Ho! Let the door be locked.
315   Treachery! Seek it out.

    [LAERTES *falls.*]

LAERTES

It is here, Hamlet. Hamlet, thou are slain;
No med'cine in the world can do thee good.
In thee there is not half an hour's life.
The treacherous instrument is in thy hand,
320   Unbated and envenomed. The foul practice
Hath turned itself on me. Lo, here I lie,
Never to rise again. Thy mother's poisoned.
I can no more. The King, the King's to blame.

HAMLET

The point envenomed too?
325   Then, venom, to thy work.

    Hurts the KING.

ALL

Treason! Treason!

KING

O, yet defend me, friends. I am but hurt.

HAMLET

Here, thou incestuous, murd'rous, damned Dane,
Drink off this potion. Is thy union here?
330   Follow my mother.

    KING *dies.*

LAERTES

                He is justly served.
It is a poison tempered by himself.

KING

She faints from seeing them bleed.

QUEEN

No, no, it's the drink, the drink! Oh, my dear Hamlet!
The drink, the drink! I've been poisoned.

> *She dies.*

HAMLET

Oh, villainy! Halt! Let the door be locked.

> OSRIC *exits.*

There's been treachery! Look for its source.   315

> LAERTES *falls.*

LAERTES

The source is here, Hamlet. Hamlet, you've been killed.
No medicine in the world can do you any good.
There is not half an hour of life left in you.
The treacherous instrument is in your hand—
unblunted and poisoned. The cruel deception   320
has turned itself against me. Your mother's been poisoned.
I can do nothing more. The King, the King's to blame.

HAMLET

So the point's been poisoned, too! Then venom, get to work.   325

> *He wounds the* KING.

ALL

Treason, treason!

KING

Oh, defend me, friends! I am only hurt.

HAMLET

Here, you incestuous, murderous, cursed Dane—
drink this poison. Is your pearl here?
Follow my mother.   330

> HAMLET *forces the* KING *to drink the poison; the* KING *dies.*

LAERTES

He's gotten what he deserved.
The poison was mixed by himself.

Exchange forgiveness with me, noble Hamlet.
Mine and my father's death come not upon thee,
335   Nor thine on me!

        Dies.

HAMLET
Heaven make thee free of it! I follow thee.
I am dead, Horatio. Wretched Queen, adieu!
You that look pale and tremble at this chance,
That are but mutes or audience to this act,
340   Had I but time (as this fell sergeant, Death,
Is strict in his arrest), O, I could tell you—
But let it be.—Horatio, I am dead.
Thou livest; report me and my cause aright
To the unsatisfied.

HORATIO
345   Never believe it.
I am more an antique Roman* than a Dane.
Here's yet some liquor left.

HAMLET
                    As th' art a man,
Give me the cup. Let go. By heaven, I'll ha 't!
350   O God, Horatio, what a wounded name,
Things standing thus unknown, shall live behind me!
If thou didst ever hold me in thy heart,
Absent thee from **felicity** awhile,
And in this harsh world draw thy breath in pain,
355   To tell my story.

        A march afar off.

            What warlike noise is this?

        OSRIC *enters.*

OSRIC
Young Fortinbras, with conquest come from Poland,
To th' ambassadors of England gives
This warlike volley.

---

346   *antique Roman* Horatio alludes to the Roman tradition, which considered suicide
an honorable death in preference to a dishonorable existence.

Exchange forgiveness with me, noble Hamlet.
Let my death and my father's not be held against you,
nor your death against me.   335

>   *He dies.*

HAMLET

May heaven free you of your guilt. I'll follow you.—
I am dead, Horatio.—Unhappy Queen, farewell.
(to the others present) You who look pale and tremble at these
>   events,
who are merely silent characters or the audience of this play,
if only I had time (which I haven't, since this cruel officer, Death,   340
is strict in arresting me), oh, I could tell you—
but let it be.—Horatio, I am dead.
You are alive; explain me and my cause justly
to those who don't understand.

HORATIO

Don't believe I'll do it.
I'm more like an ancient Roman than a Dane.
There's some liquid left.

>   *He picks up the cup.*

HAMLET

If you are a man,
give me the cup. Let go of it! By heaven, I'll take it.
Oh, God, Horatio, what a damaged reputation   350
I will leave behind if the truth remains unknown!
If you've ever held me dear to your heart,
put off the sweetness of death for a while,
and draw painful breaths in this harsh world
long enough to tell my story.   355

>   *A march is heard offstage, and a cannon shot.*

What is this warlike noise?

>   OSRIC *enters.*

OSRIC

Young Fortinbras has victoriously returned from Poland;
he greets the ambassadors from England
with this warlike shot.

HAMLET

360   O, I die, Horatio!
The potent poison quite o'ercrows my spirit.
I cannot live to hear the news from England,
But I do prophesy th' election lights
On Fortinbras. He has my dying voice.

365   So tell him, with th' occurrents, more and less,
Which have solicited—the rest is silence.

        Dies.

HORATIO

Now cracks a noble heart. Good night, sweet Prince,
And flights of angels sing thee to thy rest.

        [*March within.*]

Why does the drum come hither?

        Enter FORTINBRAS, *with the* AMBASSADORS, *with*
        DRUM, COLORS, *and* ATTENDANTS.

FORTINBRAS

370   Where is this sight?

HORATIO

What is it you would see?
If aught of woe or wonder, cease your search.

FORTINBRAS

This quarry cries on havoc. O proud Death,
What feast is toward in thine eternal cell

375   That thou so many princes at a shot
So bloodily hast struck?

AMBASSADOR

                    The sight is dismal;
And our affairs from England come too late.
The ears are senseless that should give us hearing

380   To tell him his commandment is fulfilled,
That Rosencrantz and Guildenstern are dead.
Where should we have our thanks?

HORATIO

                    Not from his mouth,
Had it th' ability of life to thank you.

HAMLET

Oh, I die, Horatio! 360
The powerful poison completely overcomes my spirit.
I cannot live to listen to the news from England.
But I predict that Fortinbras will be elected
the new Danish king; he has my dying vote.
So tell him all the occurrences, great and small, 365
which have incited my actions. The rest is silence.

He dies.

HORATIO

Now a noble heart has broken. Good night, sweet Prince,
and may companies of angels sing you to your eternal rest.

Marching offstage.

Why is the drum coming this way?

FORTINBRAS, *the English* AMBASSADORS, *and* SERVANTS
enter, with drums and flags.

FORTINBRAS

Where is the sight I am looking for? 370

HORATIO

What is it you wish to see?
If it's anything of sorrow or calamity, stop your search here.

FORTINBRAS

This heap of corpses loudly proclaims a wholesale slaughter.
Oh, proud Death,
what kind of feast is being prepared in your eternal tomb,
that you should cruelly strike down so many princes 375
at a single blow?

AMBASSADOR

This is a frightful sight,
and we've arrived too late with our business from England.
The ears that ought to have heard us are now senseless,
and we cannot tell him that his commandment has been
fulfilled— 380
that Rosencrantz and Guildenstern are dead.
From where will we receive thanks?

HORATIO

Not from his mouth,
if he still lived and was able to thank you.

385   He never gave commandment for their death.
      But since, so jump upon this bloody question,
      You from the Polack wars, and you from England,
      Are here arrived, give order that these bodies
      High on a stage be placed to the view,
390   And let me speak to th' yet unknowing world
      How these things came about. So shall you hear
      Of carnal, bloody, and unnatural acts,
      Of accidental judgments, casual slaughters,
      Of deaths put on by cunning and forced cause,
395   And, in this upshot, purposes mistook
      Fall'n on th' inventors' heads. All this can I
      Truly deliver.

FORTINBRAS
                    Let us haste to hear it,
      And call the noblest to the audience.
400   For me, with sorrow I embrace my fortune.
      I have some rights of memory in this kingdom,
      Which now to claim my vantage doth invite me.

HORATIO
      Of that I shall have also cause to speak,
      And from his mouth whose voice will draw on more.
405   But let this same be presently performed,
      Even while men's minds are wild, lest more mischance
      On plots and errors happen.

FORTINBRAS
                           Let four captains
      Bear Hamlet like a soldier to the stage,
410   For he was likely, had he been put on,
      To have proved most royal; and for his passage
      The soldiers' music and the rite of war
      Speak loudly for him.
      Take up the bodies. Such a sight as this
415   Becomes the field, but here shows much amiss.
      Go, bid the soldiers shoot.

      Exeunt marching; after the which a peal of ordnance are
      shot off.

He never gave the order for their deaths.   385
But since you have arrived here (you from the Polish wars,
and you from England) so quickly
after this bloody quarrel, give orders that these bodies
be placed in full view upon a high platform,
and let me tell the still ignorant world   390
how these things came about. Soon you will hear
of incestuous, bloody, and unnatural acts;
of misjudged accidents, and killings that happened by chance;
of deaths cunningly arranged for treacherous reasons;
and as a final result, misguided schemes,   395
which turned against the perpetrators themselves. All this I can
truthfully tell you.

FORTINBRAS

Let us hear it soon,
and let us summon the highest ranking nobles to listen.
For my part, I embrace my good luck with sadness.   400
I recall that I have certain rights over this kingdom,
which this favorable opportunity now urges me to claim.

HORATIO

I also have more words to say about that—
words from Hamlet's own mouth, which will be seconded by others.
But let's take care of all this immediately   405
while men's minds are still violently agitated, lest further
    disasters
will result from plots and misunderstandings.

FORTINBRAS

Let four captains
carry Hamlet like a soldier to the platform;
for if he had ascended to the throne, it is likely   410
that he would have proven a fine king. To mark his passing,
let him be honored by soldiers' music
and military ceremonies.
Take up the bodies. A sight like this
is fitting for a battlefield, but is most unsuitable here.   415
Go, command the soldiers to shoot.

> *They all exit marching, carrying off the bodies; then*
> *cannons are heard firing.*

Act V Review

Discussion Questions

1. What is the purpose of Scene i with the Gravedigger and his helper?

2. Why do you think Hamlet is so furious at Laertes for his manner of mourning his sister Ophelia in Scene i?

3. What do you think brings about the change in Hamlet's character and philosophy in Scene ii?

4. Why does Hamlet arrange for Rosencrantz and Guildenstern to be put to death?

5. Do you think Gertrude knew that the wine she drank was poisoned? Explain.

6. How would you describe the mood of the fencers and spectators as the duel progresses in Scene ii?

7. Do you think the Ghost would be satisfied with what Hamlet has accomplished at the end of the play? Explain.

8. What kind of leader do you expect Fortinbras to be for Denmark?

Literary Elements

1. Shakespeare often adds **comic relief** to his more serious plays. Where is this element found in Act V? Explain what purpose you think it serves.

2. **Irony** can be the opposite of what is expected. Name some elements of irony in Scene i.

3. **Dramatic irony** occurs when the audience knows more than some of the characters in the play. Look for examples of dramatic irony in Act V. Explain what makes each ironic.

4. A **symbol** is a person or object that stands for something beyond its obvious meaning. What do you think Yorick's skull symbolizes to Hamlet?

Writing Prompts

1. What if Hamlet and Ophelia had not died? Think about what their married life might have been like ten years later. Now write a scene portraying their relationship.

2. Assume you are a television or radio reporter. Write the story you would deliver about the tragic events that take place in the last scene.

3. At the end of the play, Fortinbras says, "Bear Hamlet like a soldier to the stage, / For he was likely, had he been put on, / To have proved most royal." Do you agree with Fortinbras that Hamlet would have made a good king? Explain your position in a short essay, using evidence from the play to support your opinion.

4. Describe the last, bloody scene of the play from the perspective of either Osric or Horatio.

5. Write a different ending for the play. You can write in the form of a summary or an actual scene with dialogue.

The Play in Review

Discussion and Analysis

1. Now that the play is over, you may have formed some opinions about Hamlet's character, especially as to whether or not he is an honorable young man. Reread the poem he wrote to Ophelia ("Doubt thou the stars are fire, . . ." Act II, Scene ii). Now what do you think—did he truly love Ophelia? Explain why or why not.

2. This play is full of comments about womanhood that are not always positive. In Act I, Hamlet utters the famous line, "Frailty, thy name is woman!" In what ways are Gertrude or Ophelia "frail"? If they have any personal or public power, explain what that might be.

3. Foreign powers and personalities are crucial in *Hamlet*. How do these elements contribute to the action and themes of the play?

4. Name all of the "roles" played by the main characters in *Hamlet* (mother, sister, lover, stepfather . . .). Explain how the web of relationships contributes to the outcome of the play.

5. Almost all actors, if they are men, dream of playing Hamlet at some point in their career. Why do you think that is?

6. In your opinion, which of the following is more responsible for this tragedy—the Ghost, Claudius, Hamlet, the political situation in Denmark, or fate?

Literary Elements

1. In Act I, Scene v, Hamlet says to the Ghost, "Haste me to know 't, that I, with wings as swift / As meditation or the thoughts of love, / May sweep to my revenge." Discuss the **irony** of these words in relation to the rest of the play.

2. What do you think is the overriding message, or **theme**, of the play? Be ready to defend your answer.

3. A **tragedy** is a serious work of literature that narrates the events leading to the downfall of a **tragic hero**, who is usually of noble birth. This individual's downfall is a result of a **tragic flaw** or fatal character weakness. Think about how *Hamlet* fits this definition. What is his tragic flaw?

4. *Hamlet* is rich in **conflicts**. Elements of the plot, characters, setting, and language add to the play's conflict and move the story forward. Name one of the conflicts in the play that contributes to the tragedy.

5. To see how **imagery** is embedded into *Hamlet*, find and list some of the images of deceit, death, and corruption you see. What is their dramatic purpose?

6. *Hamlet* is full of **aphorisms**, or pithy sayings, that have become familiar to English speakers. Find lines in the play that you have heard before that have the "ring of truth."

WRITING PROMPTS

1. Write a short parody of *Hamlet*.

2. Has Hamlet gone mad or is he only pretending to be mad? Write an essay that explains your opinion.

3. After viewing any film version of *Hamlet*, write a review. Good choices to see include Laurence Olivier's *Hamlet* (1948), Tony Richardon's *Hamlet* (1969), or the 1990 version of the play filmed by Franco Zeffirelli, starring Mel Gibson as the young prince.

4. Think about all the spying going on in the Danish court. What does it say about Claudius and Polonius when they eavesdrop on Hamlet and Ophelia with no expression of shame or embarrassment? Write an essay discussing whether you think their surveillance is justified. Are parents entitled to watch their children in secrecy?

5. Do some research on any of the following subjects and write a short report on your findings. You may start with an encyclopedia, but at least one of your sources should include a text about 16th-century England (Shakespeare's time).

   a. superstition and witchcraft
   b. Danish weapons and warfare
   c. history of the Danes and their relations with other European countries
   d. religion and science in 16th-century Denmark
   e. King Hamlet
   f. Elizabethan theaters
   g. special effects of the Elizabethan stage
   h. "royal" women in Elizabethan times

6. Write the lyrics to "The Ballad of Ophelia." Include a description of her tragic death.

MULTIMODAL AND GROUP ACTIVITIES

1. Divide into two teams, affirmative and negative, and debate one of the following resolutions.

   Resolved: Hamlet procrastinated needlessly.

   Resolved: Monarchy has a place in the 21st century.

2. In a small group, pretend to be the casting directors for a new production of *Hamlet*. Begin by writing thumbnail sketches of the major characters. Then choose modern actors, thinking carefully about why an actor fits that choice. You may then design a playbill or poster advertising your production, using imagery, typography, and language that gives the audience some idea of the way you will interpret your production of *Hamlet*.

3. Find a work of art based on *Hamlet,* such as a musical piece, a play, or a painting. In an oral presentation to your group or class, explain how the music, drama, or art captures the mood and events of the

play. You may need to use a DVD player, VCR, portable CD player, or slides to share this work with your audience.

4. Design costumes for some of the characters in *Hamlet*. Using the resources of the Internet or a library, examine the dress of royalty, nobles, commoners, merchants, warriors, and clergy. Sketch the garments you design, or make replicas for puppets or paper dolls. Another way to show your creations would be by using cartoon panels or computer graphics.

5. The soliloquy in Act III, Scene i begins with what might be one of Shakespeare's most famous lines—"To be or not to be." Read the soliloquy aloud, either as individuals or in chorus. Then read it again, this time having one student echo the line "to be or not to be" after every few lines or units of meaning. Or try it with one student reading the poem aloud and the rest of the class echoing this line after every few lines.

6. Read Claudius's soliloquy in Act III, Scene ii aloud, either alone or in unison with your classmates. The second time you read it, each student should be responsible for one line, but only say aloud the most powerful word in that line. Afterword, think about how these single words call to mind the themes and emotions of *Hamlet*.

SHAKESPEARE'S LIFE

Many great authors can be imagined as living among the characters in their works. Historical records reveal how these writers spoke, felt, and thought. But Shakespeare is more mysterious. He never gave an interview or wrote an autobiography—not even one of his letters survives. What we know about his life can be told very briefly.

Shakespeare was born in April 1564. The exact date of his birth is unknown, but he was baptized on April 26 in the Stratford-upon-Avon church. His father, John, was a prominent local man who served as town chamberlain and mayor. Young William attended

grammar school in Stratford, where he would have learned Latin—a requirement for a professional career—and some Greek.

In 1582, William married Anne Hathaway. He was 18; she was 26. At the time of their marriage, Anne was already three months pregnant with their first daughter, Susanna. In 1585, the couple had twins, Judith and Hamnet. Hamnet died before reaching adulthood, leaving Shakespeare no male heir.

Even less is known about Shakespeare's life between 1585 and 1592. During that time, he moved to London and became an actor and playwright. He left his family behind in Stratford. Although he surely visited them occasionally, we have little evidence about what Shakespeare was like as a father and a husband.

Several of his early plays were written during this time, including *The Comedy of Errors*, *Titus Andronicus*, and the three parts of *Henry VI*. In those days, working in the theater was rather like acting in soap operas today—the results may be popular, but daytime serials aren't recognized as serious art. In fact, many people were opposed to even allowing plays to be performed. Ministers warned their congregations of the dangers of going to plays.

But Shakespeare and his friends were lucky. Queen Elizabeth I loved plays. She protected acting companies from restrictive laws and gave them her permission to perform. Shakespeare wrote several plays to be performed for the queen, including *Twelfth Night*.

Queen Elizabeth I

After Elizabeth's death in 1603, Shakespeare's company became known as the King's Men. This group of actors performed for James I, who had ruled Scotland before becoming the king of England. Perhaps to thank James for his patronage, Shakespeare wrote *Macbeth*, which included two topics of strong interest to the king—Scottish royalty and witchcraft.

Unlike many theater people, Shakespeare actually earned a good living. By 1599, he was part owner of the Globe, one of the newest theaters in London. Such plays as *Othello*, *Hamlet*, and *King Lear* were first performed there.

The Globe

In 1610 or 1611, Shakespeare moved back to the familiar surroundings of Stratford-upon-Avon. He was almost 50 years old, well past middle age by 17th-century standards. Over the years, he'd invested in property around Stratford, acquiring a comfortable estate and a family coat of arms.

But Shakespeare didn't give up writing. In 1611, his new play *The Tempest* was performed at court. In 1613, his play *Henry VIII* premiered. This performance was more dramatic than anyone expected. The stage directions called for a cannon to be fired when "King Henry" came on stage. The explosion set the stage on fire, and the entire theater burned to the ground.

Shakespeare died in 1616 at the age of 52. His gravestone carried this inscription:

> **Good friend for Jesus sake forbear**
> **To dig the dust enclosed here!**
> **Blest be the man that spares these stones,**
> **And curst be he that moves my bones.**

This little verse, so crude that it seems unlikely to be Shakespeare's, has intrigued countless scholars and biographers.

Anyone who loves Shakespeare's plays and poems wants to know more about their author. Was he a young man who loved Anne Whateley but was forced into a loveless marriage with another Anne? Did he teach school in Stratford, poach Sir Thomas Lucy's deer, or work for a lawyer in London? Who is the "dark lady" of his sonnets?

But perhaps we are fortunate in our ignorance. Orson Welles, who directed an all-black stage production of *Macbeth* in 1936, put it this way: "Luckily, we know almost nothing about Shakespeare . . . and that makes it so much easier to understand [his] works . . . It's an egocentric, romantic, 19th-century conception that the artist is more interesting and more important than his art."

In Shakespeare's world, there can be little question of which is truly important, the work or the author. Shakespeare rings up the curtain and then steps back into the wings, trusting the play to a cast of characters so stunningly vivid that they sometimes seem more real than life.

✢ ✢ ✢

SHAKESPEARE'S THEATER

In Shakespeare's London, a day's entertainment often began with a favorite amusement, bearbaiting. A bear would be captured and chained to a stake inside a pit. A pack of dogs would be released, and they would attack the bear. Spectators placed bets on which would die first. Admission to these pits cost only a penny, so they were very popular with working-class Londoners.

The Swan Theatre in London, drawn in 1596, the only known contemporary image of an Elizabethan theater interior

After the bearbaiting was over, another penny purchased admission to a play. Each theater had its own company of actors, often supported by a nobleman or a member of the royal family. For part of his career, Shakespeare was a member of the Lord

Chamberlain's Men. After the death of Queen Elizabeth I, King James I became the patron of Shakespeare's company. The actors became known as the King's Men.

As part owner of the Globe Theatre, Shakespeare wrote plays, hired actors, and paid the bills. Since the Globe presented a new play every three weeks, Shakespeare and his actors had little time to rehearse or polish their productions. To complicate matters even more, most actors played more than one part in a play.

Boys played all the female roles. Most acting companies had three or four youths who were practically raised in the theater. They started acting as early as age seven and played female roles until they began shaving. Shakespeare had a favorite boy actor (probably named John Rice) who played Cleopatra and Lady

Richard Tarleton, Elizabethan actor famous for his clowning

Macbeth. Actresses would not become part of the English theater for another fifty years.

The audience crowded into the theater at about 2 p.m. The cheapest seats weren't seats at all but standing room in front of the stage. This area, known as the "pit," was occupied by "groundlings" or "penny knaves," who could be more trouble to the actors than they were worth. If the play was boring, the groundlings would throw rotten eggs or vegetables. They talked loudly to their friends, played cards, and even picked fights with each other. One theater was set on fire by audience members who didn't like the play.

The theater was open to the sky, so rain or snow presented a problem. However, the actors were partially protected by a roof known as the "heavens," and wealthier patrons sat in three stories of sheltered galleries that surrounded the pit and most of the main stage.

The main stage, about 25 feet deep and 45 feet wide, projected into the audience, so spectators were closely involved in the action. This stage was rather bare, with only a few pieces of furniture. But this simplicity allowed for flexible and fluid staging. Unlike too many later productions, plays at the Globe did not grind to a halt for scene changes. When one group of actors exited through one doorway and a new group entered through another, Shakespeare's audience understood that a new location was probably being represented.

Behind the main stage was the "tiring-house," where the actors changed costumes. Above the stage was a gallery that, when it wasn't occupied by musicians or wealthy patrons, could suggest any kind of high place—castle ramparts, a cliff, or a balcony.

Special effects were common. A trap door in the main stage allowed ghosts to appear. Even more spectacularly, supernatural beings could be lowered from above the stage. For added realism, actors hid bags of pig's blood and guts under their stage doublets. When pierced with a sword, the bags spilled out over the stage and produced a gory effect.

All these staging methods and design elements greatly appealed to Elizabethan audiences and made plays increasingly popular. By the time Shakespeare died in 1616, there were more than thirty theaters in and around London.

What would Shakespeare, so accustomed to the rough-and-tumble stagecraft of the Globe, think of the theaters where his plays are performed today? He would probably miss some of the vitality of the Globe. For centuries now, his plays have been most often performed on stages with a frame called the "proscenium arch," which cleanly separates the audience from the performers. This barrier tends to cast a peculiar shroud of privacy over his plays so that his characters do not seem to quite enter our world.

But with greater and greater frequency, Shakespeare's plays are being performed out-of-doors or in theaters with three- or four-sided stages. And a replica of the Globe Theatre itself opened in London in 1996, only about 200 yards from the site of the original.

The new Globe Theatre, London

This new Globe is an exciting laboratory where directors and actors can test ideas about Elizabethan staging. Their experiments may change our ideas about how Shakespeare's plays were performed and give new insights into their meaning.

✠ ✠ ✠

THE GLOBE THEATRE

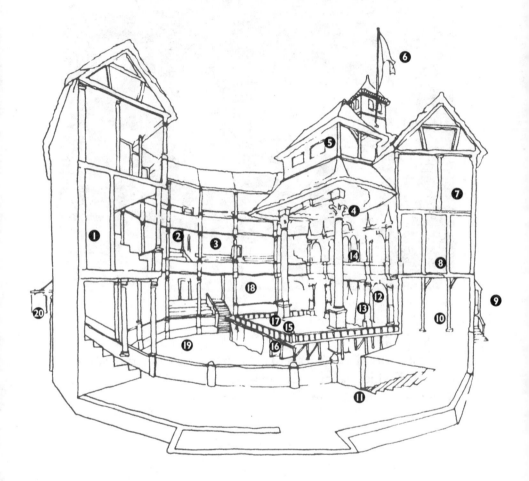

1 **Corridor** A passageway serving the middle gallery.

2 **Entrance** Point leading to the staircase and upper galleries.

3 **Middle Gallery** The seats here were higher priced.

4 **The Heavens** So identified by being painted with the zodiac signs.

5 **Hut** A storage area that also held a winch system for lowering characters to the stage.

6 **Flag** A white flag above the theater meant a show that day.

7 **Wardrobe** A storage area for costumes and props.

8 **Dressing Rooms** Rooms where actors were "attired" and awaited their cues.

9 **Tiring-House Door** The rear entrance or "stage door" for actors or privileged spectators.

10 **Tiring-House** Backstage area providing space for storage and costume changes.

11 **Stairs** Theatergoers reached the galleries by staircases enclosed by stairwells.

12 **Stage Doors** Doors opening into the Tiring-House.

13 **Inner Stage** A recessed playing area often curtained off except as needed.

14 **Gallery** Located above the stage to house musicians or spectators.

15 **Trap Door** Leading to the "Hell" area, where a winch elevator was located.

16 **Hell** The area under the stage, used for ghostly comings and goings or for storage.

17 **Stage** Major playing area jutting into the Pit, creating a sense of intimacy.

18 **Lords Rooms** or private galleries. Six pennies let a viewer sit here, or sometimes on stage.

19 **The Pit** Sometimes referred to as "The Yard," where the "groundlings" watched.

20 **Main Entrance** Here the doorkeeper collected admission.

IMAGE CREDITS